MAX GORDON PRESENTS

MAX GORDON PRESENTS

〰〰〰〰〰〰〰〰〰〰

by Max Gordon

with Lewis Funke

PUBLISHED BY

BERNARD GEIS ASSOCIATES

DISTRIBUTED BY RANDOM HOUSE

FOR MY WIFE, MILDRED,

WITH ALL MY LOVE

Contents

CONTENTS

MAX GORDON PRESENTS

1

Introducing . . .

THIS IS THE STORY of Mechel Salpeter, who became Max Gordon, who became one of Broadway's leading producers.

It is the story of one man's love for the theatre, a love that began in his early childhood and has lasted until this day, unabated and intermittently rewarded.

It is the story of an American showman who learned about show business in the hurly-burly of old-time burlesque, learned more in vaudeville during its golden days, and still more in the legitimate theatre, Hollywood and television.

The story begins in New York City on June 28, 1892, in a Lower East Side tenement at 59 Goerck Street. That tenement, like others in the vicinity, has since given way to a low-cost housing development; that section of Goerck Street now is Baruch Place, named for a great American, Bernard M. Baruch, who, oddly enough, was destined to play a major role in my career. Between the Goerck Street tenement and the hotel on Park Avenue where I now reside are the years of my life, the years of this story.

(3)

I was not yet eight when I first fell in love with the theatre, not yet eighteen when I ran away from home to become the advance agent for a burlesque show. I was twenty when I met a burlesque comedian, Al Lewis, with ambitions, dreams and a love of the theatre matching my own, and at dinner one night, laughing and talking, we formed the firm of Lewis and Gordon. With luck, hard work and good taste, that firm became, as the years went by, the foremost producer of one-act plays in the United States. We knew the glories of the Palace, the rewards of triumph in that throne room of an all but forgotten theatre form.

I was thirty-eight and no longer Lewis' partner when, broke, I set out alone in the world of the legitimate theatre. That was 1930, after the stock market crash and the onset of the Great Depression, after the death of the vaudeville I had known. In the quarter of a century that followed, I became one of the foremost producers of the time. I presented forty-five productions on Broadway—revues, musicals, comedies and dramas. Many on that list were failures, some, as we say in the theatre, distinguished failures; others were one-week disasters. But on that list also are some of the greatest hits the American stage has ever known.

Once I had four shows open in a single season, each one a hit, and all running simultaneously. My portrait has adorned the front page of Sunday drama sections and stories of my success have filled pages in national magazines.

Two of my productions, *Three's a Crowd* and *The Band Wagon,* continue to be regarded by theatrical historians as the high points in the development of the American revue. *Roberta, The Cat and the Fiddle* and *The Great Waltz* were musicals that brought abundant joy and pleasure to thousands. My plays include *The Women, My*

Sister Eileen (which subsequently became the musical *Wonderful Town*), *Dodsworth, The Late George Apley, Junior Miss, The Doughgirls, The Solid Gold Cadillac* and, of course, *Born Yesterday.*

No man, surely, has been more stage-struck than I. The theatre permeates my entire being every waking moment of my life. Three times it has broken my health, even pushed me to death's edge. It has provided me with the joys and agonies known to lovers. It has enabled me to revel in luxuries I dreamed of as a boy. For all the travail it has caused me I would not, given a second chance, choose another path. Now, more than half a century since I stood on the stage of a Buffalo burlesque house heralding the virtues of next week's extravaganza, I still feel the theatre's enchantment, its enveloping magic. The staging of a play is for me a grand adventure into a world I did not make but which I eagerly explore.

How did I get this way?

It was my dear friend, and more than one-time savior, the late Moss Hart, who said, "The theatre is an inevitable refuge of the unhappy child. The first retreat a child makes to alleviate his unhappiness is to contrive a world of his own, and it is but a small step out of his private world into the fantasy world of the theatre."

He may have been right. And yet, frustrated, depressed and forlorn though I have been many times in my adult life, I cannot recall that I was an unhappy child. True, I have shared Moss' dread of poverty—most men who have clawed and fought their way out of the Lower East Side know this feeling. Nevertheless, I cannot recollect my childhood with bitterness or heartache. On the contrary, it seems to have been in retrospect my happy time. Indeed, many are the Sundays even now, though the house on Goerck Street no longer stands, that I return to those other streets of the Lower East Side to relive for an hour of an afternoon those early days, to walk again where I had, during summer vacations, run barefoot and unattended from morning till night.

Certainly, there is nothing on either Heschel or Doba Salpeter's side to suggest that their three male children—Morris, David and I—would find their way into the theatre. My father and mother were born in the same village of Poland, a village whose name has vanished from the map. They came from poor, hard-working farm folk, and it is a virtual certainty that in their native land they never saw the inside of a theatre.

My parents were married before they were twenty, and a few years later they heard the call of the New World. Four of their children had already been born when they decided to uproot themselves and set forth for America, "the golden land." There, so they had heard, as had millions of others living in the ghettos of Europe, was the chance for freedom, the opportunity to earn a good living and provide for their children all that they themselves had been denied. With such hopes they kissed and bade farewell to parents, cousins, uncles and aunts, and set out by steerage across the Atlantic.

It did not take them long to learn that much of what they had heard was untrue. Life in the spirit-deadening tenements of the Lower East Side of New York could be no less harsh than it had been "back home"—more harsh, in fact, for those who, in their own country, had at least known the smell of earth and the feeling of open spaces.

It is true that many did ultimately fight their way from the new ghetto. But I don't think my father ever would have. To make money in America a man needs capital, and my father simply had too many mouths to feed to be able to lay away a dime. The eleven dollars he earned as a pants presser in a Montgomery Street sweatshop—I can still see him on a hot summer's day standing there, stripped to the waist, toiling from seven in the morning until after six at night—those eleven dollars were just about enough to manage the rent and keep a family of ten from starvation.

With such responsibility how could he even think of taking a chance on anything else—a pushcart, a tailor shop? What if these self-employed enterprises failed? What then?

Nor did his piety help. An orthodox Jew, who, according to the commandments of his fathers, wore a beard all of his life, my father refused to make compromises with the Christian work week. He would not do any manner of work on Saturday, the Jewish Sabbath, and, consequently, had to find employment in an establishment that kept open on Sunday. Not many such employment situations existed, which only added to circumscribing whatever ambitions he may have had. Nor, occupied as he was, did he trouble himself to learn the new language. Yiddish remained the tongue he spoke until the day he died.

Yet, disappointed though he may have been with the New World, I cannot recall hearing him complain. He seemed perfectly content, slave though he was, and being a pious man, he found much of his pleasure in the nearby synagogue, where he went on Friday nights and Saturday mornings.

My father was an excitable man—a trait, unfortunately, inherited by me. His temper could be something terrible to behold. Occasionally, he would return home from a tortured day in Montgomery Street to find that my mother, not knowing her husband had been dreaming all day of a particular dish, had prepared a menu displeasing to his palate that night. In such circumstances his temper and bellow were terrifying to eye and ear. But, like a summer storm, the thunder and lightning would soon pass. My father was the barking dog that never bit. Rant though he might, we knew that in a few moments his sense of humor would come to his—and our—rescue; that he would recognize the absurdity of his tantrum, regret the loss of his dignity, and begin to laugh.

Repeatedly he would threaten us with direst punishment, especially when some gossipmonger relayed to him the information that one of us had sneaked off for a swim in the East River or had been seen hitching rides on the back of horsecars on East Broadway. In such instances he invariably removed his strap and advanced toward the culprit most menacingly. But I cannot remember his ever using that strap. Always he hoped that the threat and the tongue-lashing would be sufficient. In a sense, they were. Although we might repeat our sins, we appreciated his love and concern for us. He, along with our mother, provided the anchors for our lives. We loved him and gave him the respect he demanded and deserved.

His outstanding virtues were kindness and compassion. He was also blessed with common-sense wisdom. We knew that no matter what trouble engulfed us we could turn to him for aid without fear of reproach or recrimination. I remember with special appreciation a certain Yom Kippur, the Jewish Day of Atonement. On this day it was customary for my brothers and me, regardless of how irreligious we might have been during the year, to pray with my father in the synagogue. Yom Kippur is an all-day observance beginning at sundown and continuing through the following day until sundown. Morris, or Cliff Gordon, as he called himself when he went into show business, had to work on that Holy Day. Somehow, he managed to get to the synagogue for a few hours, giving my father a weak explanation for his absence. My father never said so, but I think he knew what Cliff was up to. He did not push the matter, accepting the fact that his son had reached the age of independence; satisfied that, at least, Cliff had come to the synagogue.

Like my father, my mother never learned to write English or speak it. Though she lived in America for more than half a century, it remained always something of an alien land for her. She lived her life for her husband and children—cooking, baking, washing, ironing, guiding. She never saw a movie; the only show she ever saw was *The Great Waltz,* and I practically had to drag her there. Yet, for all her parochial existence, she was a woman of instinctive refinement and good taste. Neat, trim and absolutely fastidious, she could not tolerate boisterousness or vulgarity. She was a soft-spoken person and only raised her voice when my father became crotchety or one of the youngsters committed some misdeed. She was friendly but not overly intimate with her neighbors. To us she was Gibraltar. Many times I beheld her strength, and needed it, as I grew up. This strength she undoubtedly derived from the proximity with which she lived to God. Once, after my father died and she was living alone, I said that I would like to hire a housekeeper for her. "It would be good," I said. "You'd have some company." Her reply was swift and simple. "I am never alone, Max," she said. "God is always with me."

I don't believe that my father could ever tell a falsehood, and to my mother honesty was not only the best policy, it was God's law. One of my nieces recalls the humiliation she endured as a child when, on a visit with my mother to Woolworth's, she took a string of beads. When she arrived home, the theft was discovered. My mother insisted that they walk back the eight blocks to return the beads. Worse, my niece recalls, was the horrible silence that enshrouded that walk, the utter unhappiness she could read in my mother's face. I remember a day many years later when my mother said to me, "The neighbors tell me that you have four hits running on Broadway." I said, "Yes, Mama, that's true." She looked at me and said, "Tell me, Max, is it honest?"

That my parents succeeded in retaining their dignity and their trust in the verities of ethical behavior is a tribute not only to their inner strength but also to the validity of their faith. Surely it could not have been easy in the tenement jungle in which they struggled for survival. The house on Goerck Street was typical of the wretched traps in the area, many of which still stand. Upon my arrival there were ten of us confined to three rooms. The toilet, or what really was an outhouse, was downstairs in the yard. A few years later, with the help of contributions from my oldest sister and my brothers, we were able to move from Goerck Street to Cannon and then to Lewis, where the ten of us spread out into four rooms and, for the first time, the toilet was on the same floor.

In spite of the occasional verbal exchanges between my father and mother, in spite of the never-ending pressures and strains, my parents somehow succeeded in creating an environment of standards and certitudes, of love and compassion. No matter what the week had wrought, when Friday came, there was in my home an aura of getting ready for a holiday, as, indeed, the Sabbath is ordained to be. There was cleaning and scrubbing, cooking and baking, an orderly sort of hustle and bustle through which my mother moved with utter serenity. One of my special chores was to take the dough she had kneaded into a twist, or *challah* (the traditional Sabbath bread), to the community stove in the neighborhood. She may have had to scrimp during the week, but on Friday night, in addition to the Sabbath candles and the traditional white tablecloth and napkins, there was the festival chicken boiled in noodle soup, the tea and the little cakes she had made.

I have never forgotten those Friday nights during the winter, when the family gathered around the coal stove. Although my parents never actually participated—as I have mentioned, they never learned English—they delighted in listening to the rest of us singing the popular songs of the day, telling stories and playing games.

Of culture in my house, however, there was none. No one in my home had any impelling drive toward serious music, art or reading. Aside from the daily Yiddish paper that my father read after dinner, aside from the prayer books read by my father and mother, there was no other reading in my home. That seemed to have been left to me. As the baby of the family, with none of the responsibilities of helping to support the household, I was the one whose schooling was important, to whom time was given for an education. By my tenth year I had become an omnivorous, if indiscriminate, reader, a regular visitor to the library on Grand Street, and the happy discoverer of the Educational Alliance on East Broadway where I spent many Sunday afternoons listening to students debate such topics as "Is the Pen Mightier than the Sword?"

These were my roots.

2

The East Side

WHEN A MAN has passed his seventieth birthday, has fought his battles, made his fortune, and looks back on his childhood from the sanctuary of a luxurious mid-Manhattan apartment, it is easy for him to romanticize his beginnings, to create a nostalgic halo around them, to glamorize them by screening out the drab and the prosaic; or to commit the opposite mistake and screen out the brighter moments to make dominant those of deepest blue. This is especially true when he remembers mornings on which he yearned for a roll covered with poppy seeds, not to be had because the family budget did not allow for rolls with poppy seeds; or how he used to stand in the doorway of a candy factory inhaling the sweet aroma of chocolate fumes because real chocolate also remained in the realm of yearning.

The Lower East Side of my childhood was a real world, a harshly real world. I hesitate to say that I relished my childhood there. But I cannot say either that I hated it or that I lived only for that day of release, nay escape, from its soul-destroying clutches.

Spring, summer and early fall, of course, were the great times. Winters could be barren, bleak and gloomy. Not even a bright sun did much to cheer the forsaken streets or those dirty red or whatever-color-they-once-were buildings, or to relieve the melancholy hibernation. But a boy could be kept pretty busy during the week, what with going to school and after that to *cheder,* or Hebrew school, doing his homework, and trying to read.

During the other times there was plenty of life and excitement to be found on the Lower East Side. It was chattering, bubbling, vital life. On Canal Street—Suit-Hunting Avenue, it was called—the stores were bright with men's hats, ties and suits, the street alive with shoppers. In addition to us natives, who came only to stare or to dream of the days when we, too, would be dressed in what were presumably the latest Fifth Avenue fashions, there were those from other sections of the city who came in the perennial human quest for bargains. Also, there were those ex-natives who, having emigrated to the Bronx or Brooklyn, still had not learned to trust the one-price establishments like Wanamaker's and Bloomingdale's. Better to return to the old places and spend a day of warfare in pursuit of that new suit. At least you had, or thought you had, a chance to outsmart the merchant, or maybe you could catch him on a day when he needed cash and would be willing to make a quick deal. Uptown you had to pay what the ticket called for and a person could never be sure how much profit the boss was making.

Pity the unwary on Canal, Stanton or Rivington Streets. Should an unsophisticated stroller pause for a moment in front of a store where the owner operated with an outside hawker, he was bound to find himself seized by the arm and hustled inside. Once inside, there would be no end to the artifices used on him to make a sale. You had to know the ropes, keep clear of these gyp joints, and walk as close to the curb as possible.

On Hester Street summer especially had its vitalizing effects. The pushcarts, squeezed alongside each other, were more numerous than in winter, lining both sides of the street. The cacophony of venders and housewives engaged in daily combat sounded like a parrot jungle. Fresh fruits, nuts, broken chocolate, toys, dolls, vegetables, all manner of materials, ribbons, elastic, stockings—almost anything you could name—filled the carts. If you happened to be hungry, or just plain mischievous, you grabbed what you dared and ran like mad, the pushcart men desperately trying to overtake you.

Here, indeed, men laid the foundations of fortunes. Without knowledge of the language or customs, they could rent a cart for ten cents and for another dollar or dollar and a half fill it with merchandise. Many would work from five in the morning until two the next—another aspect of the jungle out of which some scratched their way to riches.

What I liked best about the summers was my freedom. No school to worry about, no homework, no special bedtime. My mother, concerned though she always was about my health and ethical behavior, had little time for the minutiae of a young boy's coming and going during his leisure hours.

On hot days when the pavements and tenements steamed, I risked the danger of some gossipmonger's tongue, the resultant threat of my father's strap, and headed for a swim in the East River. In addition to what might happen at home if my father found out, there was the danger from the neighborhood toughs and the older boys. It was one of these toughs who was responsible for

my learning how to swim at the age of six. I had run down
to the foot of Delancey Street—it was not long before
they began building the bridge there—and was hovering
around the edge of the pier when this fellow spotted me.
"Hey, Jew-boy," he roared, "how about a drink?" He
grabbed me and with a great guffaw tossed me over. I
splashed around, gulped mouthfuls of that polluted water,
and managed to keep afloat until one of the other boys,
feeling sorry for me, helped me grab one of the piles and
climb out.

Safer, although not quite as exciting as the East River
itself—nor as satisfying—was the swimming boat the city
used to tie up at Third Street and the East River. This
was a huge red barge with dressing rooms on the sides and
a sort of swimming pool in the center. It was designed to
give us kids a place where we could cool off. We used to
line up and get a fast duck in the pool, one at a time.
If you didn't get out when your turn was up, one of the
city employees would help you by wielding a sort of long
cane on your bottom. During the week the dip was free;
but on Sundays, for reasons I never bothered to investi-
gate, the city charged a nickel, and the place was empty.

When they started building the Williamsburg Bridge
on Delancey Street, a stone's throw from our house on
Lewis Street, there was no end to the fun you could have
playing in the sand or with the bricks. Another treat took
place sometimes late in the day when the drivers for the
Hecker Flour Mills Company on Corlears and Grand
Streets would unhitch their wagons and let us ride the
horses to the stables on Lewis and Houston Streets.

Once in a while, when I managed to put together
enough money for carfare, I would go up to Cannon
Street, buy some stale pies, and take the elevated train to
Coney Island. But the big event of every summer was the
outing to the Bronx. Everyone contributed ten cents to

"Itzig the Grocer" on Lewis Street who was in charge of the affair. Itzig would arrange with the streetcar people for the transportation and whatever else was needed at our destination.

On the appointed day we gathered at the corner of Delancey and Lewis Streets, a babbling band of excited, temporarily released mothers and children. There we boarded a horsecar for Third Avenue. Then, amidst scenes of seeming panic and shouted instructions about holding hands and watching out for cars and horses, we changed to the electric-powered trolley and rode the rest of the distance, all through Manhattan, up to Fort George near the upper end of the island—a paradise then of open land, trees, grass and sky. All the way we let the world know how happy we were, each in his or her own heart sensing that flush of freedom from the maze of buildings piled on each other, the fire escapes with their mattresses on which folks tried to sleep when the heat was unbearable inside, the hubbub of a crowded, volatile humanity. All the way we shouted greetings to the passers-by on the sidewalks, less fortunate than we this particular day; flirted with the girls; laughed hysterically at the frailest *bon mot;* stole a nibble here and there from our food package; sang at the top of our lungs whatever songs we knew best. The truth is that the annual outing was, in a sense, a necessary substance of our lives, something we needed to freshen our spirits.

Such were our pleasures.

We had our perils, too. It was no isolated incident that befell me that day when the hoodlum jeeringly grabbed me and with the taunting "Jew-boy, how about a drink?" tossed me into the river. In the melting pot of the Lower East Side, the poison of anti-Semitism was an ingredient not to be lightly dismissed. Jews who had fled from the oppression of the Czar, from the menace of malevolent ignorance, still found themselves being insulted in the New Land by malevolent ignorance.

The struggling Irish, the struggling Poles, the struggling Germans, still imbued with their prejudices and not yet broadened in their vision of America, were our principal tormentors. Sheenie, kike and worse epithets were not unfamiliar to our ears, and in certain areas hateful rowdies were known to laugh at old Jews on the way to synagogue, to even pull their beards and spit at them. I remember seeing my father walking peacefully along the street on the way home from work and suddenly being attacked by members of the Squares, a gang of Irish delinquents from the neighborhood. For no reason at all, they began throwing stones at him and chasing him. When he got to our stoop, his head was bleeding from a gash inflicted by one of the stones. For weeks afterward it was my job to escort my father to the doctor to have the wound cleaned and dressed.

Fortunately, the Squares and their ilk bore little resemblance to those East Side gangs of bygone days, the two worst of which were the Bowery Boys and their arch rivals, the Dead Rabbits. Old men on the East Side still told stories of the battles these two gangs waged with each other in the Bowery, the Five Points Section, or on the ancient battleground of Bunker Hill, north of Grand Street, skirmishes that sometimes lasted two or three days. The ferocity of these engagements may be gleaned from the fact that practically no weapon was barred. These ruffians fought each other with knives, clubs, fists and, when needed, their teeth.

Nevertheless, the latter-day gangs like the Squares were troublesome and occasionally battles did break out among them. But as long as they left the Jews alone, we didn't care. I, for one, was too small to get into fights with individuals or with even Jewish gangs quickly organized for self-defense or for revenge. Most of the time when such disasters threatened, I adhered to the course of prudence. I ran. But one fight I did get into with the gentiles, and even now I remember that fight with mounting excitement, because in it I and a lot of other Jews repaid our tormentors for the invectives, the insults and the humiliations they had heaped upon us.

The fight took place on July 30, 1902, the day of the great funeral for Rabbi Jacob Joseph, grandfather of Lazarus Joseph, once the Comptroller of the City of New York, and great-grandfather of Robert L. Joseph, one of Broadway's younger playwright-producers. Few funerals in the history of New York City, before or since, have equaled the one that was held that sweltering midsummer day. Estimates of the crowd ran as high as one hundred thousand persons, including those who waited on the Brooklyn side of the East River to escort the body to the grave in Temple Rodeph Sholom Cemetery in Cypress Hills.

Rabbi Joseph had been brought to New York from Vilna, Lithuania, fourteen years before. A special commission, organized by the eighteen tiny synagogue congregations that dotted the Lower East Side, had been sent to fetch him to become Chief Rabbi of the orthodox Jews in the United States. Up to that time there had not been a rabbi on whom the orthodox Jews could agree as their spiritual leader. But Rabbi Joseph was unique. His reputation had spread throughout Europe and across the Atlantic—a man of great learning, author of books propounding Jewish law, philosopher, thinker, a Demosthenes in the pulpit, who by his eloquence could move men and women to tears, shake them to the roots of their beings in sermons that sometimes were said to have lasted as long as four hours.

In addition to his duties as Chief Rabbi and his responsibilities as head of Congregation Beth Hamedrash Hagodol on Norfolk Street, between Grand and Broome Streets, Rabbi Joseph supervised the slaughtering of cattle in accordance with the regulations of Biblical law. He also governed several hundred rabbis who oversaw the purity of food supplies in general. From these various duties he derived a large income. But he died absolutely penniless. All that he had received he had passed on to the poor. It was necessary at the time of his death to award the conduct of his funeral service to the congregation guaranteeing the largest weekly lifetime pension for his widow. No man was more beloved on the Lower East Side, more revered, more respected, than our Rabbi Joseph.

We had been standing on the stoop that Monday night, my father and I, when word reached us that Rabbi Joseph was dying. From block to block, house to house, door to door the message spread. Soon the streets swarmed with people surging toward the rabbi's house at 263 Henry Street. My father and I joined the crowds. Many men carried their prayer books. They kept repeating over and over again, "O God, care for his soul, care for his soul." By midnight Rabbi Joseph was dead. An old, gray-bearded man appeared at the window, opened it, and recited from the Psalms of David. From the crowds in the streets the wailing went up. The lamentations were awesome to hear. "Our rabbi is dead. The great God has called his soul," everyone seemed to be saying at the same time. The grief was as sincere as it was general. To me, a child of ten, brought up in a pious home where one sat down to a meal with his head covered, the scene was almost overwhelming.

Finally, my father said that it was time to go home. As we pushed our way back to Lewis Street, he described, in reply to my questions, what would be taking place in the rabbi's house. The rabbi's body, my father said, would be placed on the floor with a pillow under his head. A black cloth would cover his face, in accordance with the practice of the orthodox Jewish faith. All the mirrors would be covered, along with pictures and ornaments. Candles would be placed at his head. All night long holy men would come and pray.

When we arrived home we found my mother waiting for us, her eyes red from weeping. We told her of all that we had seen. At last I climbed into bed, but there was no sleeping the rest of that night. Outside in the streets I heard people talking and crying, and I knew that all the neighborhood synagogues had been opened for those who wished to pray.

All through Tuesday the scene was the same, with people gathering on Henry Street, crying, talking and remembering the rabbi's innumerable good deeds. People seemed to be trying to outdo each other in recounting how Rabbi Joseph had aided this family or that, how in time of despair he had been a comforting angel sent by the good God. All day long people streamed into the synagogues to mourn, to utter their prayers for the departed soul of their leader. And everywhere there were rumors of the preparations that were being made for the funeral the following day.

Men spoke in awe of reports that rabbis were coming from all over the country. Someone said that more than two hundred carriages would be required, that a delegation had gone to Police Headquarters to arrange to keep order along the route of the funeral procession. There were stories of rich men bidding for burial places near that of the rabbi, and one report said that a wealthy merchant from Canal Street had offered Congregation Beth Hamedrash Hagodol five thousand dollars for the grave plot next to the rabbi's. Old men denounced these rumors and said disdainfully that no one in authority would think of listening to such nonsense.

Word that Mr. Gutterman, one of the influential Jews of the East Side, had been designated to drive the horses pulling the hearse was greeted with general approval. Someone heard that sacred sand from Jerusalem would be sprinkled on the rabbi's face before the coffin was closed. So it went, the rumors and reports, some authentic, others typical of such situations—wild, ludicrous, figments of fertile and heated imaginations.

On the morning of the funeral I was up and out of bed by seven. The sun had risen hot, and there was no doubt that this was going to be one of those sweltering days. By the time I reached Henry Street, it was already crowded to suffocation. Old men, young men, old women, young women, women with babies in their arms, boys and girls packed every available inch of standing room in both directions. Fire escapes were jammed, as were doorways and windows. Shops, stores and factories were closed. Rudely, I shoved and pushed my way to a point near the house. When I came diagonally opposite it, I ducked into a hallway and climbed six flights to the roof. Others were there before me, but I managed to secure a vantage point from which I had a view of practically everything going on below.

Suddenly there was a great din from the street, and I could see the police reserves charging and clearing a way for the hearse. In front of the house the vehicle stopped. A path was opened up to the steps as eight pious men made their way through, bearing on their shoulders an unpainted white pine box. This was the coffin, plain and unadorned as required by the Jewish religion, an outward reminder that death levels us all. After a brief wait the coffin reappeared bearing the rabbi's body. As it was borne to the hearse, the wailing increased until finally the air was filled with a volume of sound that was deafening, if not terrifying, to hear.

Men and women, unmindful of the police's repeated charges, rushed forward, all with the same idea at the same moment—to touch the coffin. Women fainted, men stumbled to their knees. Others were bowled over and mercilessly trampled in the wild and weird maelstrom. With considerable effort the police rescued those who had fallen, several of whom bled from the face and nose as they were led away. The sun moved closer and grew hotter, adding to the general discomfort. Men wiped their brows first, then their tears.

At last, someone gave the signal. The procession moved from Henry Street in the direction of Montgomery Street, where my father would be able to get a glimpse of it, his employer, incidentally, being one of the few who had not suspended business for the day. I raced down from the roof to follow the mourners. It appeared that everyone else had the same idea. Everyone wanted to keep in sight of the hearse and the remains of Rabbi Joseph as long as possible. It was as if we were afraid of being left alone. As long as we could see the hearse, we felt he was with us.

The procession moved slowly, deliberately, majestically along the appointed route. Leading the way were several hundred children from the East Broadway Talmud Torah. Solemnly they chanted in Hebrew the promise of David: "Righteousness goeth before him and prepareth the way for him." Behind them marched a solid phalanx of police, followed by thick files of mourners, many of them with long gray beards. Then came the hearse, more police preceding the horses, and others marching alongside the hearse. The two hundred or more carriages followed and then more long files of mourners.

Up Madison Street from Montgomery we moved, to

Pike Street and across to Chrystie and down to Eldridge. Finally, to Norfolk. Wherever a synagogue stood, the procession halted before its open doors as the rabbi there said a prayer and uttered a benediction. From Norfolk Street the cortege would turn down Grand and head for the ferryhouse. By this time I had become one of the mourners, marching along with the old men and chanting with them some of the prayers that I had learned in Hebrew school. With some sort of boyish pride I noted that all the horsecars whose routes took them to the ferry were tied up, unable to move because of the crowds.

As we approached Sheriff Street, a premonition of trouble came over me. There at Sheriff and Grand Streets stood the R. Hoe and Company printing press factory. Everyone knew this to be one of the neighborhood hangouts of anti-Semites; the workers in the factory had repeatedly insulted passing Jews and on occasion had even assaulted them. Hadn't anyone, I wondered, given a thought to this when the route had been laid out? Wouldn't it have been better to have gone down Delancey and then to the ferry, instead of risking some mischance? If the thought had occurred to those in charge of the funeral arrangements, I suppose they dismissed it in the naïve belief that no one would be so cruel or disrespectful as to interfere with so solemn an occasion. Besides, police protection had been promised, and the police were on hand.

It was about three minutes before one o'clock when the hearse passed directly in front of the factory. Workers who had finished their lunch were at the windows looking down and, sure enough, they were laughing, making vulgar sounds, calling out obscenities. Many of the mourners, waving canes, demanded that respect be shown. Others screamed "Shame!" Still others, in Yiddish, resorted to their own obscenities which, to be sure, were not understood by the offenders. The cries for respect only drew louder laughter, more jeers. Then from out of one of the windows on the third floor came hurtling what Mr. Hoe, Sr., later said had been some cotton waste. Whatever it was, it hit the hearse and fell off. Those in the carriages had not seen this outrage, and along with the hearse, the carriages moved down the street to the ferry.

But those of us who had witnessed the blasphemous act erupted into fury. Shouting as loud as we could, we demanded that such actions cease. In reply we were showered with nuts, bolts, bundles of paper saturated in oil, small blocks of wood, and other missiles. We became an uncontrollable mob, picking up and hurling back these objects. Some of the mourners tried to rush the doors of the factory, but in vain. Meanwhile, buckets of water were being poured from the windows. Riot police appeared, and there was not any question in their minds as to who the culprits were. They slashed at us this way and that with their clubs, shouting and wading through the milling mourners, hitting in every direction with neither reason nor restraint. One old man cried out more in anguish than in anger, "Is this Russia?"

We fought back as best we could, not so much against the police as against those hated Hoe employees. Someone in the hysterical mob yelled, "Let's get bricks," and many of us knew what he meant. We ran crazily to Delancey Street where the foundations for the Williamsburg Bridge were being set. Women filled their aprons and hurried back to the men. I grabbed as many of the bricks as I could carry and ran back to the fight. When I had unloaded, I returned for more. I don't know how many trips I made.

Meanwhile, the men in the factory had taken fire extinguishing hoses from the walls and were playing streams of water on the crowds continuing the fray. The police were directing the aiming of the hoses. It was several hours before a semblance of peace was restored to the area, though crowds still hung on several blocks away threatening to get revenge when quitting time came. The police took care of this contingency by keeping the employees in the factory for some time after hours, until they felt the danger had passed, then marching them out single file and escorting them well beyond our range.

How many Jews were hurt that day, I do not know. There were newspaper accounts of fractured skulls inflicted by the police; there were mass meetings of protest against police brutality; an investigation was ordered. I derived what pleasure I could, and it was not trifling, from the condition of the Hoe factory. It looked as if it had been struck by a cyclone. In the front of the building there was hardly an unbroken window below the fourth floor. We heard that desks, chairs and other furniture were smashed, that everything was drenched with water as a result of the fire hoses. R. Hoe and Company had to shut down for repairs.

This was our victory.

I walked the streets for days afterward with a new sense of pride and dignity. We had stood up and fought, and I had avenged many wounds—most of all, the hurt my father had suffered at the hands of the ignorant and bigoted.

Whether the Hoe employees learned their lesson, I do not know. Nor do I know whether or not there were further incidents or insults in the vicinity of the factory in later years, after the months of interrogation and the many outcries in the press following the riot. I do not know because that, as it turned out, was our last summer on the Lower East Side.

3

To the Promised Land

ONE DAY, shortly after the riot, Cliff came home and announced, "We're getting out of this dump. We're moving uptown. I've rented an apartment on 106th Street near Fifth Avenue." What had happened was simple, Cliff said. "I've got a job with the Imperial Burlesque Show—a good job. I'm going to be one of the more important comedians in the company." Then, as if anticipating my mother's question, he said in Yiddish, "Don't worry, Mama. We'll be able to pay the rent."

He paused, and then, exercising the restraint I was to learn marked the good actor, he said, "I'm going to get seventy-five dollars a week."

I think I let out some sort of shriek, in astonishment as well as admiration. My mother, her eyes still conveying disbelief, said nothing. My father sat at the table with his lower jaw slightly agape. He tried to say something but couldn't. Cliff started to laugh. "Now come on," he said. "This is good news. There is no reason for you two to sit there like that."

What thoughts coursed through my parents' minds, we never knew. But I think their silence was not altogether that of astonishment. What Cliff was calling them to was a new world, a world perhaps somewhat akin to the one of which they had dreamed when they left their native land, a world that now, after years of drudgery, they probably were not sure they could cope with. And yet I do not remember either of them objecting. I think they understood that Cliff had confronted them with the inevitable, that the time really had come to move on.

How Cliff ever got into the theatre has remained one of the family mysteries, not because Cliff didn't tell, but because oddly enough I do not recall ever asking. When he was about twelve or thirteen, shortly after I was born, it became necessary for Cliff to leave school and go to work to help the family finances. My sister Ida remembers a time when Cliff sold zithers. This pursuit may have turned him in the direction of the stage. In any case, Cliff somehow began entertaining at socials on the Lower East Side and eventually in some of the larger saloons. His bent evidently was comedy, and he did imitations of other comedians.

At first it was not easy for him at home when he disclosed his intention of making his living on the stage. My pious parents were shocked. My father, Cliff said later, bellowed as he had never been heard to bellow before, pleaded, threatened, and in quieter moments even tried the powers of reason. But Cliff had his way—it was hard to fight indefinitely someone who was helping to stock the cupboard. Cliff's ultimate success soothed my parents so that when Dave and I set out in show business we met fewer hurdles.

I must have been about seven when, after listening to Cliff telling my sisters and brother about his experiences as an entertainer, I discovered that by loitering around the swinging doors of the Atlantic Gardens, I could see and hear some of the show going on inside, a sort of first taste of what Cliff was talking about.

The Atlantic Gardens, one of the most famous of the early Bowery beer halls, was next to the old Bowery Theatre. It provided seats for more than a thousand customers and once was a most respectable place to which men and women brought their families. Later it became a hangout for the lower elements of society. The Atlantic Gardens of my time provided its beer-drinking clientele with a typical honky-tonk type of show. The dancing girls with their short skirts intrigued me, along with their high-buttoned shoes and youthful spirits. In between getting chased by the doorman, I also loved listening to the singers.

I never saw Cliff perform at the Atlantic Gardens or at the Sans Souci, another well-patronized beer hall. But his accounts of the lights, the gaiety, the dancing; his descriptions of the thugs and gangsters who had begun to make these spots their headquarters, transformed them into places more alluring to me than all the gold in some exotic El Dorado.

I was nine years old when Cliff joined the famous Al Reeves "Big Beauty" show and began earning the munificent sum of forty dollars a week. I use the word munificent advisedly, because at the turn of the century forty dollars went far, indeed. Cliff was the company's Dutch comedian when the troupe took up its stand at Miner's Bowery. After I had made life as miserable as I could for him, pestering, whining, nagging and going through all the other acts that a nine-year-old employs to get his way, Cliff finally consented to take me to a Saturday matinee, my initiation into the theatre.

Although there were a variety of burlesque shows at

the time, some friskier and more risqué than others, many, including the Reeves show, were regarded as "family entertainments"—"clean" shows in which vulgarity was kept to a minimum and remained strictly within bounds. To these, even respectable women went on Saturday afternoons. Actually, most of the fun was provided by the comics doing pratfalls and getting off *double-entendre* quips at which not even a sixteen-year-old would blush today.

When Cliff agreed to take me, I could hardly wait. As I jogged along beside him on the way to the theatre, my clammy hand clasped by his, there was no end to the questions I asked. I remember Cliff explaining that in the first half of the show I would see an act in which he played the Dutch comedian part, and in the second half I would see different fellows performing their specialties. Cliff said that in his half he would deliver a funny speech.

I was to have other thrills in the theatre in the years to come, but I believe I can safely say that none had the intensity of this "first time." To me, that afternoon, Miner's Bowery was a cathedral of art, a mysterious haven of enchantment. Even now, as I write, I cannot bring myself to admit that the girls I beheld on the stage in their then-daring tights were not queens of beauty. Yes, they were heavy—their thighs were heavy, their calves and arms were heavy, and their bosoms decidedly more ample than any possessed by certain Hollywood stars and so much admired today. But these girls were shapely, and that afternoon, and for a long time afterward, they were visions of femininity for me—gay, sprightly, buoyant, full of grace and delight.

The acrobatic team of Mazuz and Mazette had me at the edge of my seat. Incredibly wonderful they were, defying all the laws of gravity with their feats. When Charles Hoey and Harry Lee came on as the show's two Hebrew comedians, I could barely keep from falling into the aisle. Then there was Al Reeves himself, the grandest man I had ever seen. He could have modeled for the Greek Apollo. He was tall, statuesque, powerful. His clothes were sporty and he wore a large yellow diamond. Sapphires took the place of buttons on his shirt and sapphires were his cuff links, too. He told stories, did some dance steps, and played a banjo studded with diamonds.

And then, of course, there was Cliff. He appeared during the olio—that midway section of the old burlesque show devoted to variety acts. He came out in a pair of excessively baggy trousers and an ill-fitting frock coat, and was billed as a German politician. Cliff waved his arms and got all excited as he dissertated on various topics of the day, mangling the English language in the process. Everyone roared. I had all I could do to restrain myself from getting up before that motley assembly and announcing, "That's my brother!"

It was a period when unionism was making itself felt in the country. I remember Cliff beginning very solemnly, "Mine dear friends und peoble voikers. It behoofes me pleasure much to kum before youse," and getting himself worked up over the possibilities of unionism. "Imagine, mine friends," he was saying, "if dis union business keeps on, ve are going to haf a union for wives. Just imagine a union for wives—der wives are called oud on shtrike und scabs takes der places. . . ." And so it went, the audience eating it up and howling.

From that Saturday on, I was a willing captive of the theatre. I had no specific ambition, no creative inclination of any sort, no wish to act. But no one ever formed a more enthusiastic audience. I lived from Saturday to Saturday, waiting for either Cliff or one of my sisters to take me to a show. I had no particular taste or preference. What mattered was that I be seated along with a thousand other persons in front of a curtain which, when it rose, rose on a world of music and laughter, the world of happy camaraderie that existed in those days between performers and audience.

I would meet whichever sister had agreed to take me to the theatre, and together we would head for one of the playhouses on the Bowery or on Fourteenth Street. I discovered on Fourteenth Street Tony Pastor's, the Academy of Music, Keith's Union Square and Dewey's. I mixed vaudeville with burlesque, got to know the routines of many of the stellar acts of the day—the comedians, the singers, the monologists. I thrilled to the skills of the "dumb acts"—the acrobats, the jugglers, the magicians. These performers were my heroes and heroines, who made Saturday a time of anticipation and pleasure.

If my sisters did not take me, I tried to get someone on line to buy my ticket for me, since at Pastor's, for instance, you could not enter without a guardian if you were under sixteen. Once my brother Dave and I hiked two and a half miles to Fourteenth Street to see a blackface team called Herbert and Willing. Then, by one of those benighted quirks, we could find no one willing to be our "guardian." Dave and I cried all the way back to Lewis Street. Indeed, the theatre could lift the spirits, but it could also make you cry—a lesson I was to learn again much later when I challenged its citadel, discovered its caprices and its foibles, won its favors and its smiles.

It was not long before the news that we were moving spread all over Lewis Street. Those with good hearts came to offer their congratulations and good wishes. Others either stayed away or said nothing. The congratulations and good wishes we accepted as gracefully as we could, although I cannot deny that there were instances when Dave and I did not refrain from crowing a little to some certain friends. After all, our brother was a star—that's what we said he was even if it was not exactly so—a star in a big burlesque show. We did not realize that as far as some of our neighbors were concerned this was more a status of degradation than of honor.

The weeks leading up to our exodus were ones full of twelve- and fourteen-hour days of hustle and bustle. Mary, Sarah, Dora and Fanny, who by this time had married, returned to Lewis Street to help my mother get ready. New furniture had to be purchased to replace the battered, broken-down pieces that had served through the sterner days on Goerck Street and on Cannon Street. Cliff said he wanted to make things as comfortable as possible. He also wanted to be able to bring his friends home without feeling embarrassed. He instructed my sisters to exercise the utmost caution in helping my mother select furniture—the place, he said, must have taste and quality.

My father continued in the sweatshop, though Cliff had told him it was no longer necessary, that certainly after we moved uptown he would stop working. My father offered no opposition to the idea of retirement, but I think that as long as we still lived on Lewis Street he knew he would feel uncomfortable, suffer some sense of guilt, if he did not arise each morning and set forth for his daily task of pressing pants. In fact, after we did move uptown, my father, haunted by some quirk of conscience, insisted that Dave, Cliff and I could not have our suits pressed by anyone but himself. I still have a letter written from Toronto in 1912 that reads: "My dear folks: Enclosed please find $16. Five keep and eleven bank. I sent home my tuxedo. Tell Papa to press it up for me. Your son, Max."

The night before the big day was a long one, given over to the tedious chore of packing the dishes. Neighbors rang the bell to say final good-byes, took our address and promised that when they were in the vicinity they would drop in to say hello—an unlikely prospect, to be sure, and I think they knew it as well as we. But it was a necessary ritual and, at the moment of utterance, had a certain sincerity of intention.

The van arrived early next morning, and the men, moving upstairs and down with antlike studiousness, soon had snugly loaded our possessions. We all climbed aboard—my mother, father, Ida, Cliff, Dave and I. The driver picked up the reins, gave the signal, and the horses stepped forward. I sat in the back with Dave and watched the familiar sights disappear as we moved west on Delancey Street: Itzig's grocery store, the corner candy store, Allen Street, where I knew somewhat dimly that girls entertained men for fifty cents.

Dave did not say much; he was not one to air his feelings. A somewhat moody boy, he was to grow into a reticent man who preferred to drink alone at a bar, to keep his distance from others. If I did not know what was going on in Dave's mind this particular morning of our leave-taking, I certainly knew what was racing through mine. On the one hand, I could barely contain my excitement, and on the other, I trembled with anxieties and misgivings. How, I wondered, would I do in the new school? What would the teachers be like? What sort of friends would I find up there in that new world? What would Central Park be like? Cliff had said we would be nearby. Would it be anything like the park down by the East River where one day a stranger gathered a bunch of us kids and began instructing us in the techniques of picking pockets?

The van turned north on the Bowery, moved passed that venerable pile of reddish stone called Cooper Union. Many years later, after I had become one of Broadway's senior producers and had just presented *The Solid Gold Cadillac*, I was to visit this place and speak about the problems of the American theatre. Over to Third Avenue we went, and thence across Twenty-sixth Street to Madison Avenue. There stood the original Madison Square Garden, designed by Stanford White, a magnificent arena that everyone thought would last as long as the Colosseum in Rome, and which, instead, went the way of so many lovely buildings in a city that never is finished. Where it stood, there now stands the massive New York Life Insurance Company.

Up Madison Avenue we went, and all I could do was gape and gawk in awe. This was, I soon learned, the Park Avenue of its day. Residential palaces lined both sides of the street, and I came near falling off the van when we passed the Italian Renaissance mansion built by Henry Villard and now shared one-third by Random House and two-thirds by the Catholic Archdiocese. Someday, I resolved, I would live on this part of Madison.

The Madison near which we were to live was not as ornate. But the buildings were impressive enough, and the quality of the neighborhood was solid middle class. Dave and I looked around when we pulled up at 21 East 106th Street, and I think we both had the same thought: We were out of our depth, we kids from the tenements. This place was too tony for us, too hifalutin. Cliff had no right bringing us to this place.

Again, Dave kept his counsel. But when I suggested that we run upstairs to see the bathroom, he quickly agreed. Cliff had told us about the bathroom, and throughout all the long waiting for this day the bathroom loomed as the luxury of luxuries. I had up until now bathed either in the kitchen washtub or at the community bathhouse on Rivington Street.

We scurried upstairs with the moving men, almost tripping one of them. Through the door of the apartment we plunged and into the bathroom. I stopped short, felt my stomach sink and tears well up in my eyes. Somehow in the fantasy world of this apartment, the fantasy world that I had been creating, I had thought that a bathtub was a place where you could take a swim.

When Cliff appeared and heard about the wreckage of my dream, he did not laugh at my tears, nor did he berate me for lack of appreciation. He understood. He put his arms around my shoulder and said soothingly, "Everything's going to be fine. You just have patience. Now, if you'll pull yourself together, I'll take you to the matinee on Saturday." That was Cliff.

The first time he went on the road, even after those big arguments with my father and mother, he bought my father a beautiful gold watch, something Heschel Salpeter had long ago given up hope of ever owning. For my mother there was a set of earrings. Cliff found it impossible to refuse a request for a loan. Even chorus girls in financial difficulties went to him, knowing there would be no strings attached. I remember walking with him one day on Cannon Street, not long after he had joined the Al Reeves show. Money no longer was as tight for him as it had been. Before us we saw an old woman sobbing, her furniture being piled on the street. Cliff spoke to her. She said she was being dispossessed because she was unable to pay her month's rent. Cliff went to the landlord, paid the rent, and had the janitor cart the few belongings back into the house.

Not many days pass that I do not think of Cliff or mention him during some conversation. In my office, on the wall opposite my desk, hangs a large, fading portrait of Cliff in one of his characteristic poses as a comedian. At home on an end table in our living room there is another photograph, a smaller one taken a little later and in a more informal style. He has been my inspiration through the years, my beacon in triumph and defeat.

Cliff's star rose steadily during his engagement with the Imperial Burlesque Show, his act became more polished, he seemed to acquire greater skill in the delivery of his material. The audience's laughter was louder. The time had come for him to consider making the next step in his career—testing himself in vaudeville.

4

⚜︎

The Two-a-Day

VAUDEVILLE! How easy to become sentimental over it—a form of theatre that bloomed and faded in the span of half a century. Once it was every man's entertainment. Once it tickled the funnybone of millions—and plucked a little at the heartstrings with songs of home and mother.

Not that vaudeville has ceased to exist. In diluted, wraithlike form it still persists in television, night clubs and some of the larger movie palaces like the Radio City Music Hall.

The vaudeville I mourn achieved its magnificence in its own special theatres across the country—intimate little theatres in which you could almost reach across the footlights and touch your own very special performer, see every facial expression, hear every word; this vaudeville needed no special adornments to entice customers into its theatres, its banners waved proudly and its people were like no other in show business.

That the spirit of vaudeville still exists cannot, of course, be gainsaid. The late Joe Laurie, Jr., beloved vaudevillian and erstwhile columnist for *Variety*, the "Bible of Show Business," correctly predicted that the spirit of vaudeville would endure "as long as there are ambitious kids jigging on cellar doors, doing acrobatics in barns, juggling apples, playing instruments in school bands, putting on Dad's and Mom's clothes and 'playing theatre' and 'telling jokes.' "

But the big-time vaudeville that Joe Laurie, I and others loved is dead, and more's the pity.

I do not think there was ever a group of entertainers who tried so hard to please audiences as did those bygone heroes of show business. Nor were there ever audiences more generous with their applause and their laughter than those that streamed into the vaudeville houses during the heyday of the two-a-day. They were critical, and they had a right to be, as paying customers. But they were more often than not friendly, too. They applauded frequently, though not overzealously, even when they had not been thrilled or amused especially, but because they may have sympathized with the fellow "up there" who was trying to make a living.

They were friendly and their good fellowship created a rapport between the audience and the performers. They were inquisitive. They took a special delight in having an actor step out of character and speak about the cramped conditions in his dressing room or hint at the size of his salary. Like sport fans, they loved to gossip about their favorites, speculate on how much so and so made, wonder whether the dance team was in love and what problems the headliner on the bill might be having with his family or wife. It was not unusual for total strangers in a vaudeville house to exchange conversation between the acts, to voice their approval and look for agreement from the man in the next seat.

The vaudeville audience did not look for moral or spiritual uplift. It distrusted what it considered hifalutin and highbrow, though in later years these "turns" did creep into the programs. What the vaudeville audience wanted most was good straight entertainment; it was not interested in following a story through an entire evening or watching the same group of characters through three or four acts—continual conversation had no guile for its constituents. They wanted variety, and vaudeville gave it to them—variety of which there was no apparent end.

Indeed, human ingenuity can be remarkable in its diversity. There were acrobats, bicycle acts, jugglers, rope acts, trampoline acts, bag-punching and club-swinging acts. There were also the song-and-dance men, the hoofers with their own variations—the soft shoe, the buck and wing, the clog and others. There were the sketches, the "singles" who came out and sang, the larger singing acts and the smaller ones. There were the mimics and the magicians, the family acts and the animal acts. The list is longer still. But of all, it was conceded that the most challenging act, the most difficult, was that of the monologist.

Dancers sing hymns to Pavlova's art; singers melt into helplessness at the recollection of Caruso. I go speechless as I see and hear again in memory the great monologists of vaudeville. It is not because of what they had to say, but the manner in which they said it. This was their genius, a capacity for setting up a situation from which there could be no release except through laughter: Joe Welch, wearing his misfit coat and pants, his hands almost lost within his sleeves, his derby flattened on his head and over his ears, coming on stage to the music of a funeral march; Joe moving ever so slowly to center stage, facing the audience and then waiting, perhaps thirty seconds, making sure that no one failed to comprehend his plight. Then, as he continued to look over the audience with his woebegone face, he would utter that hilarious line, "Maybe you think I'm heppy?"

There were many who imitated Joe, but none came close. Joe was what the trade calls an "original." The creation of the character itself was the product of a highly gifted comic sense; the timing was expert. This was technique and talent combined, a supreme achievement.

The monologist was the direct descendant of the court jester, his task to amuse or forfeit his head. Unlike the other acts, he did not need scenery, make-up or costume if he preferred not to use them. He could come on stage in his street clothes, perform his work, and walk off without so much as raising a bead of perspiration. What he needed was material fresh as the morning dew and the nerve to go out there alone and try to make people laugh, to persuade them to forget solemnity and sobriety, to cheer them with a chuckle and a guffaw. Yet woe to him who failed. Better for him that the floor opened beneath his feet, that he be swallowed alive, anonymous and forever forgotten.

Cliff became a vaudeville monologist shortly after his engagement with the Imperial Burlesque troupe. He was signed for the Keith Circuit, and making an alliance with Aaron Hoffman, one of the greatest vaudeville writers of the time, he soon became a major attraction.

Working with Cliff's German comic style as the foundation, Hoffman developed an act called "The German Senator," which started a new style of "topics of the day" talkers. Hoffman would take current news subjects, weave a monologue around them, kid them, satirize them, and come in at them from different directions.

President Taft, for example, like President Eisenhower years later, was the butt of many jabs because of his repeated trips away from the capital. Nor did the rotund

Taft's robust appetite go unnoticed. Audiences relished hearing Cliff complaining, "Ve readt in der babers dat Preserdunt Taft ist still eading his vay from town to town. He chust goes to Vashington to get a clean collar und a shave und den he ist off again vere somebody ist giving an eading party. Py chiminy, ift Taft didn't vant to go to Vashington und stay dere, vy didn't he say so in der first place?"

By 1913, when Mexico was experiencing what some other South and Central American countries are now going through, Cliff, at the peak of his career, could command the following headline in *The Los Angeles Examiner:*

CLIFF GORDON
SPEAKS!
*The German Senator in Vaudeville Has
Something to Say about Mexico*

The something, reprinted in part, was that President Wilson had come in just in time to deal with the trouble in Mexico.

Dat's a fine coundry for presiderunts to lif in. Dere's no danger of any presiderunt serfing dree derms down der. He's lucky ift dey led him serve von.

If dey don't vant to vait until der presiderunt's term expires, somebody dakes oudt a gun und the presiderunt expires.

In New York ven dey vant to get rid of a fellow, dey hire a couple of gun men.

But in Mexico ven dey vant to get rid of a man, all dey haf to do is elect him presiderunt.

Ven a fellow runs for presiderunt down der, he has to run twice—first for presiderunt und den for his life.

Ven der citizens go to bed at nighd, dey nefer know who's going to be presiderunt ven dey vake up.

But ve vouldn't care how many presiderunts dey had as long as American citizens ver safe.

Und dat's vere Taft came to the front. As soon as der Revolution started, Taft sent a message to the presiderunt of Mexico.

He said: "You must protect American citizens."

Vat chance has a Mexican presiderunt got to protect American citizens ven he can't efen protect himself?

Some beople thought ve ought to send down a half a dozen varships righdt avay.

Dat's all very nice, but efery time a varship mofes, it costs a couple of hundred thousand dollars.

Und beliefe me, ve didn't haf to send down any varships. All ve vould haf to do vould haf been to send a couple of Third Avenue policemen down dere and dey vould haf cleaned up der whole coundry.

Der trouble vid Mexico ist dey've got the revolution habit.

Down dere efery morning after breakfast a couple of fellows get together und say, "Vell, boys, it's a nice day; let's haf a revolution."

Und by der time dey get der pistols loaded, the revolution is ofer und dey've got to start a new von. But dere's no question but vat Mexico's a great coundry. Und if dey efer get a real presiderunt, he'd only haf to do von ding to make Mexico a coundry to be proud of—und dat ist to chase all der Mexicans oudt.

Cliff never received a bad review.

One of the finest compliments he ever received was written by a critic who said that in his opinion, aside from Sir Harry Lauder, Cliff was the only monologist of the time who could get away with closing the bill, as he did on several occasions. Closing the bill on a vaudeville program was usually assigned to the "dumb acts" because, when the last act came on, many persons in the audience, anxious to beat the rush, began leaving their seats. But Cliff could hold them—that was his magic.

The fact is that it was Cliff's style, as much if not more than Hoffman's material, that gained him fame. Other stump speakers before him had talked on topics of the day. But none did it in Cliff's excited manner. It was not only what Cliff said that turned him into a hilarious comedian, but also the way he said it that not infrequently reduced many in his audience to hysterics, such incidents being faithfully reported by the reviewers.

Cliff represented the big belly laugh among monologists. He came out onto the stage in the same old getup in which I had first seen him perform, a getup calculated to tickle his listeners: the outsize, baggy black trousers; the long frock coat with ill-fitting sleeves; a dejected-looking vest; a wilted wing collar and a loosely-knotted bow tie. In the manner of the traditional orator, his left hand would be in his pocket, his right arm sometimes outstretched and furiously waving in signals of distress or rage. Sometimes that flailing arm would only be crooked at the elbow in those infrequent interludes of comparative calm. Cliff did not sing or dance or use any properties. All he did was talk. But how he could talk!

He would begin peacefully enough, his face a study in sobriety. Not a smile or even the suggestion of mirth could be detected in his countenance. As he warmed up, a certain agitation started creeping into his delivery, and the shouts of laughter from the audience actually seemed to embarrass and confuse him. The more excited he became, the higher his voice rose. The more serious he got, the more he mangled the language with his Teutonic accent and his effort to translate German idioms straight into English. He mixed up, in seeming innocence, the beginnings and endings of maxims so that they might emerge, for instance, as "a rolling stone is worth two in the bush."

The speech itself was a lesson in chaos, but to deliver it with such intensity and seriousness, to manage at the same time to make points of relevance to the day, this was the essence of Cliff's stardom.

5

∽∾⌢

Farewell Pencils, Farewell Books

ALTHOUGH Cliff kept his word and took me to the matinee to appease my disappointment over the bathtub, life did not improve for me on 106th Street—not right away.

For my father, it is true, the move brought fulfillment of those dreams he must have had when he left his shabby village overseas. He made no mystery of the pleasure he derived from being able to get up in the morning, have his breakfast, go downstairs to the nearby newsstand, purchase a Yiddish paper, and go to Central Park. He sat on a bench, reading and dozing the morning away. After lunch he took a walk or sat in the park again. The only times he picked up a pressing iron were when one of us needed his valet service. For my mother there was satisfaction in the spacious quarters, the knowledge that there was a place for everything.

I shared a room with Dave. Cliff had his own, Ida hers, and my parents another. There was a kitchen, a dining room, and what we then called a parlor. There was sunlight, and there was air, and we lived like kings—figuratively, of course. My mother still had no use for what she considered fancy frills. When Ida said one day, "Now that Cliff is making good money, don't you think you ought to get someone else to scrub the floors?" my mother's answer was, "Then what will *you* do?"

But for me the frustration presented by the bathtub had only been the beginning. The whole neighborhood made me uneasy. Everything and everyone seemed uncongenial. The kids were different from those with whom I had grown up on the Lower East Side. They were dressed better and they spoke better. I seemed totally out of place. Nor did Central Park win my confidence. I loved trees, grass and flowers. Nevertheless, even the new park seemed "fancy" compared to our old one where you could run around, make noise, and never have anyone stare at you as if you were some freak because you were enjoying yourself or being just plain exuberant.

I never told Cliff of these additional discomfitures. My sense of inadequacy, my feeling of being an alien in an alien land, happily did not last too long. Six months after our departure from the Lower East Side, Lewis Street had faded in memory, slowly but steadily, like an island seen from a vessel moving toward the opposite horizon. I learned that neat and fastidious people were not necessarily cranks and fusspots, that it was not the sign of a sissy to have clean fingernails and your hair combed, that it was not necessary to raise your voice to make yourself heard.

I made two other discoveries. One was a friend—fat, amiable Mr. Benjamin, who ran the grocery store on 106th Street and Lexington Avenue—and the other was the legitimate theatre in the form of *Way Down East*.

Mr. Benjamin loved the theatre almost as much as I did. When I was sent to make some purchases for my mother, he would tell me all about the show he had seen the week

before. On rainy days, when there were not many customers to wait on, he would go into considerable detail
about the plot and how good or awful the leading lady
had been. When Mr. Benjamin discovered that Cliff was
my brother, our bond was sealed. Sometimes he would
let his helper in the store take care of the customers while
he described for me the beauty of Lillian Russell, whom
he had heard at Tony Pastor's: "Such eyes," he would say.
"China blue and hair like gold, and the features—just perfect." Maxine Elliott was another actress who stirred his
imagination. He had seen her in *The Cowboy and the
Lady* and had never forgotten her mass of blue-black hair,
her large luminous eyes and statuesque beauty. To me,
Mr. Benjamin was both a friend and a fountain of my
favorite talk.

My initiation into the legitimate theatre I owed to my
sister Ida. Having heard much talk about *Way Down East,*
she was most anxious to see it. It was at the Academy of
Music on Fourteenth Street, and she took me with her one
Saturday afternoon.

I do not suppose that any audience could be made to
sit through a production of *Way Down East* today. I'm
sure I could not. By present-day standards the story was
as silly as the production was amateurish. But that afternoon another new realm of the theatre opened up for me.
Suddenly I found myself transplanted to rural New England, complete with snowstorm and everything else. These
were real people with real problems, and no one in the
theatre that matinee sympathized with them more than I.
There were four acts to the play, and when it was over,
I was reluctant to leave. I walked out in a semi-trance. My
face must have been flushed from the excitement because
Ida looked at me, touched her lips to my forehead, and
asked if I felt all right. I assured her I was fine, and we
took the trolley home.

I really *was* fine. What feverish symptoms I may have shown were due only to my having been terribly stimulated by the afternoon's experience.

Burlesque, vaudeville, the legitimate stage—it made no difference to me. They all added up to theatre, each in its own way a segment of make-believe, and yet, something more in sum: a way of life relieved of the monotony of most pursuits, filled with people who seemed just a little more exciting, a little more intriguing, a little more human, than the ordinary. What I could do in the theatre was not clear to me at that time. I still had no desire to act; the urge toward self-expression that drives many youngsters into the theatre had no wellsprings in me. Intuitively I must have known that there was no creative strain in me as there was in Cliff. Nor did I have the gift of mimicry. What I could—or would—do, I did not know. But of this much I was certain: There must be some place for me in show business.

Occasionally I spoke to Cliff about this determination. He would smile indulgently. "You've got plenty of time to think about your future," he would say. "First get finished with school. That's what's important."

"But, Cliff," I would offer weakly in rebuttal, "I'm fifteen. If I don't make plans now, when will I?"

"Just don't worry," Cliff would say. "You listen to me."

I listened but I resented just a little the advice he gave.

School was fine, to the extent that anything called school could be considered fine. I got used to P.S. 171 in much the same gradual way that I became used to the neighborhood, and I found that there was not really much difference between the school on 103rd Street and the old one on Lewis and Rivington. I settled down and, encouraged by several sympathetic teachers, did rather well in my studies. I was graduated with honor and some special distinction. My English teacher, noting that I was good at memorizing poems, which I delivered at top volume, recommended me to the school principal. Thus, I became one of the graduation's special attractions. I recited John Greenleaf Whittier's "Barbara Frietchie" with a zeal and fervor that won for me a gratifying thunder of applause. I can still recite "Barbara Frietchie" from beginning to end and get intensely choked up over those heroic lines.

But regardless of my scholastic achievements, the theatre encompassed my whole being. I lived it. I breathed it. Every spare chance I had was spent in some darkened playhouse, where I not only delighted in the entertainment but also developed standards of comparison. I got to know the routines and specialties of the different burlesque organizations; I saw and knew the work of every headliner in vaudeville. I fell in love, as did everyone else, with Fritzi Scheff in Victor Herbert's *Mlle. Modiste* when she sang "Kiss Me Again." I saw George M. Cohan for the first time in the musical *Little Johnny Jones,* which he had written and composed. To Cohan I succumbed like a contemporary bobby-soxer. I waited outside the stage door for a glimpse of him, and when he came out, he was wearing an ulster coat that made my eyes pop. I made up my mind that someday, when I was earning my own money, I would buy a coat exactly like that one—and I did.

On occasions when I ran out of my allowance and was reluctant to ask Cliff for an advance, I went up to the Polo Grounds and got a job at the Giants' games hawking score cards, turning the ticket stiles, or selling peanuts and popcorn. Turning stiles one day opened up to me a racket in full bloom. Every time the ticket taker had collected a fistful of tickets, a confederate would come along and take them back to the ticket seller, where they would be sold over again.

One day when my pockets were empty, Joe Welch was opening in *The Peddler*. Joe, as I have related before, was one of the greatest Hebrew comics, and I just had to see him in this show. I hurried to the Polo Grounds, where there was to be a double-header, and began working. As I ran up and down the aisles dispensing peanuts and pop-corn, the conviction grew on me that I could not wait until Saturday. I had to see Welch that afternoon. Minutes passed. The compulsion grew stronger until I did not feel I could stand it any longer. I had made enough money to buy a seat in the balcony. If I hurried, I could catch the show. I made sure the head boy was not watching, hid my basket in a corner in the rear of the stands, and took off. It was a dishonest thing to do, and I never dared go back to the Polo Grounds and ask for work again. I will not say that seeing Joe Welch was worth my tormented con-science, but I relate the story as another bit of evidence of the grip the theatre had on me.

I was sixteen and attending the old Townsend Harris High School when Cliff decided to widen his area of op-eration in the theatre. He formed a partnership with Bobby North, another fine vaudeville comic who had come out of burlesque. Their plan was to produce shows, starting first in burlesque, then moving on to regular Broadway shows. Their initial step was to gain an interest in the Behman Show, one of the higher-class burlesque companies on what was called the Columbia Circuit.

By the season of 1909–10 they were ready to branch out on their own. The first show they produced was *The Merry Whirl,* immediately hailed by reviewers as a su-perior example of burlesque production. In the prepara-tion of *The Merry Whirl,* and later *The Passing Parade* and *The World of Pleasure,* it was not unusual for Cliff and Bobby to seek my opinion. I had arrived at the point where my acumen in the judgment of sketches and other routines had gained some recognition. "Let's ask the kid," North would say, and I would reply in the jargon of the trade, criticizing situations, stage business and the like.

I was close to Cliff now, and frequently when he performed in New York and my school work was done, I would meet him after the show and come home with him. What I treasured especially about those meetings was stopping off at a delicatessen or restaurant and talking show business. Cliff would tell me how things had gone that night when he was "on," the curtain calls, the problems. Occasionally he would lecture me on taste in the theatre—he had no use for vulgarity on the stage or off, and the only times he became moody seemed to be when he had to battle Hoffman over breaches of taste. Every so often Hoffman would try to slip in a *double-entendre* or off-color quip, and when Cliff refused to tolerate it, there would be angry scenes in which Hoffman would threaten to quit. I have no idea whether or not this was Hoffman's way of seeking to maintain domination over Cliff. But I know these battles worried Cliff endlessly. In years to come I was to settle my own score with Hoffman.

Once in a while Cliff would treat me to a trip out of town over a weekend, when he was not too far from New York. Two incidents on such excursions I remember in particular, though neither involved the theatre. In Boston I slept in a hotel room for the first time. There, at the Langham, I learned that not everyone covered themselves with quilts or featherbeds when they went to sleep.

I had gone up to my room to prepare for bed. When I was ready, I began to search for either the quilt or featherbed, there being no evidence of either on the bed. At last I gave up in disgust and lay down. In a few minutes I began to feel cold. I went to the staircase.

"Where the hell are the quilts?" I called down the stairs. "I'm freezing up here!"

A bellhop came up, went to the bed, and pulled the blankets back. He showed me how to get between the sheets and pull the blankets over my body. I had never seen anything like this before.

In Philadelphia one of my childhood dreams was punctured. When I lived on the Lower East Side, there was a bakery next to Miner's Theatre on the Bowery. They used to have big coconut pies in the window, and many times I had all I could do to restrain myself from going in and trying to filch one. Many nights I dreamed of coconut pies, promising myself that someday I would buy all I could eat. As I grew older I forgot about the pies, but in Philadelphia that morning I suddenly thought of them. By the time I went down for breakfast, I had keyed myself to a high pitch of gustatory anticipation. When Cliff asked me what I wanted for breakfast, I said, "Coconut pie." There were no coconut pies, and the whole excursion soured.

How, during these years, I managed to hang on in high school remains a mystery. Townsend Harris High was designed for a pupil population that was brighter, more competitive, and more alert than that of a regular high school. The Townsend Harris program was conceived to meet the needs of its special student body, providing an accelerated study curriculum that made it possible to complete the normal four-year course in three. Many of the graduates entered the City College of New York, whose campus was shared at the time by Townsend Harris. It was Cliff's intent that I should go on to City College also. Deprived of his own schooling, he was obsessed with the conviction that it was essential for me to complete mine.

But in spite of Cliff's hopes for me, I knew that it was

foolish to continue. By the time I reached my third year—
which in Townsend Harris was actually my senior year—I
was having to force myself to attend classes. The pages
of *The New York Dramatic Mirror* and *The Clipper*, two
of *Variety*'s predecessors, were proving infinitely more intriguing to me than the complexities of algebraic equa-
tions or the interior structure of tulips.

I made several futile attempts to discuss my feelings
with Cliff and finally decided to disobey him, regardless
of the consequences. Someday he would understand; someday when I was a successful producer, he would offer his
forgiveness.

I wrote a letter to Jack Singer, manager of the Behman
Show. Singer had quarreled with Cliff and Bobby, and
their deal had been canceled. I figured that because of
the split Singer might be sympathetic to me if I told him
all about Cliff's opposition. Singer might wish to show up
Cliff in my eyes and prove to me how understanding he
really could be.

The stratagem worked. Or, at least, circumstances operated in my behalf. Singer wrote to say that his advance
man had quit. If I was serious about wanting to get into
show business, I could have the job. He explained that
while the Behman Show was in one city, it would be my
assignment to drum up business in the next city where
the show was booked. If this was acceptable, he would pay
me thirty-five dollars a week and send my train ticket.
But, he added, I must make up my mind immediately.
The show would be playing Columbus, Ohio, from January 16 through 19, go on to Wheeling, West Virginia, for
a stand, and then head for Pittsburgh for six days. Singer
recommended that I join the company in Pittsburgh,
where he would be able to give me my instructions in person. At the same time I would get a chance to see the
show, become acquainted with its special attractions, and

meet the principals in the company. Then, after a day or two, I would proceed ahead of the company to Buffalo, where the show was booked from January 31 through February 5.

If I accepted, I would not graduate with my class in June. This would add to Cliff's fury when he found out. I hesitated—but only briefly. I wrote to Singer to send me the ticket, cautioning him to mark the envelope personal. I did not mean to run away from home. But neither was I going to tell anyone until I had to.

The afternoon of my last Sunday in New York Cliff invited me to join him for a walk. This was not unusual, since we often walked together on Sunday afternoons. Our custom was to take a cab to Fifty-ninth Street and what is now called Columbus Circle. From there we strolled down Broadway, which, above Forty-seventh Street, was then a street in transition. There were still carriage factories and showrooms along the way, hotels and vacant lots, as well as some of the old buildings and cottages from the days when "The Greatest Street in the World" was only a country road.

As we crossed Forty-fifth Street and passed the New York Theatre, where Raymond Hitchcock was playing in Cohan's musical hit *The Man Who Owns Broadway,* Cliff said with a sort of chirp in his voice, "Well, Max, have you gotten over your yen to quit school?"

"No," I said, my heart jumping into my throat. "No, Cliff, I still think that makes the most sense."

Cliff's good humor drained instantaneously. I could see his lips tighten into a thin, straight line. Luckily, I was saved from the full impact of his irritation by the appearance of Hitchcock himself, walking up from Forty-fourth Street. We exchanged greetings and stopped in front of the old Criterion Theatre.

"Hitchie," Cliff began, "tell me what to do with this

kid. He wants to quit school and go into the theatre. Tell him he's wrong. He refuses to listen to me."

Hitchcock, who once had been a shoe salesman in Wanamaker's Department Store, began in his rasping voice: "Max, Cliff is right. An education is something no one ever is going to be able to take away from you."

I tried my arguments on Hitchcock, but they made no impression. The discussion went on for a while, with the familiar reiterations. As I look back now, it occurs to me that we must have been something of a picture—the three of us, two big stars of the theatre and me, trying to settle my future there on Broadway on a Sunday afternoon in January.

"Promise me," I heard Hitchcock saying, "that for my sake, if not for your own or Cliff's, you will continue with school. I know that when you have completed your education, Cliff will spare no effort to see that you get in right and will give you every opportunity to become a big man on Broadway. Now, promise."

"I promise," I lied, knowing that as soon as we got away from Hitchcock, I would have to tell Cliff everything —about the ticket and about my impending departure for Pittsburgh.

We said our good-byes and headed for home. As we neared the house (we had moved to the corner of 116th Street and Lenox Avenue, a very fancy apartment building with an elevator), I summoned my courage. I told Cliff what I was about to do. He did not interrupt as I explained my need for independence, my feeling that time was passing and I was standing still. When I had finished, expecting the worst, there again was that tight-lipped brother looking at me—this time, however, more in sadness than in defeat.

After what seemed like forever, he said, "O.K., if that's what you want, I'll take you to the train."

6

Three Squares and a Bluff

THE TRAIN TO PITTSBURGH was a sleeper, the first new experience of my new life. Two friendly traveling salesmen, having joked in the smoker about my upper berth being "in heaven," showed me how to climb into it. In heaven or not, it made little difference to me that night. I have made many journeys since. I have traveled over the face of the earth by plane and ship on missions of greater importance to my later career. Never has there been a journey surpassing this one, a trip so full of challenge and exhilaration.

I did not close my eyes all night.

I was not nervous, really. But I had absolutely no control over my imagination, now generating an assortment of diverse anticipations. Thoughts, ideas, memories tumbled over each other in disarray, none pausing long enough for elaboration: the girls I would meet, my future, my past, the diploma I would not get, Cliff, Raymond Hitchcock, my parents, my sisters, Jack Singer, the Behman Show, Pittsburgh, Buffalo, the lights of Broadway—

everything jumbled together like a pinwheel gone mad in the wind!

I have no graphic recollection of my arrival in Pittsburgh. That Monday, as far as I was concerned, Pittsburgh was nothing more than a geographic destination— its importance to the industrial strength of my country, its smokestacks and giant mills were of no significance to me. All I knew was that at 10 o'clock I would leave my hotel for the theatre and my appointment with Jack Singer.

The Academy of Music in Pittsburgh was already, in 1910, a somewhat dilapidated, dirty-reddish structure that proved no more attractive on the inside. I walked up the four steps to the box office and asked for Mr. Singer, whereupon I received some muttered instructions about going left and then right. As I turned to leave, I recognized Harry Williams, owner of the Imperial Burlesque troupe, with which Cliff had formerly played. Williams had become the owner of the Academy of Music. His familiar face and warm greeting were comforting. He listened with amusement and sympathy to my story and then took me to Singer, who sat encased in his chair behind an old desk. He was a fat, roly-poly man who, I learned later, could not tie his own shoelaces because of his girth. An assistant did it for him.

Singer must have been one of the men the burgeoning film industry copied when it began developing its stereotype of the old-time theatrical manager. A big, strong-smelling cigar gripped between his teeth, a derby on his head, his sleeves rolled up, Singer struck me as a gruff, gross sort of man, with whom someone as fastidious as Cliff would naturally have difficulty. Not necessarily over artistic taste, perhaps, but in clash of personality. I was not repelled at this first meeting, but I knew immediately that this was a man with whom my friendship could never be more than casual. If I had counted on Singer being a sort of guide and teacher, I knew now that I had better extinguish those thoughts.

Singer welcomed me offhandedly and asked whether Cliff was aware of what I had done, and where I was. I nodded.

"Well," he said, "there isn't any time to lose. We're opening here today, you know, so I have a lot to do. Later in the day, before the matinee, I will introduce you to the actors. Now, like I said, tomorrow or the day after, you will go on to Buffalo. What I want you to do there is make sure that our billboards are all covered and that our cards are in all the windows around town. You'll take some blotters with you also, which I want you to distribute in hotels. You'll learn the ropes as you go along. You must know something from being around with Cliff, don't you?"

"I guess so," I said with an almost condescending smile.

"Well," Singer said, "that's fine. Now, there is one other thing you have to do, and that is get out there on the stage between the acts and describe our show so that the customers will want to see it. We've got a great show as you'll see this afternoon. Here, take a look at the program."

I knew that Singer was not just doing a selling job on me. The Behman Show always had high standards, and whenever it came to New York, it did well. The program Singer handed me indicated that the show was called *Palm Beach,* a two-act musical comedy with book and lyrics by Ballard MacDonald and chatter by Lon Hascall, who was also the company straight man.

One item that attracted my attention was the poem just beneath the title:

> The Behman Show is here again
> In up-to-date burlesque.
> With airships, yachts and music sweet
> And scenery picturesque.
>
> Though others try and try and try,
> There's one thing we all know.
> The best they do is imitate
> The famous BEHMAN SHOW.

At the bottom of the page was an explanatory note about the reference to airships in the poem. It read:

IMPORTANT—The audience is requested to remain until the fall of the curtain on the first act as the Great Aeroplane flies through the auditorium just before the curtain falls. This is without doubt the greatest stage effect in Modern Theatricals.

Befitting its Palm Beach setting, the show was nicely costumed. Singer was no skinflint. He had been one of the first managers in burlesque who did not charge his girls for their shoes and stockings. Until about 1905 it had been customary for them to pay for these items out of weekly salaries that ranged from twelve to fifteen dollars.

I can still see the look of disbelief on old Mr. White's face when I walked into his office in the Garden Theatre in Buffalo that morning and introduced myself as Jack Singer's emissary. Mr. White, manager of the Garden, was an old-school gentleman with a gentle manner. I can still hear him saying in a slightly raised, incredulous voice, "Aren't you pretty young to be an advance man? Oh, you're Cliff Gordon's kid brother. Well, I hope you know what the duties of an advance man are."

"I think I do," I said. "It's true I don't really have much experience, but Mr. Singer gave me instructions in Pittsburgh."

"Well," Mr. White said, "did he tell you what I always

Vandamm

A portrait of my mother at eighty.

During my days as advance man for a burlesque show, I sent home this letter—evidence of both my thrift and my sense of responsibility toward my parents.

At thirty-five I had taken over the management of the Orpheum Circuit's New York office, and was shortly to embark on my career as Broadway producer.

Apeda

At eighteen Millie was as lovely as a rosebud. Under the name of Raye Dean she was appearing at the time in a vaudeville act.

Moody

Millie seemed to be or threshold of an exci career in films when agreed to marry me. of the films in which appeared was MADON AND MEN, in 1917.

My brother Cliff in a characteristic stance as The German Senator, the impersonation that won him fame and fortune on the vaudeville circuit.

Scenes from *THREE'S A CROWD* (1930), my first solo venture as a producer: the inimitable Fred Allen as he appeared in one of his famous monologues; Libby Holman, never forgotten for what she did with two songs in this show—"Something to Remember You By" and "Body and Soul"; and Tamara Geva surprising Clifton Webb in a risqué bathroom scene.

...ed and Adele Astaire as they appeared in "Hoops," a delightful song-and-dance routine ...vised for **THE BAND WAGON**, my second Broadway revue (right).

...eorges Metaxa and Bettina Hall in a moment from **THE CAT AND THE FIDDLE**, a romantic ...usical comedy with score by Jerome Kern and book and lyrics by Otto Harbach (left).

...avorting on the couch are Noël Coward, Alfred Lunt and Lynn Fontanne in Noël's amoral ...medy **DESIGN FOR LIVING**, which I presented in January 1933. It became the season's out-...anding commercial success.

★ The 1933–34 season, which proved to be the "season of the great rally" from the Depression's depths, also turned into a bonanza for me, with four hits running simultaneously. The first to open was Clare Kummer's *HER MASTER'S VOICE*, in which Roland Young and Laura Hope Crews contributed to the funmaking. Below at right: Bob Hope and Lyda Roberti in a scene from the Jerome Kern — Otto Harbach musical *ROBERTA*, Bob's Broadway debut.

Guide to the
HITS OF THE SEASON *produced by* MAX GORDON

The Musical Hit! ★ ROBERTA

The Comedy Hit! ★ HER MASTER'S VOICE

The Dramatic Hit! ★ THE SHINING HOUR

The Hit of Hits! ★ DODSWORTH

White Studio

Raymond Massey and Gladys Cooper as they appeared in *THE SHINING HOUR*, a dramatic love story by Keith Winter. Below: a scene from *DODSWORTH*, with Walter Huston in the title role and Fay Bainter as Mrs. Dodsworth. Sidney Howard made the stage adaptation from the Sinclair Lewis novel ★

This colorful and spectacular scene is, of course, from **THE GREAT WALTZ**. As Guy Robertson, playing Johann Strauss, the younger, conducts "On The Beautiful Blue Danube," the orchestra is lifted from the pit and moved backward to the rear of the stage. In the foreground the elder Strauss (H. Reeves-Smith) advances to the platform.

Ruth Gordon, as Mattie, and Raymond Massey, in the title role, meet for the first time in *ETHAN FROME*, based on Edith Wharton's tragic novel. Miss Gordon gave one of her greatest performances in this play.

Vandamm

Henry Fonda and June Walker in *THE FARMER TAKES A WIFE*, adapted by Frank B. Elser and Marc Connelly from Walter D. Edmonds' novel *ROME HAUL*.

The day after the day after Christmas, 1936, Broadway rocked with the news that a savagely satirical play about the gentle sex had come to town. It was *THE WOMEN*, by Clare Boothe Luce. Betty Lawford, playing the husband-snatcher, is shown here relaxing amid soap bubbles and foam.

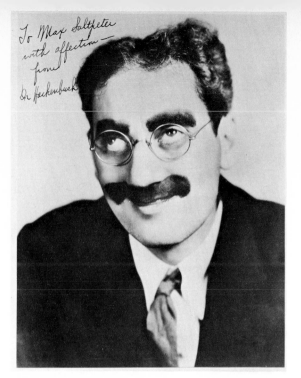

To Max Saltpeter
with affection —
from
Dr Hackenbush

This man needs no introduction. He was as mad then
as he is now, and he has always been one of my dearest friends. Seated at the piano, another zany member of the Marx family and long-time friend.

To Max
From Harpo.

Wit has been one of Noël Coward's many gifts. This inscription, not unlike an epitaph, has always amused visitors to my office.

The pixieish Jerome Kern chose to be original. Instead of autographing a photo, he sent a blank frame with inscription.

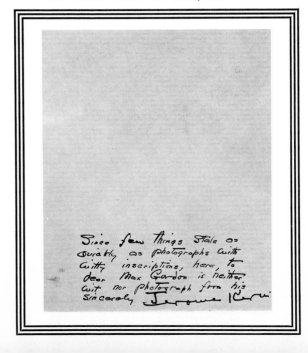

Although Bernard Baruch has preferred to concentrate his genius on world affairs, he occasionally slips away for a day at the races. Here we are doping the ponies at Saratoga one recent August.

In the summer of 1958 the St. Louis Municipal Opera Company revived *ROBERTA*, with Bob Hope in his original role, the one for which I spotted him while attending a show at the old Palace.

Bruce MacFarlane, Jo Ann Sayers (Eileen), Richard Quine and Shirley Booth (older sister Ruth) in the Joseph Fields–Jerome Chodorov comedy *MY SISTER EILEEN*, which lasted 865 performances on Broadway. Below: another great hit by Fields and Chodorov, *JUNIOR MISS*, which included among its players Paula Laurence, Patricia Peardon in the central role, and Alexander Kirkland.

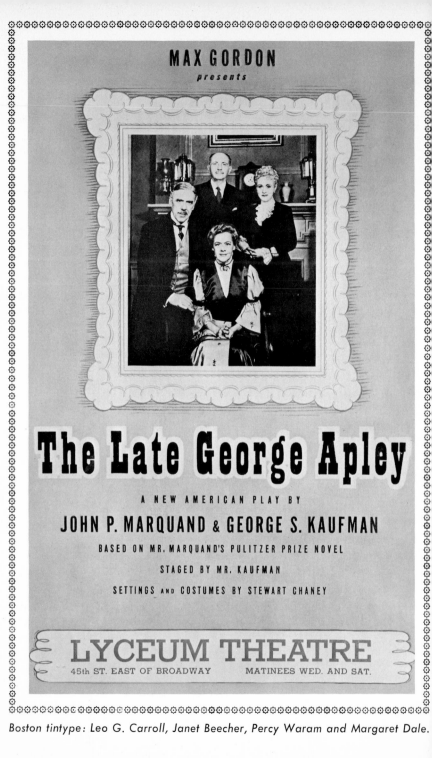

MAX GORDON

presents

The Late George Apley

A NEW AMERICAN PLAY BY

JOHN P. MARQUAND & GEORGE S. KAUFMAN

BASED ON MR. MARQUAND'S PULITZER PRIZE NOVEL

STAGED BY MR. KAUFMAN

SETTINGS AND COSTUMES BY STEWART CHANEY

LYCEUM THEATRE

45th ST. EAST OF BROADWAY   MATINEES WED. AND SAT.

Boston tintype: Leo G. Carroll, Janet Beecher, Percy Waram and Margaret Dale.

The greatest of them all, Garson Kanin's *BORN YESTERDAY*, brought laughter to Broadway through 1,642 performances, plus glory and gold to Paul Douglas, who played Harry Brock (a junk tycoon), and Judy Holliday, his not-so-dumb mistress.

Josephine Hull, one of the finest character actresses of the postwar period, and Loring Smith in a scene from *THE SOLID GOLD CADILLAC*.

Millie and I attend a recent Broadway première.

tell advance men—that it is their duty to incite the interest of the public in the show they represent?"

I liked the word incite. It was the heart and soul of the matter. I made up my mind to show Mr. White that I understood very well the duty to incite. I had worked up a brief speech about my show, and now I did a little revising to make it even more inciting. I was going to tell that audience all about the beautiful costumes in the Behman Show, about those forty lovely girls, about the show's mechanical marvels, including that bit about the aeroplane flying through the auditorium at the end of act one.

I started smoothly enough. "Ladies and gentlemen," I began, though I question how many ladies were in the theatre that afternoon; indeed, whether it was correct to call those who were, ladies in the true meaning of the word. "Ladies and gentlemen, I am here to tell you about next week's attraction, the great Behman Show, which is without a doubt one of the . . ." I got no further. A large mushy banana came hurtling from the gallery, catching me square in the face. The impact stung a little, and I was just a little shocked. What hurt especially was the humiliation and the laughter. But I refused to panic. Standing my ground, I wiped the banana from my face, smiled weakly, and began again. Whether the bum in the gallery had run out of bananas, or whether the audience had decided in my favor because I had the gumption to stand my ground, I do not know. I do know that once I started again, I was permitted to finish.

Mr. White was sufficiently impressed to congratulate me when I came off stage, and the following day the reviews spoke of how a green stripling had retained his dignity in the face of a hoodlum's attack. In fact, Mr. White informed me later, there was an increase in business, incited no doubt by interest in what sort of fellow I was.

In Buffalo I had another initiation that has stood me in good stead ever since. The brother of the comic in the show at the Garden asked me to cash a ten-dollar check for him. I did, only to discover subsequently that the check was without funds. I never seemed to catch up with the culprit, but when I did complain to his brother, I was told, "Sorry, fella. I had nothing to do with it. There's nothing I can do about it."

That taught me a lesson about cashing checks. After that when someone approached me in a similar vein, I refused. "Look," I would say, "if you want a loan of ten, say so. Pay me when you can, and if you can't, forget it. I'm through with checks."

I also learned about "leg-pulling," an earlier and perhaps cruder version of what was later called gold-digging. It was not unusual for poorly paid girls in a burlesque company, regardless of how thriftily they lived, to find themselves low in funds or in debt by the time a tour was half over. To forestall such emergencies, or to take care of them when they occurred, the girls made dates with stage-door Johnnies and teased gifts or money from them. The gifts sometimes were returned to a store for cash. Nor was there always a *quid pro quo*. Many of the older stage-door Johnnies simply liked to take the girls out. They took them to dinner, bought them presents, even gave them money in return for their company.

Some girls worked as a team. One made a date for dinner, and then the other showed up wearing what, by pre-arrangement, was to be regarded as a new hat. The first one would admire it extravagantly. Then she would try it on and eagerly ask how much it cost. She would ask her escort how he thought she looked in the hat, and when he admired her in it, she would coyly suggest that he buy it for her. Few refused, and the girls split the haul. Later, when salaries improved, these more flagrant practices diminished, though I doubt that they ever disappeared entirely.

Morality among the girls was then as it always has been, a personal matter. Some were easy with their favors, others were not. Some traveled with their mothers. Some went to church and sent money to their families from their pay envelopes. They were worldly. They swore. They talked freely with men. They fought their own battles and met the men on equal footing. Yet, there was decorum backstage and a certain modesty. A man generally did not walk into a woman's dressing room without first knocking on the door and asking, "Are you decent?"

Some companies were stricter than others, having contracts requiring members of the troupe to behave properly in hotels and on trains. There were managers who waited up at night checking the arrival of each girl in their show. Al Reeves maintained that he tolerated no nonsense from his girls. If a girl failed to show up for a rehearsal without his knowing why, he would fire her. Occasionally, he himself would take the girls out for a party at some beer garden. On taking them home he would say, "Remember, we have a matinee tomorrow. If you drank more than I saw you drink, or have a headache, don't let that keep you away from the theatre without letting me know." Girls who violated this admonition found themselves dismissed.

On the other hand, unhappily, there were managers who did not object to company members of opposite sexes doubling up on the road. There were managers who, when they found their troupe strapped for funds, thought nothing of passing their own girls along to fellows in town who had the resources to get the company to the next booking.

Fanny Brice once said that she never learned anything about life in burlesque, that most of the girls were virgins and did not go out on dates. She said that they might be ignorant, common and untrained, but they were finer in principle than many stage people she knew during her days on Broadway. Well, it all depended on where you sat, or worked. Certainly it was an odd, exotic world that included among its paradoxes such as the cultivated Thomas W. Dinkins, under five feet tall, owner of both the burlesque show "Dinkins' Utopians" and the dilapidated Bon Ton Theatre, a burlesque house. He often quoted Byron, Shelley and Keats, and urged me not to neglect my own reading.

To me, in the flush of youth, it all added up to life.

I don't think Jack Singer ever had a more conscientious advance man. I went out with the bill posters to see that our announcements were properly displayed, that our posters were on the billboards for which we had contracted. I took care of placing the advertising in the newspapers, learned about the different rates for different positions, and became familiar with the various type-faces.

I went to offices, hotels and stores distributing our advertising blotters. Everywhere I tried to create good will and interest in our show. I learned about timetables, arranged for the hauling of costumes and sets, took care of the train fares and hotel accommodations. This was the business end of show business, almost as important as knowing a good script from a mediocre one. Actually, apart from all this, I lived in the theatre. As soon as I finished my duties, I hurried out front to watch the show or went to a neighboring theatre. Almost every city had two, three or more playhouses in those halcyon days, and the choice I had was wide—melodrama, comedy, minstrel shows, novelty shows, vaudeville. I saw the good, the bad and the so-so. I devoured them all, trying to understand what made them tick, or if they did not, where the trouble lay.

I saw Nat C. Goodwin in *The Captain* and became so excited I wrote to Cliff that I thought Goodwin was one of the greatest actors I had ever seen. Some years later, after I had met George M. Cohan, I told him what I thought of Goodwin. Cohan said, "I'll tell you what I think about Goodwin. We used to go out and get drunk and raise hell together every night. I thought he was such a great actor that I couldn't call him anything but Mr. Goodwin."

I saw Laurette Taylor in *The Girl in Waiting* and I came near exploding with admiration. Here was enchantment, art, radiance, greatness. I never had cause to change my opinion. Nor did anyone thrill more to her great performance in Tennessee Williams' *The Glass Menagerie* as she remembered the glorious days when she had been a young belle of the South and gentlemen callers were frequent at her home. What I would have given to have had a chance to produce a play starring Laurette Taylor!

Once, during those beginning days with Jack Singer, my state of euphoria even convinced me that I could play the role of Dutch comedian better than did the regular comic in a show with which I had caught up in Holyoke, Massachusetts. I still had no ambition to act, but I had reached the point where I was telling everyone what was wrong with his performance. I said to Willie Fox, the comic, that if I had a chance, I could show him how to play the part. The manager heard me. "O.K., Max, want to try?" he asked. I could not retreat. For the next matinee I put on the pantaloons, the big shoes, the rummy nose. I was so obnoxiously cocksure of myself that I didn't even ask for a rehearsal. I knew all the lines, knew them perfectly. Besides, hadn't my brother been a Dutch comedian in burlesque? No one had to tell me what to do. I was going to be great. But when I got on stage, I became nervous. I lost control of my accent and forgot my lines. Humiliated, I raced to the wings, howls of laughter from the audience and jeers from the company pursuing me to the dressing room.

That experience took some of the cockiness out of me. But it hardly dampened my pleasures. Each day was filled with new wonders, new delights. Others might complain of the road's hardships, the inconvenience of moving from town to town, of unpacking in boardinghouse after boardinghouse. I thrived on it. I especially loved the boardinghouses—the good ones where for a dollar and a half a day I could get a room, gorge myself on breakfast, lunch and dinner, and in addition, get a sandwich and a bottle of beer after the theatre. Three squares and a bluff they called it, the bluff being the after-dinner snack.

I ate like a pig. I shoveled bacon and eggs into my mouth as if there were no tomorrow. I discovered that I could have lamb chops for breakfast in some places, so I did—a far cry from the cereal and milk I was lucky to get back on Cannon Street before Cliff joined the Imperial Burlesque company.

Not all the boardinghouses had the same standards. Some had poor rooms and a poor table. Some practiced such tricks as serving a troupe a chicken or turkey dinner when it arrived and another fine repast at the end of its stay. In between, the menu was terrible. But in the better places the meals were good all the time.

At Pop Teller's, in Philadelphia, for a few extra dollars a week I could get the best meals anywhere. The Four Cohans patronized Pop Teller's. So did most of the better vaudeville acts and the burlesque stars. Philadelphia boasted a half dozen or more other fine places, including Dad's Hotel, the Hurley House and Mother Green's.

Mother Irish's, on Pennsylvania Avenue, in Washington, was one of our favorite places in the capital. Here it was not unusual to see a senator or a member of the

House of Representatives enjoying himself with a chorus girl or an actress. In nearby Baltimore there was Mother Sparrow's boardinghouse. Mother Sparrow's forte was a great sense of humor plus the fact that she was a bookmaker on the side. Burlesque and vaudeville bred avid horseplayers. The moment these stepped into her place they were handed a racing form. Mother Sparrow made it both ways—for room and board and ten per cent of the bets.

Of all the places, the one I liked best was Mother Savage's in Louisville, Kentucky. There were four theatres in Louisville when I began making the rounds, and Mother Savage ran a busy place. She preferred show people and show people loved her. She was kind and understanding. An actor down on his luck knew that Mother Savage would listen and carry a tab. She knew what a temptation the nearby Churchill Downs races were. She knew that the police ignored some of the local crap and poker games, and consequently an actor could have a run of bad luck at either. She was generally filled to capacity. But if one of her regular customers arrived and she did not have a room, she would find him one somewhere else, insisting always that it be as clean and respectable as those in her own house.

Mother Savage was no prude. She knew the ways of the world. She permitted no shenanigans in her rooms, but she was not averse to telling a couple where such places could be found if she felt they were old enough to know what they were doing. She kept many a lonesome kid from getting into trouble. Once in a great while, if she liked someone very much, she could look the other way, as long as outward respectability was maintained. I knew one young reporter, now a man of great fame in journalism, who happened to be a favorite of Mother Savage's. When a girl would invite him up to her room for a while,

Mother Savage would make believe she knew nothing about it. Marc Connelly, who wrote *The Green Pastures* among other successful plays, knew Mother Savage, too. His favorite story, as well as mine in the years after, was of the time she refused to evict the owner of Magnus the Great, a brilliant performing goat. When a boarder complained of the smell, she told him to open his window.

"What?" he cried. "And lose my pigeons?"

Not all the boardinghouses were homes away from home. But those like Mother Savage's came close to filling the bill. Many actors, less fortunate than I, who autographed photographs for Mother Savage or Mother Who-ever-It-Was with the notation that her place was better than home meant it more often than not.

But it was not only the three squares and a bluff that I enjoyed. The boardinghouses were generally focal points for fun and good fellowship. After the show the members of the company would return to the house and tell jokes, sing songs, and entertain one another with their specialties, with material they might be working on for inclusion in their acts, with bits designed strictly for this sort of intimate atmosphere.

Only those who have been present at such impromptu entertainments know how exciting they can be, as each performer tries to show himself at his best before his own. In time I got to know more and more of these people, rascals some of them, to be sure, and even worse. But there was, nevertheless, about the theatrical boardinghouses a sense of being part of one big family.

These, indeed, were the golden days and nights of my life, as they also were of burlesque.

7

Lewis and Gordon

WHEN I completed the season for Singer, Cliff, having adjusted to my heresy, invited me to become advance man for one of his shows. "Might as well keep it in the family," he said, and I heartily agreed, thrilled by my big brother's compliment. And yet the elation did not last. In the ensuing months I again felt myself slipping into utter restlessness, victim of an old nettle, an old yearning. I have always been an emotional person, and in circumstances such as these I find reason powerless. As the weeks passed, the restlessness became more intense, the gnawing within similar to that which had seized me while at school—an almost frenzied need for independence, the satisfaction of knowing that I really was free and making my own way. It was not so much that working for Cliff had placed me, as it were, back under his wing. I could now, with my experience, work for anyone. It was instead a drive toward success on my own, an all but overwhelming desire to make a lot of money, to be as Cliff was, an entrepreneur, a producer—in sum, my own master. But even worse than the gnawing was the realization that I had no idea how to strike out for this emancipation. My arrangement with Cliff was the same as it had been with Singer. I paid for my own room and board and personal expenses, and I had not really managed to accumulate much of a reserve.

In this state of mind I was moping around the National Hotel in Minneapolis one night when a short, serious-looking fellow approached me.

"You're Cliff Gordon's brother, aren't you?" he asked.

How could he know that this was hardly the most propitious way to greet me, that beneath the furies that gripped me now there was also this: "Cliff Gordon's brother"? Periodically I reminded myself of what Henry Jacobs had said back in Rochester the previous season. Jacobs owned the Corinthian Theatre in Rochester, my third stop for the Behman Show. When I walked into his office, I said, "Good morning, Mr. Jacobs. I'm Cliff Gordon's brother." Jacobs exploded.

"Don't you ever say you're Cliff Gordon's brother again," he roared. "Cliff made it on his own, and if you're any goddam good, so will you. Now get the hell out of here and see that those billboards are posted."

I looked at my visitor and said, "I'm Max Gordon."

"My name is Al Lewis. I think you know me. I'm the Dutch comedian with the Vanity Fair show. I've been awfully anxious to talk with you. Could we have dinner together tomorrow night?" I said that would be fine.

We met the following evening and went to the Burtis House. The food was good, the choices many. For a quarter you could have a feast. We ate and talked.

It turned out that we came from pretty much the same background. His parents had brought him to the United States from Poland when he was three years old. Wretchedly poor, hard-working people, they had lived on the

Lower East Side. He fell in love with the theatre when he was still in elementary school, having made friends with some backstage workers at one of the neighborhood theatres devoted to cheap melodrama. After graduation he got a job as a property boy at the People's Theatre on the Bowery, eventually learned to sing, dance and project his voice from a stage, and formed a song-and-dance team with an actor named Lew Hearn.

They managed, Lewis said between mouthfuls of corned beef and cabbage, to work their way into vaudeville, had a fair amount of success, and then split, with Lewis trying straight acting in a stock company. He was happy enough for a while, he said, but some restlessness still haunted him. He turned next to burlesque, where he became a Dutch comedian. Now he realized that his acting talents were limited and concluded that his real bent lay in other areas of the theatre—directing, writing, perhaps even producing.

There was a pause when we reached the coffee and apple pie. Then I heard him saying, "Why don't we join forces? From what you've indicated, you seem to be ready for a change, too. You fit in perfectly with my plans. I think we might do well as talent agents. I know several little acts around the vaudeville circuits that we could represent. I know something about talent. You seem to have learned a lot about the business end of things. With your brother's help we ought to be able to make the right connections."

Coming when it did, Lewis' proposal seemed more than fortuitous. I saw my destiny being written before my eyes over a dinner table in the Burtis House in Minneapolis. But I parried and dodged. I had been mulling and stewing, whirling in different directions like a tiny sailboat whose rudder has come loose in tricky weather. I had no ready answer. I was assailed by doubts, fears, anxieties.

I had no money; I did not know this fellow at all. What would Cliff think of the idea? Would he help, as Lewis was suggesting?

"I need time to think it over," I said.

"Of course," Lewis replied. "Talk it over with your brother, and let's keep in touch."

Cliff adopted a reticent attitude when I discussed Lewis' idea. Aside from checking and finding that Lewis was trustworthy, he offered neither advice nor money. He said he understood and respected my ambitions and he certainly would introduce us to Joe Schenck, who at the time was head booker for the Loew's vaudeville circuit and later was to become a major factor in Hollywood's growth. But, Cliff said, the decision would have to be mine.

In a turmoil of uncertainty I set forth with *The Passing Parade,* one of Cliff's shows, in the fall of 1911. Not until midwinter did I succeed in clearing my head of all extraneous considerations and getting to the major point: Al Lewis was offering me freedom—if I really wanted it. I wrote and said I was interested in a partnership, but unfortunately, I did not think I would have sufficient funds. Actually, I was managing to save about ten or eleven dollars a week. By the end of the season I figured to have about five hundred dollars in the bank, not a great sum but it would help pay the office rent.

Lewis' reply was prompt. He had a good nest egg. We would not starve. In addition, he wrote, he had promises from a few small acts that when we were ready, they would become our clients. The positiveness of Lewis' reply, his complete optimism, helped me to make my decision. I wrote that I was ready.

In June we rented an office in the Columbia Theatre Building and began making pests of ourselves around the booking offices of the various circuits. Schenck was helpful. So were others. Actually, we did not have much to offer—a few minor acts. It did not take me long to realize that potential clients were not breaking down our doors. It would require time to build a reputation in the profession—time, patience and money.

We did not starve. But neither were we in sight of riches and security. We received five per cent of the price paid for an act, which would not have been bad if we had enough acts or if the few we did have commanded better deals. An act rating three hundred dollars a week brought us fifteen dollars. The arithmetic was as simple as that.

I was not exactly exuberant over our situation. Nor was I in any sense discouraged. Impatient, fretful, anxious—yes. I was all these things. But not discouraged. In the brief time that I had been associated professionally with show business, from the many conversations that I had heard between Cliff and his friends, I had learned enough to know that the road to success on either side of the footlights could be long and rugged. Besides, this was an intensely exciting period in the development of vaudeville. For someone as stage-struck as I, it was intoxicating. Indeed, for a while now vaudeville had been gaining in professional esteem and public acceptance. A whole army of talented men and women were singing, dancing and making merry on stages across the country. And determined men were battling to expand their interests.

Martin Beck, who had been instrumental in developing the strong Orpheum Circuit in the West, was preparing to invade New York, preparing to open his new Palace Theatre on Broadway and Forty-seventh Street. To everyone's amazement, Beck had gone to Paris and persuaded the great Sarah Bernhardt to undertake a tour of his vaudeville emporia at a salary of seven thousand dollars a week. She insisted, so the story went, that she be paid at the rate of five hundred dollars a performance—in gold—before she went on each day.

It was a tremendous coup for Beck, whose progressive policies had already stirred more than a ripple in vaudeville circles. He believed it was essential to hire the finest artists—dancers, actors, musicians—even if on occasion they might fail with a vaudeville audience. He believed that a bill must have variety, change of pace, something for everyone.

Beck's feat in persuading Bernhardt to play in vaudeville was likened to getting Paderewski to compose ragtime or Rodin to model sand statuary in Atlantic City. She was regarded as the greatest tragedienne of her time— if not, in fact, of all time—a human monument to the art of acting, a connecting link, an observer said, with the heroic days of dramatic poetry, the illuminator of the great works of French writers from Racine to Rostand. When Mark Twain saw her, he said, "There are five kinds of actresses: bad actresses, fair actresses, good actresses, great actresses and Sarah Bernhardt."

On street corners and on sidewalks, in restaurants over their coffee, wise men buzzed and wondered, spoke with awe and admiration of Beck's conquest, speculated as to whether Bernhardt would "go" in vaudeville, knowing at the same time what acclaim and what crowds she had drawn when she made her earlier tours in legitimate theatres. But, they asked, would the vaudeville public buy Bernhardt, would, indeed, the lovers of the legitimate theatre, a bit snobbish toward vaudeville, be willing to take a surrounding bill of comedians and the like in order to see Bernhardt in excerpts from her triumphs?

The wise men also raised questions about Beck's wisdom in building the Palace "so far uptown." Willie Hammerstein, who managed the major vaudeville house in New York, thought the Palace would be dead in two years.

Others were willing to wait and see. More than even this, though, many wondered what tough, foxy, battle-hardened Edward Franklin Albee was going to do about this invasion—Albee, who once had been an "outside" ticket man for a circus, who now had built the giant, powerful Keith vaudeville circuit in the East, who had helped shape and formulate policies for the equally powerful United Booking Office, who, in time, was to become the czar of American vaudeville.

Albee, it was pointed out, had always feared the ambitious Beck, a man who had come to this country as a member of a German acting troupe and when it broke up had taken a job as a waiter at twelve dollars a week and tips in Chicago's Royal Music Hall. Albee did all right, though. When it became known that Beck would not be able to get any acts through the United Booking Office because Willie Hammerstein had the franchise on all vaudeville from Forty-second Street to Columbus Circle, Beck's backer—a wealthy Westerner—ran out. Cornered, Beck went to Albee. The upshot was that Albee gained control of the Palace, with Beck retaining twenty-five per cent, and the booking went through his office.

None of these machinations, of course, affected the struggling firm of Lewis and Gordon. But, seeming to be part of them, speculating with the veterans on street corners and in the restaurants, trading bits of information and rumor, bragging a little and dreaming—all this kept me from becoming too discouraged about our own slow progress.

We had gone through another meager week when I decided to speak to Lewis about an idea that had been steadily injecting itself into my consciousness. I wanted to start producing one-act plays. It was not an original idea —one-act plays were being done in vaudeville, but their introduction had been somewhat recent. What attracted me, as I pointed out to Lewis, was the fact that as producers, we would own the property, make the deals, pay the actors. "This five-per-cent agent's deal," I argued, "is strictly piker stuff. If we could produce one-act plays, we might make some real money." Lewis was agreeable.

As novices, however, we were unable to get a decent property. Hoffman was overcommitted and did not have the time. Other top-flight writers were wary of entrusting their work to us. After weeks of futile effort Lewis suggested that we try a comedy act he had heard about from an English actor. The act, Lewis said, was an English pantomime, a sort of burlesque of a fire company. We found Billy Ritchie, the English actor who controlled the American rights to what was called *The London Fire Brigade*. When Ritchie finished describing it to me, I thought it had possibilities. It was all about a fire brigade that goes to a fire with the engines going the wrong way and the firemen getting tangled up in the hoses. Lewis footed the $750 production bill. When we had the act in shape, we got a booking in a Trenton theatre. The story is short. After the first performance the house manager ordered us off the bill. *The London Fire Brigade* was an ignominious disaster. No one laughed; there was not a titter in that benighted theatre that afternoon.

We rode back to New York, blasted the audience, blasted the manager, blasted Ritchie. I said to Lewis, "Don't worry, Al. If it's the last thing I do, I will see to it that I get back the $750 for you. If I spend the rest of my life doing it, I'll pay it back."

Lewis smiled wanly. We were in trouble. I could see that he was trying to figure out what to say about our future together. After what seemed like hours he said he thought the firm ought to continue. The best thing, he said, would be for him to go back to trouping, while

I kept the office open and continued to book the acts we had.

The failure in Trenton had been a bitter blow, and it was some time before I could see it in perspective. I felt miserable about Al's going back on the road, something from which he thought he had escaped when we formed our partnership; miserable that so much of his money, as well as what little I had, was down the drain. I aggravated myself for weeks after the fiasco, called myself a fool for not realizing that *The London Fire Brigade* was nothing more than claptrap—I who had been so sure of myself, who had spent my life picking flaws in the works of others, who had been certain that such mistakes need not happen.

In clearer moments I realized that doing the act had been Lewis' suggestion, that he could not accuse me of poor judgment, that, indeed, though I had failed to recognize the act for what it was, it had not been solely my responsibility. Nevertheless, self-recrimination had the upper hand. Every time I thought of that miserable afternoon in Trenton, I experienced a sinking feeling in my stomach and a tightness in my throat. It did not occur to me in these irrational interludes that this was hardly the way to take failure in the theatre, that if this was to be my way, I had better get out. Had I such wisdom then, how many days and nights of misery I would have saved myself, how much torture of mind and body. Surely I should have known that in show business failure comes to most more often than success; that years of striving are often destroyed in a single night, and fortunes lost; that those in the performing arts—actors, managers, writers and the rest—are subject to the whims and fancies of what the late Oscar Hammerstein 2nd called "The Big Black Giant"— the public, the audience upon whose acceptance all stood or fell.

8

You Can't Follow Sarah Bernhardt

THE OPENING of the Palace on March 24, 1913, provided a temporary antidote for my misery. A heady sort of excitement permeated the Broadway air, and like a soothing ocean breeze, it helped me if not exactly to forget, at least, to stop dwelling neurotically on our Trenton debacle, on my missing both Cliff and Lewis who were on the road, on being alone.

The opening was gala, the theatre a jewel. From the curved marble rail in the rear you could hear a whisper from the stage, and wherever you sat in the eighteen-hundred-seat theatre—still one of our largest—you could see the stage clearly. The seats, which since have given way to red plush, were upholstered in a beautiful flowered cretonne. The two crystal chandeliers suspended from the ceiling bespoke the grandeur of royalty.

As for the program, Beck, in spite of his troubles, put

together a diversified bill. The Eight Palace Girls, performing a gay and stirring dance, opened the show. Mc-
Intyre and Harty had been on the bill for the matinee
but because of a conflict with another act were replaced
for the evening performance by Taylor Holmes, an excellent monologist, who was also a legitimate stage star. In
addition, there were Ed Wynn, a rising young comic at
the time; Milton Pollock & Co., in a George Ade one-act
comedy called *Speaking to Father;* a wire act involving
the Four Vannis; an exotic dancer named La Napierkow-
ska, whose squirming gyrations and undulations were supposed to result from her having been stung by a bee; Otto
Gygi, billed as a Spanish court violinist, who turned out
to be the hit of the show; and a large "flash" act, *The
Eternal Waltz,* involving thirty persons.

On the whole, though, the show was a dismal failure.
Certainly, none of us realized that we had witnessed a
historic event or that the Palace would come to supplant
Hammerstein's five blocks away, on Broadway and Forty-
second Street—Hammerstein's, where the truly big acts
would be always and forever.

Somehow, men never seem to learn the lessons repeatedly written in history—that power wanes, thrones
crumble, and new heroes rise upon the scene. In three
years the Palace became the White House of vaudeville.
No theatre in the country, in this century, ever wove itself into the fabric of show business lore as did the Palace.
It endured for a generation. In that short span it became
an international treasure chest, a legend celebrated in
fiction, in drama, in Hollywood.

The sidewalk in front of its lobby became known as
the Palace Beach. It was the meeting place for the big and
the small, the employed and those who hoped to be noticed by some Keith booker and given a chance. Those
"at liberty" might not have the price of a cup of coffee;

they might be on the point of eviction, but that would not deter them nor weaken their spirit. They would parade up and down, dressed in their best, not for a moment thinking of pawning the diamonds they flaunted. The good front was what counted, what was needed—the positive key to opportunity.

Success at the Palace came to mean many things: the top, major league, prestige, money. After scoring at the Palace, many acts left its dressing rooms to go into musical comedy, the theatre, films. I myself, many years after that opening night, found a young comic on the Palace stage and hired him for my musical *Roberta*. His name was Bob Hope.

I did not miss a bill at the Palace, and when, for its fifth week, the management booked the gifted young English singer Jose Collins, I was delighted. She had leaped into recognition three seasons before as the Countess Rosalinda Cliquot in the musical *The Merry Countess*. Those of us who appreciated quality immediately became her most ardent worshipers. She was to open at the Palace on April 21, the day that Cliff was to appear at the Majestic in Chicago on the same program with Sarah Bernhardt.

Bernhardt's tour, which was to end two weeks later at the Palace, had turned into a grand success. Everywhere audiences thronged the theatres and critics cheered. Her Floria Tosca in Victorien Sardou's tragedy was called a demonstration of "sublime genius"; her Marguerite Gautier in *La Dame aux Camélias* was hailed as an "ineffaceable memory"; her Lucrezia Borgia "will live always in our minds"; her portrait of a queen consumed with an unholy love in Racine's *Phaedre* was "superb"; and "watching her varied characterizations has readjusted our standards of acting."

Cliff wrote that he was going to have to follow her on the bill, a sensible enough arrangement from the theatre's standpoint. Cliff would offer comic relief to the heavy dramatic fare. But he wondered, and I did, too, how it would work out. He was not sure that he could do it, he wrote, but he would try.

My concern for Cliff receded into the background as I settled into my seat at the Palace, anticipating the appearance of Jose Collins. The program was excellent—amusing songs and chatter, a tabloid musical comedy, a notable animal act, an entertaining playlet, a clever impersonator, and then Jose and her partner, Maurice Farkoa. Farkoa sang a song about the difficulties of the English language that proved most diverting, and twenty-one-year-old Jose was an unalloyed pleasure, she alone worth the price of admission. Beautifully gowned, with exquisite manners, she was like a lovely apparition. Wisely, she did not try to strain her sweet voice, nor did she resort to any artificialities. Had I the chance, I would have been on my knees before her, humbly expressing my admiration.

I left the theatre in a state of enchantment. It was not until I boarded the subway that I began to wonder how Cliff had gone in Chicago. Back home I still wondered as I sat in the dining room with my mother and father, having a snack. The telephone rang. It was near midnight, rather late for a call. A fearful premonition and anxiety seized me. I reached for the receiver. The voice on the other end said tentatively, "Hello. Is this you, Max?"

"Yes," I said nervously, "this is Max. Who is this?"

"Listen, Max, this is Dave Lewis, of the team of Lewis and Fields. I'm in Chicago, Max. I've got bad news."

I felt all my nerves knot. I tried not to faint.

"Is he dead?" I do not know what made me ask that question—as if I already knew what Lewis was trying to tell me.

"Yes, Max," the reply came back, "he's gone. He was

found dead in his hotel just before the evening show. I don't know all the details, but Jack Singer is here with the Behman Show and he's taken charge. Get hold of Aaron Hoffman and let Bobby know and other friends of Cliff's. Jack will wait for instructions tomorrow on what to do, after you and Aaron decide. I'm sorry, Max."

I tried to control myself as I faced my mother and father and told them. Before I had finished, my father was crying—I had never seen him cry before—and I felt myself sobbing, too. My mother sat stolidly in her chair, immobilized, gazing ahead, her eyes fixed, as it were, on eternity. Inside of her, I thought, she must be praying; surely, God must be with her now in this hour of her great sadness. She never cried that night.

How I myself got through that night I do not know. I found Hoffman in a saloon on 125th Street. I called Bobby North in St. Louis where he was with a show. I called as many friends of Cliff's as I could at that hour. It was five in the morning when, in Cliff's office, I met with Hoffman and Louis Epstein, manager of *The Merry Whirl*. It was decided that the best thing would be for me to take the morning train to Chicago to bring back the body. I was on the train when I received a telegram notifying me that new arrangements had been made. Singer had been instructed not to wait for me but to send Cliff's body on immediately. I was to stop in Pittsburgh and await the body there on Wednesday morning.

The train arrived at Union Station at 5:30 A.M. With me were several of Cliff's friends. Singer thoughtfully had sent his property man with Cliff's remains. I relieved him and brought Cliff to New York on Wednesday evening. Hoffman, Epstein and others were at the station. The plan was to take Cliff to our apartment. Funeral services had been scheduled for the following day in the synagogue

across the street. The burial would be in Washington
Cemetery in Brooklyn.

The turnout for Cliff's funeral was impressive. There
were editorials in the trade press, one of which I saved. It
appeared in *The Player* and read: "When Cliff Gordon
passed away, the amusement-seeking public lost one of its
best caterers. Cliff brought a lot of happiness into this
world, and he dispensed it freely during his theatrical
career. The world has lost a great entertainer, and the
great beyond has gained by it. His mission on earth was
to make us smile, and he succeeded beyond all expecta-
tion, and while his passing has left many of us sad at
heart, he left us a legacy of memory, wreathed in smiles."

Those who could not attend sent wires or notes. One I
have never forgotten. It came from Nat Wills, a great
monologist and entertainer, a rival and admirer of Cliff's.
It read: "Is there anything I can do for you?"—the hand of
one human being reaching out to another in time of
trouble. Ever since, I have offered that hand in my own
messages to friends in time of distress.

The services and burial were mercifully brief. We returned to our home to observe the days of memorial required by the Jewish faith. Friends came to share our
sorrow, to support us in this hour of need.

Bit by bit, piece by piece, I reconstructed what had
happened to Cliff, my beloved brother and mentor, who,
at thirty-three, had died alone in a hotel room in Chicago,
away from those who had cherished him so much—those
parents, brothers, sisters and friends who would have
rushed to his side at the first call.

It is true that Cliff had not been feeling well for a
considerable period. He had been tired and had complained of severe headaches, for which he had been given
some medicine by the family doctor. But when he was not

in the grip of these headaches, he was fine. Everyone who saw him before he left on the tour recalled that his spirits were high. He had arrived in Chicago in the morning, gone straight to the Hotel Sherman, registered, refreshed himself, and immediately went to the Majestic for rehearsals.

At the matinee Sarah Bernhardt had given a great performance in *La Tosca,* and the audience, first reduced to tears, had then burst forth in cheers. It was Cliff's turn then to entertain them as "The German Senator." Lyman Glover, manager of the Majestic, told me that Cliff went on, determined to make the audience laugh. However, at about the same time he was seized by one of those fearful headaches resembling cramps in the brain. Valiantly he strove to work himself into his monologue, but after five minutes he knew he was not going to make it. The audience, shaken by Bernhardt, failed to respond. Cliff walked off at the finish of his act to no applause and remarked to Glover that the audience was stolid and mirthless.

"I couldn't get 'em," he told Glover. "Any comedian who tries to follow Bernhardt is bound to die."

"Never mind, Cliff," Glover said. "Maybe you'll feel better tonight. It's a tough spot, but try again."

Unaware that his remark, intended as a theatrical observation, would become ironic truth, Cliff returned to his hotel. He left word at the desk to be called at eight o'clock. That night when the bell sounded in his dressing room, there was no answer. Glover hurried to a telephone and called the hotel. "Mr. Gordon is not in his room," he was told. He insisted that they had better force the door. But the end had come. The doctor who was summoned found the bathtub half filled with water. A hot bath apparently had induced the fatal heart attack.

I had thought that by understanding how Cliff died I would find some relief from the pain of my loss. But it did not help. Instead, the image of his lonely death, his passing in agony and defeat, seemed only to deepen my despair.

I went to my office in a state of stupor and accomplished nothing. I kept asking the age-old question, "Why?" I remember one day sitting with Louis Epstein and saying, "Louis, tell me, did it happen? Did this really happen?" And one day I said the same thing to Eddie Clark, a vaudeville actor, who assured me, "Time heals all." I had no faith in that, and in fact, as time passed, my wound seemed to grow deeper.

The realization that responsibility now was mine, that my brother Dave and I would have to carry on in Cliff's place and take care of our parents, drove me into a panic. Cliff had left eighteen thousand dollars in cash, more than enough to sustain us in any immediate difficulty, more than enough certainly until that day when I would get on my feet in the theatre. But this fact was never able to penetrate my consciousness. Whatever fears and insecurities were born in me in the days of my early, crimped childhood on the Lower East Side suddenly erupted full-grown, like the dragon teeth that sprang up as soldiers in the mythological fields, and no less terrifying or destructive.

Intensifying these fears was a lack of confidence in myself, the first signs of which I had noted as an adolescent and had forgotten in the exciting years that followed. It did not matter that from every side friends predicted great things for me in the theatre, that Minnie Hoffman, Aaron's wife, had told me in the presence of my mother that Aaron was sure I would be as successful in the business end of the theatre as Cliff had been in the artistic. I was captive of a sense of inferiority that was destined to hound and torture me for the rest of my life, a sense of inadequacy and uncertainty that even now rouses itself

some mornings to wreak, as it were, some ancient venge-
ance on my dignity and my identity.

My weight went from 150 to 118 pounds. For months
I could not stir myself to look after more than routine
details. I listened and heard only vaguely the advice and
admonitions of friends on how I had to snap out of my
lethargy. From the road Al Lewis kept up a steady stream
of notes. He reminded me that Cliff would not approve of
my behavior, that we owed it to Cliff's memory to make
good now, that now, more than ever, it was imperative for
us to push forward with our hopes and our dreams. That,
Al wrote over and over again, would have been Cliff's way.
We could do no less.

Just when the break came, I do not know. Whether it
came one morning as I opened my eyes after another fitful
sleep, or whether it burst upon me somewhere on some
street corner as I stood wondering which way to turn, I
do not recall—if, indeed, I ever really knew. What I do recall is that one day all the things that people had been
telling me began to have meaning. I was like a vessel that
had pushed through a fog bank into open sea, blue sky and
sun. I could almost feel the strength of life returning.
The mists of despair fell behind. My will and spirit revived. If I could not yet laugh easily, I could at least
harness and direct my energies.

I began making the rounds again, letting people know
that I was ready to go on. Everywhere Cliff's memory
opened doors and men promised their help. Among the
most sympathetic was John J. Murdock, general manager
of the Keith Circuit, right arm of the mighty Albee, and
one of the truly great men behind the scenes of vaudeville.

He had started in show business in the Nineties as a
stage electrician, but it had not been long before he

became one of the more important entrepreneurs in vaudeville, buying theatres, running them, organizing booking
offices, developing talent. Shrewd and sharp in his business
dealings, he had a reputation for knowing how to make
his enterprises pay. He could be as cold as a professional
poker player, as tricky as a fox, as patient as a cat waiting
for the right moment to make its kill.

Murdock was an odd little man who lived to the age of
eighty-five but looked old at fifty. He would sit at his
desk cross-legged, toy with one of the many assorted knick-
knacks he kept in his desk drawer as he discussed a matter
with an employee or a visitor, and take frequent gulps of
goat's milk, a bottle of which he always kept handy on the
top of his desk. Later in life he was told that he had cancer.
He decided that honey was a cure for the malignancy and
took to keeping a container of it on his desk, eating from
it throughout the day. He became rabid on the subject of
honey. He studied every aspect of bee culture. He even
devoted part of his Mamaroneck, New York, estate to
raising bees so that he could always have a fresh supply of
honey. When some doctors came to him with the theory
that a serum against cancer could be developed from thor-
oughbred horses, Murdock was an easy target. It is believed he spent close to a million dollars buying thorough-
breds on which the doctors conducted their experiments.
Whether or not Murdock ever had cancer, I do not know.
The fact is he outlived his doctors.

It was generally known that Murdock did not place his
trust in many men. But the few who won his confidence
could count on his unwavering loyalty. He also liked giving young people a chance. He had been fond of Cliff.
The day that I walked into his office and introduced myself, he seemed to transfer this affection to me. Sipping at
the goat's milk, he listened as I told him of my grief over
the loss of Cliff, of my newly found resolution to continue

in show business, and of my desire to concentrate on producing one-act plays.

"I am on my own, now," I remember saying. "I don't want you or anyone else to do anything special for me. All I want is a chance." He listened intently and when I finished, he said, "Now you go ahead and when you are ready, you just let me know. I will give you my personal attention."

With such encouragement from Murdock and others I picked up the threads of my life.

It was about this time that Aaron Hoffman completed *Straight,* a one-act melodramatic play he had begun shortly before Cliff's death. As I read it, I felt that it packed emotional strength and a heart-warming conclusion that could be most effectively developed in a theatre. Somewhat nervously, I suggested that he let me produce it, pointing out how much it would mean to me in prestige. When Hoffman surprised me and agreed, I could hardly wait to write to Lewis for his approval.

Al agreed that the play had strong possibilities. He also agreed that it would be a coup of some proportions for us to produce a play by the man considered by many to be one of the best in vaudeville. But, he wondered uneasily, where would we get the money? I had the answer. I would ask Bobby North. North loaned us a hundred dollars for the set and costumes, and I put the play into rehearsal.

When I thought it was ready, I called Murdock, who, true to his word, personally telephoned the booker of the theatre in Yonkers and asked him to give me a tryout. Unhappily, *Straight* did not "play." Unaccountably, it went dead in front of an audience. I gave Murdock a lame alibi and pleaded for another chance. Again he arranged a booking, this time in a Brooklyn theatre. But *Straight,* it seemed, was ill-starred. Our engagement was cut short.

Unhappy, dismayed, humiliated though I was, I refused to give up. I must have suspected that something more than the play was at stake, that what was being tested was my faith in myself, in my judgment. I told Hoffman that the play had to work, that I would find a way. For several days after the Brooklyn fiasco I mulled over the problem and, after repeated readings, concluded that my evaluation of the script was sound. The fault was not in *Straight.* It was in the actors and the director who had staged it.

I was walking down Broadway trying desperately to think of someone who could fill the leading role when I encountered an actor named Arthur Sullivan. In him I realized was embodied the strength the part required. I grabbed him by the arm and told him he had to read *Straight.* A day or two later he called. He thought the part was fine and was willing to see what he could do with it. I made another decision. I called Ben Teal, who had directed *The Merry Whirl* for Cliff, and told him I wanted him to redirect *Straight.*

We went back into rehearsal, but I did not have the nerve to call Murdock again. On my own I managed to persuade the manager of a theatre in Hoboken to give me time. When the curtain rose on *Straight,* I held my breath. Twenty minutes later I breathed again like a human being, or at least like a human being who knows the joy of success and vindication.

Straight had made it. It had turned out to be everything I thought it could be. The play remained in Hoboken for three days; then the Loew's Booking Office ordered it to its American Roof on Eighth Avenue and Forty-second Street to finish out the week.

Fortified with my good news, I ran into Ray Hodgdon, son of the general manager for the Keith Circuit and himself a booker for the Keith theatres in Pittsburgh, Cincinnati and Indianapolis. Hodgdon remarked that he needed an act for the Davis Theatre in Pittsburgh, a house managed by Eugene Connolly. A man gifted with both superior taste and a reputation for being hard to please, Connolly was also famous as the manager who closed Lillie Langtry (whose first name is often misspelled), the great English actress known as The Jersey Lily, after her first performance in his house.

I told Hodgdon about the success of *Straight* and that it was playing the American theatre. "Let me take you to see it," I said, and we went there together. When the curtain came down, Hodgdon said, "O.K., Max, you go to Pittsburgh. If the act goes over there, I'll book it in the rest of my theatres."

After the act opened in Pittsburgh, Connolly wired his pleasure and volunteered the comment that *Straight* was an "American classic." I said a silent prayer of thanksgiving. Nothing, I vowed, could stop me now.

That in the years to come there would again be lapses in self-confidence, that show business would give me many heartaches, never occurred to me in this hour of triumph. It was enough to know now that I had proven myself, that I had scored in spite of the setbacks and without the help of my older and somewhat more experienced partner.

The account of my faith in *Straight* and its ultimate success was not lost on my colleagues. For days after *Straight* moved from the Loew's Circuit to the Keith, it provided a source of conversation and speculation. Wherever I went, other agents, producers and bookers gave me either a literal or figurative pat on the back. I knew the sense of achievement that revitalizes a man's self-respect.

The most important and longest lasting of the repercussions involved Hoffman himself. He came to the office after Lewis had returned from the road and spoke of my good work in his behalf and of his appreciation. He said that after the years of association with my brother Cliff it seemed fitting that he continue with me. He suggested that we arrive at a business arrangement whereby he would be a silent partner in the firm of Lewis and Gordon, that for a fifty-per-cent interest he would be willing to turn over to us all of his vaudeville plays.

We jumped at the offer—perhaps a little too eagerly. I knew that Hoffman would not be easy to live with, that it would not be long before he let us know how much we owed him in gratitude, how deeply we were indebted to his talent. Through his long relationship with my brother this ego need had been a constant source of irritation and pain. Yet, in spite of this knowledge, I realized that Hoffman's was a most flattering gesture toward two tyros. It needed no great intelligence or perspicacity to realize how valuable an alliance with Hoffman could—and did—turn out to be. Hoffman, even if he tried, could hardly write a failure in vaudeville.

Other writers noted the vote of confidence he had given us. They saw the taste and standards with which we produced his plays, heard about the integrity and sound business procedures on which we insisted, and began sending us their plays. We became, in three years, vaudeville's leading producers of one-act plays. In five years we had a virtual monopoly on the best talent. Hardly a month passed that one of our acts was not on the boards of the Palace. Under our management the leading stars of the legitimate stage, as well as those of silent films, went out on tours of the two major circuits, the Keith and the Orpheum: Judith Anderson, Theda Bara, Mary Nash, Henry Hull, Clara Kimball Young and Roland Young.

We were at the top, we made money, we had position

and respect. And Al Lewis, as the producer, was mainly responsible for our success. The firm of Lewis and Gordon represented class, style and quality. How many one-act plays we actually produced over the years, I do not know. Nor can I now describe more than a dozen in detail. But there is one for which I do have a special fondness: *In the Zone,* by Eugene O'Neill. It is a moving play, a poignant one, about a seaman whose mail is rifled by his shipmates. We picked it up among a batch of one-act plays that we had purchased from the old Washington Square Players, a Greenwich Village group that meant much to the development of the young O'Neill and to the American theatre itself. From its ranks the Theatre Guild was born.

Shortly before we were going to produce *In the Zone,* O'Neill sought us out. He wanted an advance of fifty dollars against his royalties. When I asked him why, he said that he wished to marry. *In the Zone* proved to be an artistic success on the Orpheum Circuit, but I did not hear from or see O'Neill again until many years later.

The meeting was arranged by Richard Madden, one of the country's leading play agents at the time and O'Neill's personal representative. O'Neill, Madden said, had been talking about the old days of vaudeville, about the glorious days of George M. Cohan, and had expressed a wish to hear some of the old Cohan songs. Madden said he could think of no one other than me who would remember some of those songs. When I started to say something about not being much of a singer, Madden stopped me. "Look," he said, "that's not really important. You may not have heard it, but Gene's a very sick man. He's got Parkinson's disease. Now, if you could see your way clear to visit him and sing some of those songs, you would be performing a great act of kindness."

O'Neill was gay enough as we talked and grew senti-

mental and nostalgic. Among the songs he wanted to hear
was the one about a young Negro who says:

> I'm gonna get right up
> And put on all my clothes,
> I'm gonna go round
> And take in all the shows.
> I'm gonna ride around in an open carriage,
> And if ah meets mah girl, there's gonna be
>   a marriage.

Another song I sang to him that night had never been
published. In it Cohan described his ambitions to be a
playwright and confided these to a friend, asking his advice. His friend answered:

> Go get a flag,
> Because you need it, you need it, you know
>   you do.
> Go get a flag
> And always save it and wave it, and they'll
>   stand for you.
> Hire a lot of chorus girls
> And fire these bum legits,
> Get yourself a Yankee Doodle gag,
> Put some real songs in your shows
> And sing the damn things through your nose;
> For Godsake, go and get a flag.

It was one of those odd evenings that occur once in a
lifetime. I remember it with a strange mixture of amusement and sadness.

9

Enter Millie

I DOUBT that there is any man who can ever call his success in a given endeavor strictly his own. There is always some stroke of chance, someone outside himself who opens a door, pushes the right switch, sees the promise of the future. In my case that single man was John J. Murdock, who, through it all, enjoying it all, remained true to his promise. That little old man, who, between his sips of goat's milk, had assured me of his interest in my career, never wavered in his faith or his loyalty. Whenever there was a problem to be solved, a special need to be answered, he was there ready to help.

Although *Straight* had been booked into Keith theatres, that good fortune alone did not provide the open sesame to the sacred sixth floor of the Palace, where the United Booking Office, under Albee's dominion, held forth. There sat the men who could make and break agents and acts. They were the men who booked the different theatres around the circuits. Only those with franchises—or, to put it more bluntly, permission from Albee himself—were allowed into this special heaven. Without a franchise an agent would first have to send his card in and then wait all day in the hope that he would be seen. This step-by-step process could consume days, sometimes weeks. But a man with the special blessing called a franchise could walk into the office, march from desk to desk, and book a full season's tour in a day.

Murdock saw to it that I was admitted to this holy of holies. Later, when I became bold enough, I pointed out to him that while this arrangement was fine, I was still limited to booking only our own plays. I had other acts—not many, of course—but I said that if I could book them, also, I would be able to make more money and consequently be able to produce more one-act plays. Murdock understood and arranged this, too. When, once, I foolishly got into a battle with Albee over the price I wanted for a play and was practically thrown out of his office, it remained for Murdock to smooth the ruffled feathers and save my neck. How close my neck had been to the knife, I found out some time later at the opening of the new National Vaudeville Artists clubhouse. Albee was there and when we came face to face, he smiled and said, "You know, Max, I've had a note about you on my desk for three years. But I'm tearing it up tonight."

Oddly enough, and to Murdock's great satisfaction, Albee and I became good friends after that night. Soon I was dining with him and spending weekends on his yacht. And it was Albee, eventually, who was responsible for my producing the act that gave me the greatest satisfaction I received during my entire career in vaudeville; more, perhaps, than that derived from the success of *Straight*. It was the act I produced for the late great Eddie Foy, Sr.

The great old Foy act, "Eddie Foy and His Seven Little

Foys," had disbanded. The man who once could point to a thousand imitators seemed to have come to the end of the line. When Albee heard of his plight, he called me to his office. He said, "Max, we've got to do something for Eddie Foy, Sr. Get some of your writers to write him an act, a one-act play. Maybe we can get him a tour."

I called in Eddie Burke and Tom Barry. "Albee wants an act for Foy," I said. "If we can come up with a good one, he'll book it for the Palace and the circuit."

Burke and Barry delivered a script that caught the essence of show-business sentiment. They had Foy playing a stage doorman who sees two youngsters come off the stage in a heated argument. The boy is accusing the girl of stepping on his lines and all the rest of it. As the stage doorman listens, it appears that the youngsters are going to break up their act. He calls them to him and tells them that they are repeating the story of his life—that jealousy and stupidity cost him his own career. He warns the two that if they don't stop their bickering, they also will wind up failures—the boy, perhaps, nothing more than a stage doorman. At this point the stage doorman remarks that he used to do a dance not unlike the one the boy does and shows it to them. The dance, of course, was the famous old Foy soft-shoe. By the time he is finished, the youngsters are making up and walking back through the stage door arm-in-arm.

Foy opened the act in one of the small out-of-town theatres. It was a smash. We brought it to New York, to the Jefferson Street Theatre. I went up to Albee and told him the time had come for him to see what we had. As soon as the act was over, he congratulated me and everyone in sight and, on the spot, booked it into the Palace.

The Monday afternoon that Foy opened at the Palace and went into his dance, the regulars, along with the rest of the crowd, were stamping and whistling and cheering.

To use an old show-business term, they were tearing the house down. I went backstage to Foy's dressing room when it was over. He threw his arms around me, tears streaming from his eyes. "Max," he said, "they didn't talk to me at the Astor yesterday; they hardly knew me. But they'll talk to me now. Max, you'll go to heaven for this."

Although Murdock's original promise to help me was a reflection of his regard for my brother Cliff, this alone might not have kept him on my side. What probably did were my industry, ambition and devotion to my work—traits that were dear to his heart.

The fact is it never occurred to me, either during those years of apprenticeship in burlesque or during those that saw Lewis and me ride to the crest of our success, that I had no private life. Nor, if it had occurred to me, would it have made much difference. Nothing seemed to matter more to me than show business. I took girls out from time to time, those from the burlesque shows and others from among the many I met and knew in vaudeville. But none made any impression on me. They offered their fleeting pleasures and were quickly forgotten. My mind was much too occupied with the myriad details and mysteries of the trade, with the demands and requirements of our firm. Wherever our acts were breaking in, there I was, and when, as it sometimes happened, we had a dozen or more in preparation simultaneously, life was for me an endless tour of theatres in New York and out of town.

I soaked up all sorts of information, became a reservoir of facts and fancies, knew practically everyone performing before the footlights, knew everyone maneuvering in the back offices. I don't think there was an act of quality that I did not know, hardly a theatre in the East with which I was not acquainted. My eyes and ears became sharpened to the significance of movement, the nuance of voice. I could watch and listen to a scene and know exactly when it would reach its peak of impact. I could, as I did one night, bend down to retrieve a package of matches as I watched the team of Ball and West, and without seeing Ball, or hearing his voice, remark to my brother Dave, "He's going to blow that laugh, for sure." And he did. My ear told me that the actor had waited just a fraction too long after his cue.

I lived for show business from the moment I opened my eyes in the morning until, weary from the daily rounds, arguments and excitements, I closed them again at night. The truth is that they were never really closed for long, and there were those who called me "the agent who never sleeps." Clients knew that after shows they could always hunt me up at Shulem's restaurant on West Forty-seventh Street or at the Friars, where I frequently found myself in the company of George M. Cohan and Max Winslow.

And then, one day I had a new interest, a new dream.

Lewis and I had gone to Amsterdam, New York, for the break-in of one of our acts. Although the act had gone well, Lewis decided to stay an extra day to improve some minor points. There was no need for the both of us in Amsterdam. I figured I might as well return to New York. Boarding the train almost simultaneously with me was a vision of feminine beauty—delicate, with doll-like features, soft, glistening darkish-blonde hair, rosebud lips. There was a freshness and innocence about her, a dignity and bearing that overwhelmed me, literally robbed me of my breath. I took my seat, not far from the one she had chosen, still smitten, still amazed and awed. Somewhere, too, memory told me I had seen this vision before. But where? For what seemed endless miles, as the train rolled downstate, I tortured my brain for a clue.

Unable to restrain myself any longer, I walked to her

seat and in my most courteous tones began, "Pardon me. My name is Max Gordon. I don't usually do this sort of thing. But haven't we met?" Even as I uttered the words, I knew how ridiculously trite they sounded. Only my sincerity supported me.

She looked at me, not frostily, but with a sort of cool disdain. "No," she said, "I don't think so," and turned back to staring at the passing scenery.

Avoiding the questioning glances of some of the other passengers, I returned to my seat to renew the search of memory. At the point of hopelessness, I suddenly knew. I knew for sure. My heart leaped with the certainty as I started back to where she sat. We had met months before, for a fleeting moment, in the office of Laurence Schwab, a booker for some small vaudeville theatres in Pennsylvania, the same Laurence Schwab who was to team with Frank Mandel and give Broadway such wonderfully exciting musicals as *Good News, The Desert Song,* and *The New Moon.*

"Excuse me," I said, once again sensing all eyes in that car fixed on me. "Excuse me, I'm really not trying to be fresh or forward. But I know we've met. Laurence Schwab's office. You must remember. You visited him with a letter or something. And I was there. It was only a moment, I know. You were leaving."

Her look of annoyance gave way to amusement. A smile began to shape itself around her mouth.

"Yes," she agreed, "I guess we really did meet, didn't we? I do remember meeting someone in Mr. Schwab's office. I had gone to see him about work."

I sat down next to her. The remainder of the trip was spent in getting acquainted. I told her of my connection with show business. We talked about vaudeville, whom we liked, whom we did not. I told her all about Cliff. In an effort to make an impression, I boasted about the firm

of Lewis and Gordon. I learned that she was a singer and
dancer in a "girl act," so called because these acts, popular in vaudeville at the time, usually consisted of about
eight girls, costumes and scenery, a comic, and perhaps a
few other entertainers. She had been in Amsterdam because that was where she grew up, and her parents still
lived there. Her stage name was Raye Dean, her real name
Mildred Bartlett, and she had been in show business only
a short time. She was seventeen when she had gone to
New York to visit family friends and decided to stay.
Having appeared in some of her high school's musical
productions, she thought she would try making her way in
show business.

Sooner than I wished, we arrived in Grand Central
Station. I had hoped the journey would never end. All
the time that we talked I, like a gay child on a holiday,
dreamed that the train would keep going to no destination
at all. Yet, each passing station had drawn me back to
reality and too soon it was over. I took her to the rooming
house where she lived, thinking all the while that no girl
I had ever met was like this one, no other girl had ever
spun such enchantment or so excited my imagination.
Before leaving, I extracted a promise that she would permit me to see her again. She kept her promise in her
fashion, and it was not long before I knew I was deeply,
irrevocably in love.

It was not an easy courtship. I soon discovered that
Mildred, or Millie, as her friends called her, had other
suitors, some far more affluent than I; she was often on
the road; and there were the pressures of my own enterprises to keep us apart. Neither could she be said to be
particularly encouraging. Friendly, yes, and gay and utterly charming. But she maintained a disconcerting reserve, a disturbing detachment that I found terribly difficult to overcome. There were periods when, for days on

end, I would call her only to be told that she was out, or that she was on tour, or that she was in church—a variety of excuses that seemed designed to mock me, though I never knew and could not deny their veracity.

Once, when I asked for a date and she said she was going to a baseball game at the Polo Grounds with "a gentleman friend," I went, too, not so much to spy on her—how could I in such a crowd?—but just to know that I was where she was. Nor did it, incidentally, help me that day that I had asked Lou Holtz, the comedian, to go with me, or that we found ourselves by the wildest of accidents seated ten rows behind Millie and her gentleman friend. This circumstance induced Holtz to rise up periodically and yell at the top of his lungs, "Has anybody seen Max Gordon?" Nor did the six months I spent in the Army help. Although I did not go overseas, and although I did succeed in wangling more than a normal allotment of weekend passes, I was hardly in a satisfactory situation to press my cause.

Yet, even after my discharge I did not seem able to make much progress. Once, during an especially discouraging time, I went to Rita Boland for help. Rita was Holtz's wife. She was appearing with Millie in a Ziegfeld show at the Coconut Grove, atop the Century Theatre, overlooking Central Park.

"Rita," I said, "please see this girl and find out if I have a chance. I'm madly in love with her, and she hardly gives me a tumble. You've got to find out for me tonight because the suspense is killing me. I'll wait for you in Rector's after the last show."

That night I sat in the rear of the long room that George Rector had opened on Broadway and Forty-eighth Street, less exclusive than the original Rector's he and his father used to run. It was two o'clock in the morning when Rita arrived. She halted momentarily at the door as my heart seemed to halt with her. She searched the room until she saw me and shook her head from side to side. Spotting friends at another table, she joined them, leaving me in black despair. She did not have the heart to tell me, I discovered, that Millie was, if not exactly disinterested, hardly overwhelmed by my attention.

Millie has never explained to me what it was that changed her mind in my favor, or how it came about that some time after Rita's inquiry she permitted me to see her more frequently. Nor have I asked. I like to think that, in addition to my persistence, the sincerity of my love became evident to her and she, in turn, realized that she had more than mere affection for me.

The fact is that I never formally proposed to Millie. The time simply came when we knew that we would marry. Yet, even that knowledge, though it delighted me beyond description, was not without its problems. Millie by this time had achieved some position as an actress both on the stage and the screen. She had enjoyed a six- or seven-month engagement in Chicago in a play called *Experience,* played with Effie Shannon in *Suppressed Desires,* and appeared in *Friendly Enemies.* On the screen she had performed in *Madonnas and Men,* with Edmund Lowe, and *A Message from Mars,* with Bert Lytell. It dawned on me that I might marry a star, that sometime I might find myself in a position where my wife would be supporting me. The thought was utterly repelling, and yet not without foundation. In my short experience I had seen men marry stars and lose them because of the unequal status that so deeply challenges the male ego.

One day I was to meet Millie at a movie studio. We had made an appointment for a certain time, but something had delayed the filming of the day's scenes. I found myself waiting, as it were, outside the stage door. As the minutes and the hours passed, my irritation increased, along with my conviction that this could never be a satisfactory arrangement for me.

"I cannot be a stage-door Johnny," I told her later at dinner. I asked her whether she would consider giving up her career for our marriage. I told her I could never stand the idea of her supporting me, of her earning more than I did; that I could never stand being her husband rather than she my wife. Millie looked at me for a moment or two. My heart sank deeper and deeper. When she replied, a smile punctuated her lovely cheeks.

"Max," she said, "I hope you haven't been bothering yourself about that. But I'm glad you mentioned it. No, I really don't mind leaving the stage. In fact, I think I planned to. I want to be your wife, that is enough ambition for me." I swelled in appreciation, too full to tell how happy she had made me. I was to learn that this was truly Millie. In the years that followed, her loyalty and fidelity to that ambition helped me through many crises, helped me to live.

A problem before our marriage not as easily solved as the one I have just described was the difference in our religious faiths. Millie, although raised as a Baptist, had no qualms about intermarriage. For me, it was not so simple. True, in moving into the theatre world I had not so much lost touch with my religion as to have become detached from it. I had arrived at a conclusion not dissimilar from Millie's: that religious faith was a matter of private conscience. As long as two persons respected each other's beliefs, religious differences could be bridged.

For me, the dilemma was how to tell my parents, how to explain to those two pious old Jews, without breaking their hearts, that I was in love with a Christian girl, that I needed this girl from "the enemy camp." Over and over again, tossing on my pillow in the dark hours of the night,

I wondered how I would be able to confront them with the news, remembering as I did the gasp of horror in my mother's voice, the look of revulsion in my father's eyes, whenever a neighbor or relative reported an intermarriage; knowing also that in many orthodox families a son or daughter marrying outside the faith is often looked upon as dead, requiring, indeed, the traditional mourning observance.

The problem was not so complex for Millie. She had demonstrated her strength and independence when she had left home to fend for herself in the big city. I did not possess this degree of independence. I will not say that my attachments were deeper or that I loved my parents more. That would be evaluating, judging that which I have no right to judge. Although I had moved into a world my parents never did comprehend, I had continued to live with them, as had Cliff when he was alive, as had Dave, as had my sisters until they were married. I doubt that it ever entered any of our heads to leave home and live alone. If it did, we had suppressed the idea at its birth. Not because we did not desire such freedom, but because each of us knew how much such a move would hurt our parents.

The problem had not been resolved when Millie and I decided to marry in the spring of 1921. For my sake we were married by a rabbi. This, I hopefully told myself, might help to assuage the pain my parents would suffer on that inevitable day when they would know.

Millie and I were married on May 23, 1921, with Bobby North and his wife as witnesses. We had made no plans for a honeymoon, partly because of my business commitments, but mostly because I had not yet been able to face my mother and father with the truth. Instead, I announced that I had to go out of town for a few days. We went to Atlantic City, where a new play by Aaron

Hoffman, *Just Around the Corner,* was having its tryout. We went to the Shoreham Hotel for three unforgettable days, saw Aaron's play, walked along the ocean shore and were in our own glorious heaven. On our return I moved into Millie's two-room apartment on West Sixty-seventh Street. Moved in, that is, half literally and half figuratively. Every night for more than a month, as if our marriage had not taken place, I returned to my parents' home. It was a ridiculous arrangement. Yet, coward that I was, I kept postponing the inevitable. Millie put an end to my procrastination by announcing that we could not go on this way.

"Max," she said to me one night in a voice I had never heard before, a voice that was stern and at the same time touched with an edge of sadness, "Max, either we are married or we are not. You cannot continue this childish masquerade. If you don't tell your parents, I will."

The tone of her voice told me that there was no longer room for discussion, that it would be useless to plead for more time—I had really had all the time a man could rightfully expect. Millie was right. I had been behaving not like a man who has presumed to take upon himself the adult responsibility of marriage, with all the duties implied in that responsibility, but instead, I was behaving like a frightened, ineffectual child. Millie was right. I promised I would do as she demanded.

Toward evening of that day, trembling and miserable, I walked toward my parents' home on West 116th Street. I tried to prepare myself for the ordeal. As I neared the house, I saw my mother approaching, her arms laden with the day's shopping. I hurried to help her. I kissed her and was taking the bundles from her arms when she said to me in Yiddish, "Max, my child, is it true that you have married a gentile?" The question, unanticipated as it was, uttered as it was, in gentleness and anxiety, sent a quick chill through my heart. The tears rushed to my eyes. "Yes, Mama, it is true," I said, and poured out the story of my love for Millie. The tears overflowed. I was crying like a child.

Once again I had miscalculated. For, just as this remarkable woman had sat stonelike and dry-eyed the night I had told her of Cliff's death, she now betrayed none of the emotionalism I had feared. We walked upstairs and there I told my father. Again my fears proved baseless. These two grand old people had heard of my marriage. They had agreed between themselves to accept it. With tears still streaming down my face, I heard them forgiving me, saying that they would like to meet my wife.

The following Friday night, the eve of the Jewish Sabbath, I brought Millie to my parents' home. There was the traditional white cloth on the table in the dining room, the *challah,* or festive bread, beneath a white napkin awaiting my father's blessing, the candles in the majestic little candelabra with their flickering flames. My sisters were there with their husbands, Dave was there, and everyone was spruced up and polished; everyone just a little nervous and apprehensive over this meeting with my wife, this girl from another world.

Whatever her own apprehensions were, Millie presented an appearance of outward calm. She kissed everyone, including my father with his long gray beard. It was not long before her charm and the ease of her manner warmed and relaxed us all. The reserve gradually melted. The evening was pleasant and memorable. When it was over, I almost smothered Millie in my gratitude. I never had any fear that she would fail. But to have her turn the meeting into such a triumph was something for which I had not bargained. In later years my mother referred to Millie as a Jewish angel and the affection between them grew deep. It lasted as long as my mother lived.

After that Friday night I moved into Millie's apartment. When, after my father's death, I rose every morning and went to my mother's house to breakfast with her, Millie understood and approved. No matter where we lived, as long as I was in New York, I continued this practice—a strange ritual, perhaps, for a grown man. But I enjoyed it, and it gave my mother great pleasure. It was a small payment I made for all that she meant to me; it was little enough atonement for whatever pain I may have caused her.

I should have been the happiest of men. I had married the girl of my dreams, the anxieties that had bedeviled me because of our religious difference had proven baseless, and I was a successful man traveling "up." Indeed, not only were Lewis and I in vaudeville's front ranks but we had also achieved our ultimate goal first dreamed of at the Burtis House dinner. We had invaded the legitimate theatre in association with Sam H. Harris, one of Broadway's greatest producers. Beginning in 1920 with Aaron Hoffman's superb hit, *Welcome Stranger,* and for five years thereafter, we had been involved with Harris in such productions as *Six Cylinder Love,* which opened three months after my marriage; the sensationally successful *Rain,* in which Jeanne Eagels gained a measure of her immortality; *Secrets; Easy Come, Easy Go; The Family Upstairs;* and *The Jazz Singer,* which Lewis directed himself, and in which George Jessel added to his own fame by portraying a Jewish cantor's son who preferred to do his singing in the theatre rather than the synagogue.

As newcomers to the Broadway theatre we had done extremely well. Still, I was not content. I was dissatisfied, restless. Every day I went to the office and on the daily round with an odd sense of failure, an insidious unease, eating away within me. My dissatisfaction was not a mysterious malady. It was induced by frustration, the knowledge that I really had no great voice in any of our successes, that I had been gradually but effectively shunted aside, that I had been repeatedly made to feel unimportant and inadequate. It was not a new feeling exactly, nor had it arisen when we expanded our activities to the theatre. Actually, I had been living with it for a long time, but I had succeeded in submerging it beneath those layers of the subconscious from which it only erupted intermittently to cause me anguish.

It was my marriage that was the catalyst, that seemed to bring all the rancor to the surface, that seemed to sharpen my awareness. Like most normal men, I wished my wife to think of me as an important man, to recognize the image that I had of myself. But in my heart I knew that the image was without reality, that my contributions to the firm of Lewis and Gordon had been restricted to the minimum.

I conducted the business of the firm, but the gratification and the recognition that rewards creative effort were denied me. Not that I had any great hankering to be a director in the full sense of that word. But my experience over the years had given me good reason to believe that I knew something about stagecraft, that I knew something about what would be effective on the stage and what would not, that I knew something about acting. Nevertheless, I had noted the increasing number of occasions when suggestions I made were disregarded by both Lewis and Hoffman. More often than not, I suspected that I was being merely tolerated. This was never made clear to me in as many words. The treatment was more subtle—indifference, disinterested shrugs of the shoulder, impatience, shriveling replies, patronizing attention.

For years I tried to tell myself that these were fantasies, the imaginary hurts of an insecure and uncertain young man whose vanity played him tricks. There were occasions when I had the distinct impression that I was like a pup trailing at the heels of its master. I tried to rationalize and put my feelings in order and perspective. But time only intensified my hurts, gave greater substance to my suspicions.

Not too long after the success of *Welcome Stranger,* we had a financial disagreement with Hoffman which left both Lewis and me smoldering. One day, in a burst of temper and boldness, I sought out Hoffman. I told him that we had decided to sever our business relations with him. I told him also what I had previously feared to say— how I detested his need to dominate people, how he had made Cliff miserable, how he had made me miserable, and how I was not going to stand for his abuse any longer. We arrived at a financial settlement, and I told Lewis what I had done. Lewis blanched, but I assured him that we could get along without Hoffman. The next day I took off for Europe, somehow convinced in my mind that from now on I would no longer feel inferior.

How naïve I was. Lewis, alone, was more difficult for me than Hoffman. He seemed to brush me aside and make it bluntly plain that he was the boss. Repeatedly I made suggestions for which I received no credit. I was, in my eyes, an appendage, a fifth wheel. The vista of the years ahead was not a cheerful one.

This was my state of mind that day early in 1926 when I received a call from Marcus Heiman, head of the Orpheum vaudeville circuit. It was a call that was to change the course of my life. Heiman, a well-spoken man whom I had known rather casually through my friendship with John J. Murdock, wondered whether the firm of Lewis and Gordon, so successful in vaudeville, would be interested in expanding its scope. Specifically, would it like to take over the management of the Orpheum's New

York office and also head the production department? The offer, Heiman said, carried with it a yearly contract providing for a weekly remuneration of five hundred dollars.

In 1926 this was a considerable sum of money, which, when added to our other income, would come close to putting us on Easy Street. Al, however, said he was not interested. His ambitions had been fanned by the success he had scored as the director of *The Jazz Singer*. He said that he felt his talents and interests could best be served by his continuing in the theatre.

I did not argue with him. In his rejection lay my freedom. If only Heiman would agree, I could be my own man again. Nervously I called Heiman and explained to him why the firm of Lewis and Gordon would not be interested. But, I quickly added, I was available. Heiman seemed startled but did not press any questions. He said that my suggestion was perfectly fine; he would be delighted to have me and the five-hundred-dollar-a-week contract still held. He said that he was particularly impressed by my reputation for honesty, relating that when he had asked Murdock whether he could trust me, Murdock had told him that he would give me his wallet and never count the money.

I told Al of my decision. A chapter of my life had ended, and a new one was about to begin.

10

❧❧❧

A Curtain Falls

HOW MYSTERIOUSLY THE WHEEL SPINS.

Not only did 1926 mark the end of Lewis and Gordon. It also marked the beginning of a new era in the entertainment world. It was in that fateful year of 1926 that sound effects and music were successfully applied to the screen, an achievement whose reverberations were to overturn a world. A year later dialogue was introduced in the film version of *The Jazz Singer,* and the stampede and panic, of which there had already been rumblings, were unleashed in full force. Pitiful and tragic were the consequences for those unable to cope with the new development.

Surely everyone knows that many of the kings and queens of silent films toppled from their thrones, that many desperately sought aid from speech teachers and failed, that many could not memorize lines and emote at the same time, that stars like John Gilbert found the timbre of their voices unsuited to the mechanical monster that had been conjured up to destroy them. Suddenly and

(109)

mercilessly they were severed from the source of their fortunes; pitifully and yet understandably they were tossed upon the junk heap of defeat.

Suddenly, also, Hollywood knew that in addition to photogenic actors who could speak with clarity and credibility, it needed writers who could create dialogue as well as plots. It was obvious that it must now turn to the legitimate stage and vaudeville. By 1928 the race was on in full cry. Directors, actors and writers were sought, courted and tempted. The financial blandishments were difficult to resist, the promises not unlike a vision of paradise.

Symptomatic was the pleading call I received from William Fox, who had been a friend of Cliff's when Cliff was a humble performer in East Side clubs and at stag socials. Fox himself had been a performer who early had seen the possibilities in the silver screen and had gone West. Now he was calling to ask for help in rounding up actors, directors and literary properties for his projected Movietone productions.

It was a tempting opportunity, but I was still under contract to Orpheum, having signed for five years. I reluctantly turned him down. I suggested that he ask Al, who after our parting had gone on to stage and co-produce with Sam Harris one of the most successful plays of the period, *The Spider*. Al took the job. In time he himself went West. In the years that followed, he gained many film credits for such productions as *Merton of the Movies, Meet Me in St. Louis* and *Torch Song*.

Little did I realize when I was rejecting Bill Fox's offer that my own fate was being sealed in vaudeville, that the liberating decision I had made in 1926 was headed for disaster. In that strangely fateful year a man named Joseph P. Kennedy embarked on a career in show business that was to have profound effects upon it and indirectly upon me.

The father of the future President of the United States, Joseph Kennedy had been president of a bank at the age of twenty-five, subsequently an assistant general manager for the Fore River, Massachusetts, plant of Bethlehem Shipbuilding Corporation, and at thirty-one he was manager of the Boston branch of the New York banking firm of Hayden, Stone and Company. Now he had decided to go into business for himself. Through his various connections he put together one million dollars to gain control of R-C Pictures and the Film Booking Offices from their British backers. The official statement said that the overseas interests felt the development of the companies could best be carried out under resident control. Kennedy renamed his acquisition the F.B.O. Pictures Corporation and became its president. A year later Pathé, Inc., asked him to become a special adviser, and it was not long before he became chairman of the board.

Hollywood was soon aware of Kennedy's methods of operation, and many of its citizens did not like them. Marcus Loew was supposed to have asked, "What's Kennedy doing in the movie industry? He's not a furrier." Until Kennedy's entrance into the film colony everyone had been accustomed to the lavish hand of former New York furriers and cloak-and-suiters who had so shrewdly seen the potential in the film business. They seized upon movie-making with relish and imagination and never concerned themselves with the costs. Money was to be made, so money could be spent. Why not be a little extravagant? Into this wonderfully mad never-never land came the Irishman from Boston with different ideas. He had, as was observed by one bitter onlooker, an accountant's approach to movie-making. He slashed at overhead like a maniac let loose in a film-cutting room. Kennedy the banker wanted to know why and how and wherefore.

Whatever the older Hollywood citizens thought of the upstart's methods never disturbed Kennedy. He continued to operate as he saw fit. Early in 1928 came the announcement that he and David Sarnoff, then vice-president of the Radio Corporation of America, had concluded a major deal. R.C.A. and its affiliate companies, General Electric and Westinghouse, had acquired a substantial interest in Kennedy's F.B.O. Pictures. The announcement put the picture clearly:

This affiliation opens to motion pictures for the first time the tremendous resources and potentialities of radio. It will give the movies the use of all present patents and prospective developments of sound reproduction and synchronization, radio broadcasting, television, etc., of the Radio Corporation of America, the General Electric Company, and the Westinghouse Electric and Manufacturing Company.

A complete revolution of present-day entertainment may easily develop as the result of the close affiliation between the important leaders of motion pictures and the powerful engineering organization of the radio group. The services of the technical staffs of the three greatest electrical companies in the world thus become available to the motion picture industry to help that industry in its constant endeavor to give the public a new and better entertainment.

The first important development of the combination will be the presentation of a new method of sound reproduction and synchronization perfected by General Electric. The officials of the Radio Corporation of America feel that the method and apparatus excel all previous efforts in the direction of "talking movies."

The Radio Corporation and its associated companies have been experimenting with and developing a method of sound reproduction for use in connection with motion pictures for several years and as it reached perfection decided upon a direct affiliation with an established motion picture company as the practical way of putting it into general use.

No one reading that announcement could miss the point. Those of us in vaudeville and the theatre knew that the difficulties already in evidence would deepen. The competition would be deadly, with the odds obviously against us. By May, Albee was announcing that Kennedy had become associated with him and Marcus Heiman in the management of the Keith-Albee-Orpheum Circuit through the purchase of a large interest in the common stock by Kennedy in association with a financial group that included Blair and Company and Lehman Brothers. Albee also used the occasion to deny rumors that he would retire from active management of the circuit with which he had been associated for forty years. Controlling interest in the company, he pointed out, was still held by the Keith associates. Nevertheless, shortly afterward a new office was created, chairman of the board, to which Kennedy was elected. Periodically throughout the summer Albee and Kennedy issued statements about how they were going to revitalize vaudeville. New theatres would be built, new talent would be recruited, new writers, directors and producers would be found. There was even talk about a revival of "big-time" straight vaudeville programs in theatres across the country, where vaudeville had been compelled to share time with films. And even then Kennedy was not finished altering the face of show business.

With the coming of October also came the biggest news of all—the formation of a new corporation, Radio-Keith-Orpheum, with David Sarnoff as chairman of the board. Kennedy netted a million dollars for his part in effecting the merger.

The announcement of the merger also carried the news that Hiram S. Brown, president of the United States Leather Company, would on January 1 become president of RKO, continuing as a director and member of the executive committee of United States Leather. That was the beginning of my downfall.

Brown was an excellent leather man but knew nothing about show business. I had occasion to voice my criticism of the move to Sarnoff. He replied stiffly, "I want a businessman in the job. A business needs a businessman."

"That's fine, Dave," I said, "but how is a fellow like Brown going to know how much talent is worth, how much, for instance, to pay someone like Fred Astaire?"

"Don't worry," Sarnoff said, "we've got a great board of directors."

"O.K., Dave," I retorted. "But tell me, who's going to write the jokes?"

The whole approach seemed foolhardy to me. And I was not the only one. There were others in show business who felt that the appointment of Brown was a mistake. Brown, I am sure, heard of my sentiments. It was inevitable that he would; I had enemies in the organization. There were those who were jealous of me, of the fact that I, an outsider, had been brought in by Heiman to take charge of the booking and production. The shift in power, the change of command, gave them an opportunity to revenge themselves.

When I walked into my office in the Palace Theatre Building, after a trip around the circuit, and discovered a barrel of sawdust and a broom standing there, I knew that my time had run out. I immediately went to Brown's office and demanded to know the meaning of this outrage. He looked at me and there was no sign of warmth in his eyes. "Well," he began, "what do you want to do about it? You don't seem to fit in here. From what I gather, you can't get along with anyone."

"I don't get along with them because they are a bunch of incompetents," I shouted. "And now I'm going to show you, Mr. Brown, what I'm going to do about it."

I took out of my pocket the contract that still had two years to run and tore it up. "This is what I'm going to do about it, Mr. Brown," I said and walked out of the office.

It was a good exit. But whatever satisfaction my histrionics had given me was purely temporary. When I had cooled off and the glow of my performance dimmed, I was faced with the cold fact that I was out of a job.

I was really only a little ahead of most of the others. All the grandiose schemes and hopes for a revival of vaudeville that Albee, Brown and Kennedy had trumpeted in the daily press, shortly after the formation of RKO, turned to nothing. In three years vaudeville as I had known it—pure vaudeville, straight vaudeville, big-time two-a-day vaudeville that had flourished and brought such joy and pleasure and satisfaction to millions—had come to an end.

Few of us suspected the doom being written. But when it came, it all seemed so obvious. With the development of talking pictures and radio, it was impossible for vaudeville to carry on. The movie houses, with their great seating capacities, began booking the headline acts and paying salaries that made it impossible for the smaller vaudeville houses to compete for talent. As the number of vaudeville houses shrank, the exodus of actors and writers increased. Westward, they went, following the sun to Hollywood's promised land.

Veterans who knew the Palace in the days of its greatness still recall with incredulity the night the last two-a-day reserved-seat non-film house in this country called it a run. Only a few hundred were there to attend the last rites. The orchestra seats were half filled. There were no farewell speeches. There were no tears. Apparently no one really cared. Vaudeville in the true tradition had outlived its time.

The next day the Palace went to a four-a-day policy, a

one-dollar top, and no reserved seats. For a while there was a pickup in business, but in a few weeks it really was over. After that the Palace showed vaudeville and films.

For me, the months following my departure from Hiram S. Brown's office were filled with desperation. I had just about awakened to the reality of my needs, adjusted to the idea that I had to start all over again, when the world turned over. It turned over on October 24, 1929—Black Thursday—the day when the stock market crashed, thereby signaling the beginning of the most dreadful depression in American history. Like everyone else in show business, I had been "in the market." I had been in for years, ever since Aaron Hoffman used to come into the office with his cash profits and announce, "Here comes Santa Claus."

Through those crazy Twenties, like everyone else, I had been convinced that prosperity would go on forever. To be sure, I had experienced losses. I had been trapped once in a "bucket shop" deal that cost me close to ten thousand dollars. But that was nothing to become dismayed over. There was plenty more money to be made, and I made it in show business and in the market. I remember playing golf with Groucho Marx one day in Great Neck, Long Island, and remarking, "Marx, why should we really work at all? Here we are playing golf and having a wonderful time, and I've already made three thousand dollars today in the market."

When Marcus Heiman offered me the post with Orpheum, he had given me in addition an option on five thousand shares of stock at thirty dollars a share. When the merger with the Radio Corporation of America took place, I sold the stock at forty and made a neat fifty thousand dollars. This is the way it had been. And then there was that Thursday. Groucho says I called him up, and in a voice that sounded as if it came from the grave, I said, "Marx, the jig is up."

Even then I had been a bit more fortunate than many others. I owned securities outright in several cases. But the devaluation left me terribly pinched. Millie offered to pawn her rings. But I could not bear that thought and refused. We moved to a less expensive apartment. We ate our meals at home. We saw only our closest friends.

I picked up a few acts, which I could still book in the Keith offices, and produced an act or two. I was, to put it plainly, grubbing—I who had once been a kingpin in the Orpheum Circuit, who with Al Lewis had produced some of the best one-act plays in vaudeville, who had even sipped a bit of the elixir of success in the Broadway legitimate theatre.

It was not an easy comedown. I think that what kept me from going under at this point, aside from Millie's unflagging devotion and encouragement, was the grim knowledge that there were other men in considerably worse straits, men who had been stripped of every material possession they owned and had nothing to which they could turn for their livelihood. At least I could sustain myself with the thought that in show business you never know when the dice will come seven—tomorrow, next week, next month, next year. Somewhere in some nondescript theatre I might find an extraordinary talent or act that would take me back along the road from which I had been routed.

By the spring of 1930 it was only too clear that the cold, deadening tentacles of the Depression were to be at the country's throat for some time. Along with that chilling fact, the growing popularity of talking pictures, which had been spelling the doom of vaudeville, was also writing an unhappy future for the legitimate theatre. The number of playhouses in New York began to dwindle; permanent stock companies throughout the country—the backbone of the theatre and an invaluable training ground for its actors—were succumbing. The number of touring companies was reduced. Woe was the word wherever you listened to Broadway show people talking about show business.

Such was the deepening gloom when, in the drama section of *The New York Times,* I read an announcement that sent signals flashing through my head. Dwight Deere Wiman, William A. Brady, Jr., and Tom Weatherly, who had earned a well-deserved success with their revue *The Little Show* in the spring of 1929, were announcing plans for a second edition. But they were not re-engaging three of the first production's stalwarts: Clifton Webb, Libby Holman and Fred Allen. If they had any reasons other than the desire for new faces in addition to new talent, they did not say. But the thought of these three performers being free simultaneously, following their superb performances in *The Little Show,* tantalized me.

In a state of great excitement, I put in a call to Marcus Heiman. Following the merger with R.C.A., Heiman had sold out his interest and joined Judge Erlanger, Charles B. Dillingham, and Saul Baron in Erlanger Productions. "Marc," I said, "did you see the item in the *Times* today?"

"What are you talking about?" he snapped impatiently, and I knew that I had called at a wrong moment. He was in one of his irritable moods. But my enthusiasm overrode my judgment, and I persisted.

"Marc, I mean the item about Wiman, Brady and Weatherly not taking on Webb, Holman and Allen for *The Second Little Show.*"

"So what?" Heiman shot back.

"Well, Marc, why don't you hire them? You could build

a show around them for the Erlanger Theatre. It's empty, isn't it?"

"Yes, Max," Heiman replied, "but we're not interested. Walter Batchelor was up here the other day. He's their agent, and he has the same idea. He says they'd like to do another revue together. He wants our help. But we don't have any confidence in him as a producer."

"Marc," I pressed on, "I'm only trying to be helpful. You ought to reconsider. These people were sensational in *The Little Show*. Webb is great, you know that. He can sing and dance. Holman's the most exciting torch singer in the business, and Allen has practically ripened overnight. He is going to be one of the great comedians. In fact, Marc, he's terrific already. I think there is a big public that will go for them in the right kind of show."

"For heaven's sake, Max, I told you we're not interested," Heiman replied, and after a split second added, "Why don't you do it?"

Perhaps my excitement was responsible. Perhaps I was too sensitive. Perhaps I thought I detected a note of derision in Heiman's voice. If not that exactly, then a challenge. In any case, I got angry.

"Well, dammit, I will," I said and hung up, startled at my reckless audacity. Where was I to get the money for a show? The question seemed ridiculous to contemplate. The stocks that I had managed to retain had depreciated to the point where they were worth no more than about five thousand dollars. What I had left in the bank was piddling. Most of the people I knew were in the same fix. "Angel" auditions, so popular now in raising money for shows, were not in vogue then. Producers gambled their own funds on their judgment, or had a small coterie of reliable associates to back them.

The fact is that even if the custom of holding an audition for so-called angels had been popular, I doubt that I would have subscribed to it. I never have. There is something humiliating to my old-fashioned mind about dozens of men and women coming to your home—or to a hotel suite—drinking your liquor and eating your petits fours while you keep hoping some of them will part with a few hundred dollars. It is almost similar to passing the hat, like some London back-yard minnesinger or itinerant busker in Leicester Square. In later years, when I became an established producer and the costs of launching a show made it prohibitive for an individual or even a small group of investors to put up all of the necessary capital, I sent out letters to acquaintances inviting their participation.

Aside from the question of raising the money to make good on my reply to Heiman, there was that equally delicate question as to whether Webb, Allen or Miss Holman would even listen to me. I probably could get to Allen. He and a fellow named York had teamed years before in a vaudeville act, Allen and York, and my brother Dave had been their agent. But how would I get material? And what about Batchelor? Would he be willing to step aside?

After a few days of indecision I concluded that the questions were not so awesome. I told myself, with rising confidence, that I could not be hanged for trying. Boosted out of the doldrums by Heiman's challenge and awakened by a realization that I had nothing to gain by inaction, I became aware of a new purpose. A whole new career was possible, a career in the legitimate theatre on my own. Now I had a chance to prove myself.

I called Batchelor, who quickly filled in the picture. He, as I had suspected from my conversation with Heiman, had no source of financing. He would be delighted, he said, to step aside if I could raise the money. As soon as I hung up, I called my brother Dave and told him of my plans.

"Look, Dave," I said, the pitch of my voice rising as it generally does when I am excited, "I've just spoken to Batchelor. He says it's all right with him if I can raise the money. I'm still not sure that I can, but I have some ideas. What I need now more than money is assurance that Webb, Holman and Allen will go along with Batchelor and me. So, do me a big favor. Speak to Allen. He knows who I am. But maybe the others don't. He can talk to them and tell them about my record, about my background with Cliff, about Lewis and Gordon and the acts we did in vaudeville. Ask him to tell them how I've always stood for taste in the theatre, how Cliff used to insist on it even in burlesque, and that they can be assured of a first-class production. You know, have Fred build me up."

Dave and Fred did their jobs. The only stipulation was that Howard Dietz and Arthur Schwartz, who had contributed to *The Little Show,* be retained, Dietz to write lyrics and compile the material, Schwartz to do as much of the music as possible. I said I was only too willing to go along with such an arrangement. In no time at all everyone was signing contracts, I was making announcements to the press, and I found myself walking west on Forty-first Street to see Attilio Giannini about money. Giannini was the manager of the Forty-first Street branch of the Bank of America, from which some years before Lewis and I had borrowed $50,000 for one of our projects. We had repaid the loan promptly, and our reputation for integrity was unassailable. It had occurred to me that I ought to try the bank again.

Altogether I estimated that I would need $125,000 to do the kind of show I had in mind. If I could get $25,000 from the bank, I felt reasonably certain that I could persuade Heiman to get the Erlanger interests to go along with another $25,000. Certainly the package I had put together was attractive enough. With $50,000 in hand I could go to the set builders and costumers and get credit for the remaining funds, which, assuming the show was a success, I would be able to repay as we went along.

Giannini proved more affable than I had hoped. The speech I had nervously prepared was not needed. We spoke for a while about show business, the merger that resulted in the Radio-Keith-Orpheum corporation, and naturally, about the collapse of the stock market. We agreed that the situation was not bright, but like a lot of other financiers at the time, he was optimistic that the country would right itself in due course. When I explained the purpose of my visit, he was cordial. "Yes," he said, "come back when you actually need the money, and you will have it."

My calculation about Heiman and the Erlanger company proved accurate. In a mood of great elation I sat down with Dietz and Schwartz to make plans for what would be *Three's a Crowd*. It was agreed that we would strive for an intimate revue of the finest quality, surpassing, if possible, even that of *The Little Show*. What we desired was a production that would delight the eye and yet not be ostentatiously elaborate, whose content would be sharp, witty, sophisticated and intelligent. Not only did we feel that this would be the best type of show in which to display the talents of our principals, but it also represented our determination to underscore and widen the break *The Little Show* had made with the big revues of the Twenties.

These lavish entertainments first blossomed in the period before our entry into the First World War. After the Armistice they came into full bloom, an evident answer to the entertainment needs of many Americans who preferred checking their brains along with their hats when they entered the theatre. It was a time, as economists and historians know, of unprecedented prosperity. A good many of us naïvely believed that the free enterprise system had solved forever the problem of the business cycle, that good times would never end, that the nation stood on the threshold of the glorious day when there would be a chicken in every pot and two cars in every garage. It was also, as every sociologist and reformer knows, a period of debauchery, short-skirted Charleston-dancing flappers, roadside inns, jazz and bathtub gin. To a large segment of the populace—drunk with the philosophy of easy come, easy go—the notion of thinking in the theatre was undiluted nonsense. The butter-and-egg men, sugar daddies, Babbitts and stock-market millionaires, when pleasure-bent, demanded reflections of opulence, lavish display, comics, smutty sketches, good tunes and plenty of beautiful girls—mostly undressed.

Nothing in show business satisfied these requirements like the revue. It almost seemed that anyone who could assemble the ingredients could get the money to put on the show. The best known of the revues at the time were, of course, the *Ziegfeld Follies,* which Florenz Ziegfeld had first introduced at the Jardin de Paris; *The Passing Show,* produced by the Shuberts; *Artists and Models,* also sponsored by the Shuberts; *George White's Scandals;* and *Earl Carroll's Vanities.* On these productions and others of their ilk money generally was spent with the hand of Croesus. These were the entertainments in which some of America's most beloved artists cavorted: Marilyn Miller, Eddie Cantor, Bert Williams, Eddie Dowling, Fanny Brice, W. C. Fields, Charles Winninger, Van and Schenck, Will Rogers, Gallagher and Shean, Bert Wheeler, Frank Fay, Phil Baker, Ann Pennington, Willie and Eugene

Howard. Much of the best of our light music was contributed to revues, and Ziegfeld had in his stable at one time or another Irving Berlin, Victor Herbert, Harry Tierney, Rudolf Friml and others.

Indeed, I should not wish to trade my memories of these productions, certainly not those of some of their highlights. I roared with everyone else in 1920 when Fanny Brice, my old favorite from burlesque, who had made her debut in the *Follies* of 1910, came on as an East Broadway vamp and also played a skit with W. C. Fields. In that 1920 *Follies* there were also Van and Schenck singing "All She'd Say Was Uh Hum," and there was Berlin's "Girl of My Dreams" and Victor Herbert's "The Love Boat." The next year's edition brought back Fanny Brice making everyone laugh as she sang "Second-Hand Rose," and then making everyone cry as she sang "My Man," reminding us of her own unhappy private life, her marital problems with her husband Nicky Arnstein. I never have forgotten John Charles Thomas' Broadway stage debut in *The Passing Show* of 1921, his lovely baritone sweetening all of the cavernous Winter Garden, or Willie Howard doing his inimitable take-off on Frank Bacon's long-running hit vehicle *Lightnin'*, or Marie Dressler making ribbons out of the mystery melodrama smash of the day, *The Bat*. I treasured the thrilling musical score Ray Henderson, Buddy de Sylva and Lew Brown created for *George White's Scandals* of 1926. Four major songs came out of that show. They were "Black Bottom," danced like mad by Ann Pennington, and unleashing a dance craze that swept the nation; and those present-day standards "The Birth of the Blues," "The Girl Is You," and "Lucky Day."

Oh, there were great moments in those revues, great stars and great talents. But on balance, they and the others that imitated them were entertainments that in varying degrees catered to the sex-hungry and the thrill-seekers.

The Passing Show, competing with the *Follies,* always seemed determined to be just a little more daring than the Ziegfeld productions and came very close to total nudity, as did the *Vanities* and the *Scandals.*

When the Shuberts introduced their *Artists and Models* in 1923, one startled critic wrote, "Never before in an American revue has a similar degree of nudity been obtained." The girls paraded the stage with naked breasts; there were shows also in which the girls' only attire were girdles of beads. There was one edition of *Artists and Models* in which, to justify the title, the chorus boys were arrayed in smocks and other raiment of artists—the girls who impersonated models needed, as one observer noted, no particular costumes at all.

Through this wild, crazy period in the American theatre considerable sums were invested and frequently squandered on revues and musical comedies. There were some isolated efforts in the revue field to cater to sophisticated audiences who might be more interested in wit and fun than in smut and nakedness. There were the early vivacious editions of *The Greenwich Village Follies,* the exuberant *Garrick Gaieties,* and the delightful *Grand Street Follies,* all on modest or moderate budgets, trying to keep alight a torch testifying that shows did not have to be vulgar and expensive to afford entertainment; that taste and a point of view could provide amusement and pleasure. These revues in their livelier and better editions specialized in simplicity and economy. They depended more on satire and parody than on skits and sketches, foreswore elaborate settings and opulent costuming, and endowed their songs, lyrics and dance routines with a special éclat and smartness.

The Little Show was in that tradition, with a little extra something added. It respected the minds and standards of the more discriminating theatregoers. It was presented with the sort of impeccable skill that generally marked the slick class of the more pretentious, lower-aiming revues. It was, in short, a worthy target for *Three's a Crowd*, and was never really out of my mind during the months of preparation in that feverish summer of 1930.

Assembling a revue, large or small, is never an easy task. It involves many talents, diverse bits and pieces that have to be fitted together, plus an all-important subtle factor in the theatre called pace. The truism that you never really know what you have until you see it on a stage goes double, I think, for a revue in which there is no story line to hold the spectator's interest. You pick and choose, relying on your mind's eye and your mind's ear, on your judgments of who has talent and who has not, hoping all the time that the songs you admire will fill a theatre as effectively as they do a room, that lines will sound as hilarious to the paying customers as they do to you and your friends, that the performers on whom you have placed your heart and substance will not let you down.

I listened to Dietz as he described his concept of the form the revue ought to take, listened to him read his sketches, heard Schwartz play his songs. I read the lyrics, churned with ideas and suggestions, hypnotized myself with confidence that all would be right when the curtain went up, knowing deep inside at the same time that all could go wrong. I booked the Erlanger Theatre in Philadelphia for our out-of-town tryout and set October 15 for the New York première at the Selwyn Theatre on Forty-second Street.

In mid-August I went to the Bank of America to collect the money Giannini had promised. I was shown into his office and instantly sensed that I was in great trouble. Gone was the affability of our earlier meeting. Instead, there was a decided reserve in his greeting, not even a trace of a smile. He came to the point quickly. He had been wrong about the economic picture when we had spoken earlier. No, the bank was not in trouble, but the policy-makers had decided to tighten credit. He was sorry, but he could not authorize the loan. I looked at him aghast. When I found my voice, it came out like a screech, disclosing the panic that had seized me.

"You can't do that, you can't do that," I repeated several times, realizing even as I uttered the phrase how ineffectual and childish it must sound to this man across the desk. "We've made all our plans. I've signed people to contracts. I've got obligations. I've made arrangements for theatres. You can't do this to people. You can't do this to me. You can't."

"I know how you feel," he replied, "and I'm terribly sorry. But I am afraid that is the way it has to be."

With the greatest difficulty I restrained myself from leaping at his throat. I had never been so overcome with frantic desperation. I forced myself to remain seated, gripped the arm rests of the chair, and began to plead. I said that I had been brought up to be a man of honor, that his bank need have no fear—I would pay back every cent of the loan no matter what happened short of death. I must say in fairness that he listened. He could have pushed a button and had me thrown out. But the volubility of my outpouring, the sincerity of my pleading, his own realization that he himself had impelled me on my course apparently combined to break his resolution. He looked at me, a faint smile on his lips, and said, "All right, I will give you the money, but if you don't pay it back, I'll shoot you."

11

✤

A Curtain Rises

By THE END of August we were ready for rehearsals. Among those who had been signed to support our three stars were Portland Hoffa (later Mrs. Fred Allen), Margaret Lee, Tamara Geva, the exquisite and exotic Russian dancer, the California Collegians (including Fred Mac-Murray), Harold Moffet, Amy Revere and Marybeth Conoly. For the dance numbers we hired Albertina Rasch, who had come to New York from the Imperial Opera Ballet School and contributed outstanding dance routines to *Rio Rita* in 1927, *The Three Musketeers* the following year, and in 1929 to *Show Girl* and *Sons o' Fun.* She was, indeed, to go on to greater fame and can be counted among the pioneers who helped clear the way for such choreographers as George Balanchine, who brought their concepts of ballet to the theatre in subsequent years.

For our sets I placed my faith in a complete unknown, a young designer named Albert R. Johnson. I had seen a play called *The Criminal Code,* for which he had designed the sets, and I was amazed at their effectiveness in

creating the play's mood. They had a sharp simplicity that
I could not resist. Although none of us knew him or had
heard of him before, we sent for Johnson. He arrived—a
boy of eighteen. But I did not hesitate. I told him what
we wanted and offered him a contract.

I think the closest Dietz and Schwartz came to a disagreement with me in those planning days was over the
naming of a director. I had seen the work that Hassard
Short had done on several of the big musicals and revues
of the time and insisted on using him. Dietz and Schwartz
argued against Short for the very reasons that I felt were
his recommendations. They said they thought he might
not be able to fit into their younger and more modern
ideas, that he might be too chichi and extravagant. Irving
Berlin, for whom Short had worked on the *Music Box
Revues,* as well as Sam H. Harris, whom I had consulted,
urged me to stick to my guns. They both thought highly
of Short and said his experience might prove of special
value to us. I won the argument.

Short did prove invaluable. Not only was he able to
comprehend the point of view we hoped to establish, but
he also enthusiastically endorsed it. One of his contributions to *Three's a Crowd,* in addition to his excellent
management of the company on stage, was his abolition
of the traditional stage footlights. Instead, to our great
satisfaction, he lighted the show from the balcony—the
first time, I think, that anyone had ever done so in the
musical theatre.

As for the material, I was full of optimism. Dietz, a man
after my own heart, was a tireless worker, fastidious and
exacting in his standards. Schwartz, tall, lean and intense,
composed a song that gave me chills every time it was
sung by Libby Holman during rehearsals. It was called
"Something to Remember You By." There was another,
an import from England, composed by Johnny Green,

with lyrics by Edward Heyman, Robert Sour and Frank Eyton—"Body and Soul."

Fred Allen had a sketch that doubled me up, a travesty on Admiral Byrd, much in the news those days for his polar expeditions. The sketch had Allen returning from one of these explorations, a great public hero. He delivered a lecture on his experience, with blank lantern slides. I can still hear that dry, nasal voice, intoning in mock solemnity a series of side-splitting observations. I can still see Fred staggering around the stage in his moth-eaten fur parka shouting, "Snow! Eternal snow!" On my urging, Groucho Marx, with whom I had been close friends in vaudeville—we had practically grown up together in its service—wrote a highly amusing sketch with Arthur Sheekman, called "The Event." Altogether we had more than a score of scenes and songs. As we headed for the Erlanger Theatre in Philadelphia, an air of cheery confidence pervaded the company.

The first bit of trouble to pop up was my utter dislike of the set for the first act finale. It was supposed to be a garden. When I saw it, I turned to Schwartz in complete disgust and said, "It looks like a Coney Island casino on a Sunday night with no business." It was Johnson's only error. When he redesigned the set, it turned out to be magnificent. The other problem came from a completely unexpected quarter—the failure of "Body and Soul." Instead of being one of the reliable high peaks of the production, it was one of the valleys from which the show had difficulty recovering its pace.

Libby had come out on opening night bathed in the exciting magic of Short's lighting arrangement, but instead of tearing the house apart, she left it only mildly aquiver. Different effects were tried on successive nights, but none helped. Each night after the show Libby would sit in her dressing room with tears streaming down her cheeks. "You can make it 'Two's a Crowd,' " she sobbed one night in despair as she threatened to quit.

One day Dietz went to New York. On the way back, the story goes, he met Ralph Rainger in Pennsylvania Station. Rainger had composed "Moanin' Low" for Libby, one of her big moments in *The Little Show*. As we heard it later, Dietz grabbed Rainger and started to explain what was happening to Libby in Philadelphia. "You've got to go back with me to Philly," he told Rainger, "and I will not take no for an answer. The song's a hit, sure as I'm talking to you. But right now it doesn't seem to fit Libby or Libby doesn't fit it. I don't know which, and yet we're all convinced this is her song."

Rainger said he was sympathetic, but he could not possibly go to Philadelphia. Dietz evidently was not listening. He just kept pushing him to the train, in through the door, and into a seat. Fortunately, Rainger was good-humored about his being shanghaied. He listened to the song played by the orchestra, asked Libby to sing it, and went to work. He reorchestrated the entire number. In place of the ending that Green had written, Rainger substituted a kind of rising crescendo. Even Libby was encouraged. The song sounded great at rehearsal, and that night she stepped out on the Erlanger stage with new confidence. Before the last note had sounded, the audience was shouting, stomping and demanding an encore.

The morning after the New York première I sat in my office letting myself soak in the reviews and the praises they sang. We had opened against Kenneth Macgowan's and Joseph Verner Reed's beautiful production of Shakespeare's *Twelfth Night*, starring Jane Cowl, and of course, all the first-string critics had felt conscience-bound to pay homage to serious theatre and classical art. But the second-string reviewers set up such a hullabaloo about the virtues of *Three's a Crowd* that in quick time the regulars were visiting the Selwyn and seconding the reports their assistants had filed. They agreed that *Three's a Crowd* was a grown-up revue, devoid of conventional routines. It had beauty and grace, they said, a high sheen, a civilized sophistication, and as one veteran reviewer wrote, "a little good, clean-cut gentlemanly dirt unmarred by vulgarity or exhibitionism." A sample of the "gentlemanly dirt" was a bathroom scene in which a young woman stumbles upon a young man taking a bath. Superficially it appears that they are strangers. But when she accidentally goes to the bathtub and glimpses the young man's anatomy, she recognizes him as an old-time acquaintance. Altogether, it was the opinion of many that we had surpassed *The Little Show* in every department—quality, style, humor and song.

I had taken a wild chance on myself and had come through. I was, at last, an independent Broadway producer. Every day for a week after the opening of *Three's a Crowd* I stood across the street from the Selwyn, gazed at the marquee, and came near blowing up with pride as I read again and again, "Max Gordon Presents." Occasionally I wondered how it would have sounded had it read, "Mechel Salpeter Presents." What's in a name?

Success being its own reward, I wanted more. It was not long after the opening that I sat down with Dietz and Schwartz to discuss plans for another show. Dietz, who was actually in the advertising field at the time, was full of ideas. After considerable talk we decided to do another revue similar in concept and intimacy but on a larger scale.

Dietz thought he would like to do a show in which he wrote all the lyrics, Schwartz wrote all the music, and one man did all the sketches. This, he reasoned, would help create a definite unity instead of trusting to luck in assembling the show. He agreed to handle the over-all supervision. But he made two stipulations. He wanted George S. Kaufman to write and direct the sketches, and he wanted Fred and Adele Astaire to head the cast. Involved principally with plays and musical comedies, Kaufman had found time to contribute a sketch to *The Little Show,* one of its best. Fortunately, the idea of doing all the sketches for a revue appealed to him.

We announced our plans for *The Band Wagon,* with Hassard Short as director, Albertina Rasch, choreographer, and Albert Johnson doing the sets. We chose Kiviette and Constance Ripley for the costumes. Dietz, as agreed, was over-all supervisor of the production. But his other credit caused a bit of a flurry. He requested that his name come ahead of Kaufman's in the place where the program read "A Revue by." He was so insistent on this that without consulting Kaufman, I said, "O.K. Let's toss for it. I'll call for George." I should not have taken that responsibility. But Dietz seemed anxious, and I was afraid to cause a row. I gambled on things coming out right. They did. Dietz lost the toss, and I never had to face the problem of what might have happened had it worked out the other way.

In addition to the Astaires we hired Frank Morgan and Helen Broderick to underscore the comedy, and Tilly Losch, the brilliant Austrian-born dancer who had been acclaimed in her debut here, in 1927, as dancer and choreographer for Max Reinhardt's repertory.

In late February, shortly before we were to go into rehearsal, I found myself walking along West Forty-fifth Street with George Kaufman. "I hear you haven't got the money for this show," Kaufman said.

"Who told you?" I asked sort of stupidly, knowing that he was right.

The Erlanger firm had agreed to put up a small sum,

enough to enable me to go ahead with the preliminary arrangements. I had become so enmeshed in planning for the show that I kept putting off the fact that the bulk of the financing still needed to be raised.

"One of the boys at the *Times* told me," Kaufman replied. "Is it true?"

"Don't worry about the money," I stalled. "The Erlangers have plenty of money." I was sorry I said that, but it was too late.

"I'm not dealing with the Erlangers," Kaufman snapped. "I'm dealing with you."

Shaken by this brief exchange, I managed to separate myself from Kaufman a block or two later, and headed for the Selwyn. Although *Three's a Crowd* was a hit, it had not yet fully recovered its investment. The continuing Depression dissuaded me from approaching Giannini. At the Selwyn I mentioned my problem to the box-office treasurer who promptly announced, "Oh, I can get you the money."

"From where?" I asked, hardly believing what I heard.

"Oh," he said, "from the speculators, the brokers."

"Really," I replied and walked away.

I went to see Louis Lotito, then treasurer at the New Amsterdam Theatre, and now president of City Playhouses, Inc. I told him what the Selwyn man had said.

"That's right," Louis replied. "Haven't you heard of the 'buys'?" I had not. I had in some respects remained totally naïve about certain business techniques in the legitimate theatre. Louis looked at me, a smile wreathing his pleasant Italian face.

"Max, it's hard to believe," he remarked.

"Well, that's the way it is."

Lotito said he would get the money for me. The big brokers would advance the money, in return for which I would agree to let them have certain designated tickets each week, choice locations, of course. And each week, before paying for the tickets, they would deduct a portion as payment for the loan. Within two weeks Lotito handed me checks totaling ninety-nine thousand dollars.

Meanwhile, Kaufman was turning out his sketches, and Dietz and Schwartz, secluded in a room at the St. Moritz Hotel, were industriously creating the words and music. I shall never forget the Sunday Schwartz telephoned.

"Max," he yelled, "we've just finished a knockout."

"Sing it for me," I said. "I can't wait."

Schwartz sang "I Love Louisa." I nearly jumped through the mouthpiece. In my exuberance I proclaimed, "Boys, it's a pleasure to go broke with you."

Schwartz and Dietz had two other songs that I loved: "Dancing in the Dark" and "New Sun in the Sky," and what I was trying to tell them over the telephone was that the way things were going, even if the show failed, I would be happy, having had the pleasure of being associated with it and its talented people.

Rehearsals began in March. They were a happy time. The performers, all top grade, went about their assignments with a professional assurance that was a delight to behold. There were few moments of temperament, everyone evidently having the utmost confidence in the others. I haunted the theatre, cheered by what I saw and heard. Johnson's designs for the sets connoted the style and dash we were after. Mme. Rasch, as usual, was working with her dancers in businesslike fashion. Short had charged the atmosphere with excitement by suggesting that we use twin revolving stages to enhance our effects, making them part of the action instead of using them for changing scenery. I bought the idea on the spot. Never before had a revue in America used a revolving stage, much less two of them.

As had been the case with *Three's a Crowd*, we approached the Garrick Theatre in Philadelphia in a mood of calm confidence. There had been something about *The Band Wagon* from its inception that seemed to mark it for success. The first indication that this feeling was valid came at the final dress rehearsal. Noël Coward, who was in the audience, could barely restrain himself. He was, of course, an early devotee of the smart sophisticated revue, and as *The Band Wagon* unfolded, he kept yelling "Bravo!"

Encouraging as was his demonstration, it was also unnerving. I expected a hit, but I had not anticipated such a reaction from one of the theatre's most sophisticated practitioners. Could Coward have been exaggerating his appreciation out of politeness? Did I dare believe that what I had assembled here, helped edit and co-ordinate, had actually been touched by the wand?

I faced the opening night in Philadelphia with rising agitation. That first night could have been the New York première. Because of the people involved, especially because of the Astaires, a little army of Broadway professionals descended upon us: producers, actors, lyric writers, authors, newspapermen. I stood in the back of the theatre hardly able to believe my ears. Each number brought its own reward. Shouts of "Bravo" and "Encore" reverberated through the old Garrick. Even the revolving stages won their own cheers, as they deserved. Short and Johnson had integrated them into the action in all sorts of imaginative ways until they seemed to create a poetry of their own. In the finale they turned in opposite directions, one of them bearing a carousel, while on the other the Astaires danced as they had never danced before, and the orchestra played that contagious polka, "I Love Louisa."

When the houselights went on, the buzzing in the aisles and later in the lobby signaled a smash hit. By the end of the performance I was in a complete daze. I remember that Oscar Hammerstein 2nd, whom I knew slightly, graciously sought me out to say that he thought this was the best revue of our time. I did not go backstage. Instead, with Millie, I walked around the block and then into the alley behind the theatre. I was sitting on the fire escape steps when someone came to say the company wanted to see me. I went backstage, still stunned. Millie apologized for me, saying that I was tired, and took me back to our hotel.

Neither of us slept that night. Mostly, I sat at the edge of my bed. Over and over again I kept saying that this was not possible, this thing that had happened tonight. I kept saying, "No, it can't be true," with Millie reassuring me that it was true, and in the next breath I was saying, "God, how happy Cliff would have been for me tonight. How proud he would have been. This is what he would have wanted me to do. This is what he would have done had he lived."

Through the night I talked of the plays I would do in the future, the big, big plans. Millie wisely tried to remind me that there was still New York, a sobering enough thought, but I did not see how we could miss.

The remainder of the Philadelphia engagement was a sellout. We spent the time putting the finishing touches to the show, increasing the pace here, changing it there. As we faced opening night in New York, June 3, 1931, at the once glorious home of the musical theatre, the New Amsterdam, now a movie grind house, Kaufman observed in his saturnine way that he wished we had left the show in Philadelphia and brought the notices to Broadway. No one paid any attention to his gloom, convinced that he was as confident as the rest of us.

The New York première was a dressy affair, most of those in the orchestra arriving in white ties and tails. I myself was in full dress. For those of us who had gone through the excitement of the Philadelphia opening, the cheers that greeted *The Band Wagon* were just a little anticlimactic, though most enjoyable. The following morning I read and reread Brooks Atkinson's review in *The New York Times*. It was a review that was to give me great satisfaction and solace through the years. It still does. It read:

After the appearance of *The Band Wagon,* which was staged at the New Amsterdam last evening, it will be difficult for the old-time musical show to hold up its head. George S. Kaufman and Howard Dietz have put the stigmata on stupid display by creating a thoroughly modern revue. It is both funny and lovely; it has wit, gaiety and splendor. Brilliantly written by Mr. Kaufman and Mr. Dietz, brilliantly staged by Hassard Short, brilliantly acted by the Astaires, Frank Morgan, Helen Broderick and Tilly Losch, and brilliantly scored by Arthur Schwartz, it is a long step forward in the development of a civilized art of stage revues.

The authors are not unmindful of what they are doing. In the first number they travesty briskly all the set pieces of formula musical shows—the moonlight serenade, the blackout, the waltz number and the dance routine. "Nanette" lampoons the close harmony hokum; and in "Where Can He Be?" Miss Broderick laughs off the sleazy coquettishness of the hackneyed leading lady.

But *The Band Wagon* comes bringing gifts of its own. Nothing the *Chauve-Souris* has brought here surpasses the impish "Hoops" number that Fred and Adele Astaire sing and dance in their freshest style. A jovial stein song, "I Love Louisa," substitutes for the flamboyant old first-act finale a whirling merry-go-round flourish. In three extraordinary numbers Tilly Losch raises musical show dancing to the level of fine art. One is a cloth-of-gold bit described as "The Flag." There is macabre splendor in "Dancing in the Dark." And the ballad of "The Beggar Waltz," with Fred Astaire, puts the revolving stage to use as an instrument of narrative beauty. Albert Johnson's gay settings, the smart costumes, the imaginative lighting give these decorative numbers a lean grace that is modern without being bizarre.

But the authors of *The Band Wagon* are satirists. Look to their sketches for the most malicious and expert wit of the season. "For Good Old Nectar" brings the old grads' cheering section into the college classroom and substitutes for the football hero the history champion. "The Pride of the Claghornes" turns topsy-turvy the most hallowed traditions of the South. "Pour le Bain" applies cultured salesmanship to the marketing of bathroom appliances. There is a perverse lament for the business depression, and a skimming parody of a Fred Allen parody in *Three's a Crowd*. No devastating wisecracks, no smutty jokes, no heavy-handed gags, and no laboriously assembled jests—the satire is adroit, informed and intelligent. You need not check your brains with your hat.

This wryly tempered fooling requires skilled performers. *The Band Wagon* has just that sort of band. Frank Morgan's dignified futility and his accurately pitched voice do as well by the grandiloquent Southern Colonel as the blandly esoteric announcer. Helen Broderick's venom is subdued and deadly. For several years the Astaires have been the most engaging pair of dancers on the musical stage. *The Band Wagon* is the best vehicle they have had. They ride it jauntily, and Fred has ripened into a comedian whose spirit is as breezy as his stepping.

The other reviews were similar in tone. I called a ticket broker, Harry Kaufman. "Harry, how is it?" I asked. "Is it going to be O.K.?"

"Are you crazy?" Harry answered. "It's an absolute sensation."

I took my hat and went down to the Pennsylvania Station, where I boarded a Long Island Railroad train for Great Neck.

I wanted to play golf—alone.

12

Jerome Kern

No MATTER how intense the glow of achievement, it has
the unhappy and inevitable tendency to dim and cool.
Those of us who find life unsatisfactory without this comforting warmth are constantly compelled to seek its renewal. This need has been one of the plagues of my life.
Though I think I live better with it now than I did, it
remains a constant spur in my flesh. By the end of June—
during which I had been warmed by the inner pleasure
of seeing my two hits playing simultaneously on opposite
sides of the street—I was casting around for new conquests.
I had contributed two milestones to the American revue,
and I should have been content to rest for a while, to
conserve my strength and harvest my rewards. But I could
not. Having worked with some of the great talents in the
theatre, having proved to myself and the world that I
knew my business, I strained to push on.

I spoke to Max Dreyfus. "I would like to try a musical,"
I said. "I would like to try one with Jerome Kern."

I was not being ingenuous, although Dreyfus could have

interpreted it that way. Dreyfus was a close friend of Kern's and at that moment one of the most important men in American music. As a boy he had come to America from Kuppenheim, near Baden, with dreams of becoming a pianist and composer. He had taken a job with the music publishing firm of Harms, Inc., where he was a pianist, arranger, errand boy and occasionally even a salesman of music. In his own cool and detached way he came to the conclusion that he lacked the talent to realize either of his dreams. He became instead a businessman. In time he was able to buy into the company and become its prime mover. It was under his direction that Harms ultimately was able to take over the publishing firm of M. Witmark & Sons, which for years had been supreme in the field.

Dreyfus brought to his new calling something unusual in the music-publishing business—his musicianship. This enabled him to understand, ferret out and nurture talent. Kern was one of those to come under his wing. Young, unknown, and good-looking, Kern walked into Dreyfus' office bearing an armful of unpublished melodies and a desire to imbibe the atmosphere of the music world. Dreyfus listened to Kern's work, sniffed the prospects, and took him on. At first he assigned Kern to selling sheet music through the Hudson Valley. Then he encouraged the young composer by publishing some of his melodies, arranging for him to accompany Marie Dressler in her vaudeville engagements, and helping him get composing assignments for Broadway shows. The two formed a fast friendship. Kern eventually had all his music published by Harms and became an important executive in the company.

My desire to produce a musical by Kern stemmed from two salient facts. The more obvious one was his eminence among the theatre's composers. In 1905, when I was still dreaming about going into show business, Kern had already produced the well-received "How'd You Like to Spoon with Me?", his first song to be interpolated into a Broadway show, *The Earl and the Girl.* In 1910, the year I ran off to join the Behman Show in Pittsburgh, Kern had revised the music for *Mr. Wix of Wickham,* and Alan Dale, then drama critic for the *New York Journal,* was inquiring in print, "Who is this Jerome Kern whose music towers in an Eiffel way above the average hurdy-gurdy accompaniment of the present-day musical comedy?" And in 1914, when Victor Herbert heard Kern's songs for *The Girl from Utah,* which included "They Didn't Believe Me," Herbert announced, "This man will inherit my mantle." The predictions and acclaim that continued to greet him as he turned out such numbers as "Till the Clouds Roll By," "Who?" and "Look for the Silver Lining" were further substantiated by *Show Boat,* for which he wrote what can only be described as a cornucopia of a score.

My other reason for wanting to do a musical with Kern was more personal. It sprang from a sense of adventure, a feeling that having been involved in probing new approaches to the revue, I should like to help explore new pathways for the American musical. In 1927 *Show Boat,* written with Oscar Hammerstein 2nd, had given Broadway a musical with a new dimension. Called a musical comedy, it was much more than that—an authentic musical play, the kind the more astute and demanding critics of the American theatre had been talking about for years. Its characters were human beings with whom it was possible to sympathize. *Show Boat* told a completely logical and poignant love story; it utilized a true native background for atmosphere and setting. Above all, it had an artistic unity. Music, dance and comedy were integrated and developed out of the basic plot.

Doing *Show Boat* had been Kern's idea. He had persisted in the face of opposition, first from Edna Ferber
who had written the novel, and later from his friends. Miss
Ferber could not comprehend how her account of life on a
show boat plying the Mississippi could be decked out
with chorus girls and the conventional tricks of musical
comedy. She had no use for anything that might debase
what had become one of the most popular novels in
American fiction. But when Kern outlined his ideas to her
and promised a new form of musical, she was wise enough
to share his dream. Meanwhile, Kern's friends argued
that the average Broadway theatregoer went to a musical
in search of girls and lighthearted entertainment. He
would not be interested in Kern's ideas of art or what a
musical could or should be.

None of these arguments had deterred Kern, or Hammerstein, who had more than willingly enlisted to adapt
the book and write the lyrics. Hammerstein's beliefs
about what direction the American musical should take
agreed completely with Kern's. Together they formed an
indomitable barricade against the nay-sayers.

It is hardly necessary to tally the results. They gave
Broadway and America a pioneering effort and a classic,
laying the groundwork for what was to become America's
undeniable contribution to the world's theatre. Kern's
great dream opened the way for such creative artists as
Rodgers and Hammerstein, Frank Loesser, Leonard Bernstein, Alan Jay Lerner and Frederick Loewe. Kern himself bequeathed to the world songs it has never forgotten.
Edna Ferber, when she first heard the words and music for
"Ol' Man River," said that as the music mounted and
mounted, her hair "stood on end, the tears came to my
eyes, and I breathed like a heroine in a melodrama."

The sheer music of *Show Boat* overwhelmed me when
I heard it for the first time. But even more I was mag-

netized by the possibilities I sensed had been opened to the musical theatre. My remark to Dreyfus, therefore, was not so much ingenuous as deliberate. Dreyfus could say a word in my behalf to Kern. And he did. A few days later I received a call inviting Millie and me to dinner in the Dreyfus home in Bronxville. "Kern would like to see you," Dreyfus said. "He will be there."

Elated as I had been on getting the call, and though I had prepared myself on every phase of Kern's career, I could not quell my mounting nervousness as the train carried Millie and me to Bronxville that Saturday. It was not yet dark, and the countryside of suburban homes, open fields, and the gentle little Bronx River that runs part of the way along the tracks was pleasant to see. But I was not paying too much attention. I felt like a schoolboy headed for the examination that would determine whether or not he received his diploma. There was no doubt in my mind that I had been summoned to pass muster. As we rolled passed Fordham, Woodlawn and Mount Vernon, I kept wondering how to avoid failing the test, whether I should keep my mouth shut for the most part, letting what I had done on Broadway speak for me, or whether I should try to impress him with the range of my background.

These questions and others swirled through my head like dry leaves in a wind as we alighted from the train in Bronxville and headed toward the Dreyfus home. The home itself was everything that could have been expected. Though others in the nation had been badly hurt by economic pressures of the dislocated times, there was no sign of it here. A huge, handsome old house, it was set well back from the road, among tall trees, lovely shrubs and dazzling flowers. The grass was a lush, healthy green, unharmed yet by summer's heat.

I tried to be simultaneously earnest and casual as I was introduced to Kern, a man of medium height, his hair graying and receding, his nose strong and sharp, his clothes well tailored and immaculate. Through his heavy spectacles I saw eyes that were alert and impish, while his mouth spread in a warm smile illuminating his whole countenance.

He congratulated me on the success of *The Band Wagon,* which he had just seen. I told him how sorry I was that Broadway had not heard anything new from him since *Sweet Adeline,* which he had written with Hammerstein. A more conventional musical than *Show Boat,* it had opened in September, 1929, and full of nostalgia and heavy with sentiment, it suddenly became an anachronism in the face of the dire events that shook the nation the following month. It closed after exhausting its heavy preopening sale.

Throughout dinner, one of those typical German repasts that seemed to go on for hours, Kern kept up a marvelous flow of conversation, his nimble and informed mind leaping from one subject to another with astounding ease. No one could deny that here was a man who had devoted his life to a study of the theatre and to his art, who had traveled widely and delved into a variety of subjects on which he could speak with professorial authority. Clearly a sophisticate, a *bon vivant* and lover of life, he presented a picture of dignity and sedateness that always appeared to be tempered by that pixieish smile.

I listened in rapt attention, made occasional comments, and saw my hopes, like a toy sailboat, drift farther and farther away. I could hardly meet the requirements of this urbane man who seemed to have been to the manner born. Indeed, I gathered that he had been reared in an upper-middle-class home of culture and refinement. His father, born in Baden-Baden, but brought up in New

York, had earned a comfortable living, first as president of a company that had a contract to water the city's streets, and later as head of a merchandising firm. In addition, the elder Kern had made wise investments in real estate.

Kern's mother was a cultivated woman, Kern said at one point, who enjoyed giving regal parties and dinners. She was a good amateur pianist, and music, books and theatre discussions had been a regular diet in his home. As he talked, I wondered how I could expect to cope with such a man, I, a first-generation American who had foolishly cut off my schooling, who had carefully and at times painfully acquired the necessary social graces instead of absorbing them into my bloodstream from childhood. It was only too evident that Kern regarded taste and "class" as virtues of the highest importance. Although I felt that I could satisfy any demand in the first category, I was not at all certain that he would think I measured up in the second. Not if he had any trace of the snob in his veins.

After dinner the cigars were passed. We were about to adjourn to the drawing room when Kern caught me by the elbow and indicated that he wished me to follow him. We went upstairs and into a bedroom. He closed the door and began to talk.

"I did not wish to say this downstairs in front of the others," he began, "because I thought I might embarrass you. However, Dreyfus knows how I feel. I think you are going to mean a great deal to the theatre. These are bad times, and the old producers are falling away. You can be the theatre's white hope. No, don't protest, there is no need for modesty here. I have seen *Three's a Crowd* and, as you know, *The Band Wagon*. It is clear to me that you are in the tradition of Ziegfeld and Charles Frohman. You are like me, a devil on details. You spare nothing to make a production as right and as attractive as possible."

I managed a "thank you," which Kern brushed aside with a wave of his hand. He continued, "Dreyfus tells me that you are now interested in producing a musical and that you would like to do one by me. It happens that I am working on one with Otto Harbach. I would like very much to invite you to my home next week—I live here in Bronxville, too—and we'll discuss it further. You can listen to some of the music I have completed. If you approve, we can talk terms."

It was difficult to stifle a desire to say that I did not have to hear anything, that I was ready to talk terms that moment. Never had I expected it to be as easy as this. I held back because I sensed that this man would not approve of what might be construed as immature eagerness. Though he might be vain, he was a thorough professional who would not regard this as a compliment.

"I am thinking," he went on, "in terms of another musical which, like *Show Boat,* would attempt to explore new paths. I think the American public is ready to accept musical theatre that is more than routine claptrap. *Show Boat* has encouraged me to think that it is possible to work artistically and with greater integrity in the medium than may have been imagined. Otto has an idea for a musical that I think lends itself to serious treatment. You should know that we have been talking about eliminating chorus girls, production numbers and formal comedy routines. We are striving to make certain that there will be a strong motivation for the music throughout."

It sounded fascinating, adventurous. I told Kern of my enthusiasm and that I agreed with his estimate of the public's taste, citing that as my own reason for having undertaken to do quality revues.

Signing contracts for what was to be *The Cat and the Fiddle* was, as I had expected, a formality. For the remainder of the summer I made periodic trips to listen to the progress of the show and made preparations for what we decided would be an October première at the Globe Theatre. Harbach, who had first worked with Kern on *Sunny*, in 1925, set his story in a music conservatory in Brussels. There he had a young American girl, partial to American-style popular music, fall in love with a fellow student, a serious Rumanian composer. The Rumanian had completed an opera. At first the difference in their musical tastes threatened to keep them apart. But through the plot's diverse machinations, they each came to see value in the other's musical propensities and point of view. By the final curtain they were, of course, happily united.

Dealing with human beings and music, the story stimulated Kern to range widely. He incorporated a fugue into the score; inspired, he wrote the memorable *canzonetta* "The Night Was Made for Love," which formed a sort of unifying thread throughout the play. In addition, there were those characteristically lyric and lovely melodies: "She Didn't Say Yes," "Poor Pierrot," "One Moment Alone," and "Try to Forget."

We signed Bettina Hall for the role of Shirley Sheridan, the American girl, and Georges Metaxa for the role of Victor Florescu, the Rumanian. Others in important parts were George Meader and Odette Myrtil, with Jose Ruben directing. Rehearsals began at the end of August. In early September I sent *Three's a Crowd* on what was to be an extended tour across the country.

Not all, however, was exhilaration and pleasure. Kern was a terror. When he said at our initial meeting that he was a devil on details, he was not exaggerating. He gave me early samples of this demoniacal drive, particularly in his composing. He would sit at the piano with his music manuscript pad on a writing desk attached to the keyboard. This saved him the trouble of leaning forward to make his notations on the music stand itself. He wrote his notes in pen and ink. When he completed enough bars, he played them to get an idea of what he had written. More often than not both palms came crashing down on the hapless keys. But when he wrote something that pleased him, he rubbed his hair in great agitation and excitement. He often said that composing resembled fishing —"You get a nibble, but you don't know whether it's a minnow or a marlin until you reel it in. You write twenty tunes to get two good ones—and the wastebasket yearns for the music."

So exacting, so prolific, and so bottled up with melody was this man that frequently he wrote two different tunes for a given point in a story. Those discarded but too good to be thrown away were filed for future use. The true depth of Kern's fastidiousness and energy, however, I did not glean until after we had gone into rehearsal. He was tireless in his drive for perfection. It seemed that he hardly needed any sleep at all. No detail escaped him. The slightest misplacement of the tiniest prop was enough to send him screaming down an aisle shouting invective left and right.

Mere details? Hardly. Oscar Hammerstein 2nd once said, talking about his own experiences with Kern's theatrical fanaticism, "He proved to me that while people may not take any particular notice of any one small effect, the over-all result of such finickiness produces a polish that an audience appreciates." This insistence on perfection did not disturb me. I wanted perfection as much as he did. But what caused me anguish, what tore at my heart and my gut, was Kern the man—the many-sided man who could be, when he wished, everything other than the gentle, sophisticated individual I had met in Max Dreyfus' home that Saturday night in Bronxville.

He could be maddeningly irritating, constantly counter-
ing almost any suggestion with an impertinent "Why?"—
a deliberate tactic calculated to unnerve the questioner.
I have heard it said that he once told a young conductor,
"Young man, if you wish to accomplish anything in this
business, you must remember that it is extremely important that you meet any suggestion with the word 'Why?'
and say it loudly and in an annoying manner. That way
you're a little ahead to start with, and in the end you'll get
your way."

This trait, along with his almost neurotic need to be
right, did not help matters. Our clashes were frequent and
intense. I did not have the guile or the finesse to convert
him to an idea by advancing it in such a way that he
would believe he had originated it. There were horrible
moments when, as if in a nightmare, it seemed that again
I was being bullied by Aaron Hoffman, again I was in
Al Lewis' shadow. Nevertheless, such was the nature of
this man that there were days when I could do no wrong,
when he professed love and admiration for me, trumpeted
my virtues as if I were, in truth, the white hope of the
theatre he had said I was.

The complexity and paradoxes of this genius—for he
was indeed that, as the music library he left behind testi-
fies—were revealed also by his pixieishness. For all his
urbanity and sophistication, which overawed even his
poor timid wife Eva, he was, when the mood was upon
him, a latter-day Peter Pan, a man with a child's heart,
who refused to grow up. He could, when so inclined, step
out on the balcony of a hotel suite and deliver a speech
on the virtues of temperance to a startled group of celebrants emerging from a night club across the street. Once
in London, strolling with some friends, he came upon a
group of workers laying the foundation for a pavilion. He
blandly announced that plans for the building's construc-

tion had been canceled. Everyone, he said, could go home. And they did.

Nor did I escape. He knew how much I abhorred obscenity and lewdness on the stage. He had heard, also, that I had argued vehemently against the "Pour le Bain" sketch in *The Band Wagon,* in which Helen Broderick, after inspecting various bathroom appliances in a swank salon, hinted to the salesman that there had been no discussion of another type of fixture. The salesman, always with a line of poetry at his command, replied, "Heard melodies are sweet, but those unheard are sweeter." This became one of the show's biggest laugh moments, but it never appealed to me. Kern roared when he heard of my objections. In one of his puckish moods he wrote a lewd sketch which, with the aid of several members of the company, he inserted into a rehearsal one afternoon in Philadelphia. I was almost frantic with rage before I understood that the scene was a joke at my expense. Kern, never more gleeful than when one of his gags succeeded, was beside himself with laughter. Tears streamed down his face. Ten minutes later he could become moody and miserable. He was completely unpredictable. No one knew from one moment to the next what to expect from him. He was not easy to live with.

The Cat and the Fiddle opened on schedule, captivating both critics and public. I had my third straight hit and Broadway gulped. Members of the theatrical fraternity, envy smudged all over their faces, wondered, "How does that Gordon do it?" while on tablecloths in the Rialto's restaurants they figured my profits.

How little Broadway or the world really knew or ever knows of a man's life. Three straight hits—but I was borrowing money on which to live. *Three's a Crowd,* which had run eight full months at the Selwyn, managed to just about make back its investment, including the monies that Giannini and the Erlangers had advanced. But the tour had proved a dismal failure.

The Depression and talking pictures had all but engulfed the road. Evidence of the downward economic slide had been accumulating on Broadway. Before the season was over, the hitherto all-powerful Shuberts were in financial trouble. Actors were begging for work. Bankers, trying to protect their theatre mortgages, began producing shows. Conditions away from New York City were worse. *Three's a Crowd* ran into disaster signals on its first stop, no more than thirty minutes from Manhattan. In Newark, where the potential gross had been figured at approximately thirty thousand dollars for a week's playing time, we did exactly ninety-two hundred dollars. When the pattern was repeated in the following stand, I hurried to the company and announced that the show could not continue under these circumstances. Everyone agreed to a salary cut. *Three's a Crowd* went on, taking checks in cities when the banks closed, making no money at all, winding up with Webb, Allen and Holman receiving salaries of fifty dollars a week instead of the fifteen hundred dollars for which they had been under contract. Better a bird in hand than the breadline or selling apples.

Nor had *The Band Wagon* repaid its investment when *The Cat and the Fiddle* opened. I was the talk of Broadway, the wonder boy with the Midas touch who had to "touch" friends and associates to keep afloat.

There is a Saturday morning, five months after the opening of *The Cat and the Fiddle,* that is as vivid in my mind as if it had happened yesterday. It was the day on which I set aside two tickets for Noël Coward to see the show.

Coward and I had met for the first time less than a year

before, not long after the opening of *Three's a Crowd*. Millie, Hassard Short and I had gone to London to see a new musical, *Evergreen*, by Richard Rodgers and Lorenz Hart, being tried out in the West End. The Erlanger people thought I ought to see it with a view toward our producing it together on Broadway. However, I was not terribly impressed by *Evergreen*, and it never did get to Broadway.

While in London we went to see Gertrude Lawrence and Coward in his big hit *Private Lives*. Short knew Coward and suggested after the performance that we go backstage and say hello. Coward greeted us most graciously and, after we were seated, looked straight at me and asked how I liked the play. "I liked it," I said, unenthusiastically.

"I can see that you really didn't, Mr. Gordon," Coward remarked, without the slightest rancor.

"But I did," I protested, taken aback by this forthright Englishman.

"All right, Mr. Gordon," he said chidingly, "I can see that you didn't. Now tell me the truth."

"Well," I began, "since you've asked me for it, I will tell you. I really liked the show until the last act. In that act you play a scene with Miss Lawrence for about fifteen minutes, and I must admit that you do get a lot of laughs. But you overplayed the scene, and with that laughter I felt the sincerity of your play go right out the window. I didn't believe either one of you, and I was sick of both of you by the time the scene was finished."

Jumping up, Coward exclaimed, "My God, these Americans certainly put their finger on things. It's true. I have felt that I was losing the audience—I knew I was losing the audience—but I didn't know why. They were laughing, and as you say, they were the wrong kind of laughs. I can't tell you how much I thank you."

The next morning, as I was preparing to leave, Coward

visited me at the Savoy Hotel. Again he was profuse in his thanks. "I wanted to tell you," he said, "that I've followed your suggestions. I rewrote the scene overnight, and I've called rehearsals for this afternoon."

I did not see Coward again until that night in Philadelphia when he was practically jumping up and down in his seat at the dress rehearsal of *The Band Wagon*. He had come to America to make plans for the production of *Private Lives,* in which he and Miss Lawrence were to repeat their roles on Broadway. About six weeks after the opening of *Private Lives,* I was walking on Broadway when I met Clifton Webb, a close friend of Coward's. "You ought to go up and see Noël," Webb remarked. "He's asked about you."

I had wanted to, of course, but in spite of my London brashness, I was still in awe of Coward. Webb's nudge helped. Coward was happy to see me, and we went for a drive. As we rode along, I managed to say that someday I would like to do a play with him, to which he replied, "Well, someday you might."

By one of those mad coincidences, on the Saturday for which I had arranged Coward's tickets to *The Cat and the Fiddle,* I awoke to read in *The New York Times* that he had written a new comedy called *Design for Living.* It was, the story said, a play about three people "who love each other very much," and Alfred Lunt, Lynn Fontanne and Coward were to appear in it in New York the following January.

"Good God!" I hollered to Millie across the breakfast table so that she jumped with fright. "Here, read this. This is the biggest thing in show business." I grabbed the telephone and called Sam Harris, who had become a close friend and confidant. "For heaven's sake, Sam," I bellowed, "did you see that news about Coward this morning? What do you say to that combination? Boy, how would you like to produce that one? A dream, isn't it?"

That night I went to the theatre intending to greet Coward after the performance. The curtain had gone up. The first person I encountered in the lobby was the show's press agent, Howard Benedict. He gave me a big grin and an enthusiastic, "Hello, boss. Congratulations. Coward said to make sure you see him after the show. He's going to offer you his new play."

"Wise guy," I replied, angered by what seemed a pretty poor joke. "What do they need me for?"

"Well, all I know is what I told you." Benedict said.

After the performance I asked Coward what was going on, and he laughed. "I've got to run along now, Max. See me Tuesday at 12:30. I'm at the Waldorf."

I sweated out Sunday and Monday. Max Gordon presents Noël Coward . . . the tantalizing idea gave me no rest. A coup. What a combination—almost worth a right arm.

I drove Millie out of her mind as I babbled about the prospect. On Tuesday I was at the Waldorf. I found Coward in bed, attired in a colorful robe, having breakfast. The man knew how to live.

"Noël," I began, "I must do that play. I hope you were not fooling."

"No, Max," Coward replied, "I wasn't. But do you know the terms? We'll each want ten per cent of the gross as salaries. I'll want another ten per cent as the author. We'll put up twenty thousand dollars, and you will put up ten thousand. It will have to be a limited engagement —twelve weeks. I get bored after that, and besides, I've other things to do. What do you say, old boy?"

"It's a deal," I said, offering my hand. Coward took it, saying, "You don't want to think it over, do you?"

"No," I said. That handshake was the only contract we ever had.

I asked for the courtesy of using his telephone. I called Millie to tell her the news. When I hung up, Coward was smiling from ear to ear, a mixture of amusement and amazement on his face. "Wonderful, wonderful," he said. "You know, I thought you were going to call the press." He was to mention the incident many times in later years, and always with admiration.

13

❦

Disaster, with Music

NOTHING ENDURES, cynical poets wail. Certainly the state of euphoria induced by my triumphant encounter with Noël Coward did not. A few all too brief weeks of excitement, the Broadway buzzing, the ego satisfaction of sideward glances as I entered a restaurant, the sense of soaring onward and upward, the vain, deluding human assumption that what was happening to others around me would never happen to me—a few all too brief weeks and it was all over. The cloud to which I had ascended vanished into thin air.

In the joyous excitement following the opening of *The Band Wagon,* I had agreed to do another revue with Howard Dietz and Arthur Schwartz. In retrospect it was a foolish thing to have done. There is a saying about going to the well once too often. But there is also a fairly general tradition that a producer goes along with successful writers. My agreement was not only natural but almost obligatory. Dietz and Schwartz had given me two hits in a row—in the case of *Three's a Crowd* it was not their

(157)

fault that conditions on the road were such that the show failed to make money.

In the spring of 1932, as the Depression slipped further and further into what was to be its darkest period, getting money for the new show, *Flying Colors,* was impossible. Bankrolls—what there were of them—had gone into hiding. Brokers on whom I had counted were in trouble. There was talk of surprisingly few new productions. Many producers who kept going figured that the only things to do were revivals. At least the royalties could be eliminated in the case of classics, and old sets were available.

My own personal financial position deteriorated. As a successful producer I had convinced myself that it was necessary to keep up appearances. At the same time I was intent on trying to protect stock market securities I had purchased on margin. The result was an accumulation of debts reaching close to one hundred thousand dollars. On the face of it my behavior appears now to have been the epitome of vainglorious folly. Actually, it was not an extraordinary or wildly illogical position.

I had gone into producing on borrowed money. There was nothing wrong with this. Businessmen frequently do, expecting to repay their obligations from profits. I had expected to begin repaying my debts with the profits from *Three's a Crowd.* This turned out to be a miscalculation. But *The Band Wagon* did close its engagement with a ninety-thousand-dollar profit, half of which was mine, and *The Cat and the Fiddle* had just about cleared its investment at the time of my meeting with Coward. Running strongly, I figured it would go a long way toward my making good my intentions. But this was not to be. Instead, unable to raise the required capital for *Flying Colors* from outside sources, I was forced to use my profits.

Because of the economic climate we decided that although we would try to do another sophisticated, modern revue for essentially the same audience that had admired *Three's a Crowd* and *The Band Wagon,* we could not afford to make it too restricted for the general taste. Hence the decision to present the revue on a somewhat larger scale than *The Band Wagon.*

We signed Clifton Webb, always good insurance. He could dance, act, clown and sing. Indeed, one critic had said of him, "Little or no scenery is needed when Webb is on the stage—he is his own production." From *Three's a Crowd* we brought back the fetching and excellent Tamara Geva. We hired the incomparably funny Charles Butterworth, who could give the appearance of a man always in need of someone to help him cross the street, whose grasp of any subject could be as feeble and confused as an American tourist in a five o'clock Paris traffic jam. To round out an excellent cast, we signed Vilma and Buddy Ebsen.

Dietz decided, with my agreement, to seek a fresh talent for the large dance numbers. After watching some of the work of the able but then, from a Broadway point of view, completely inexperienced Agnes de Mille, we gave her the job. We also decided, for a change of pace and because of his heralded flair for the spectacular, to give the scene designing assignment to Norman Bel Geddes. Dietz himself would handle the general direction.

We went into rehearsal in August. It was hot and I was nervous. Nor did it help my anxiety to discover that the mercurial Kern, reunited with his former partner Oscar Hammerstein 2nd, had written a new show, *Music in the Air,* which, without a word to me, he had given to another producer. As I have indicated, there is a general tradition for producers and writers to continue their relationship after they have enjoyed success together, unless that relationship has been an unhappy one for business or personal reasons. Kern never had given me any reason to believe that whatever disagreements we had during the tryout period of *The Cat and the Fiddle* had lingered. On the contrary, he had sworn undying fealty to me following an incident that occurred in the Globe Theatre not long after the opening of the show.

The theatre had been in the process of changing ownership. On the Saturday night of the week in which the transaction was made, I went to the box office to collect the show's share of the gross receipts and discovered that someone had appropriated the till. I had no money on which I could put my hands. Phone calls to the various members of the Erlanger firm, which had a forty-per-cent interest in the show, proved futile. The actors had to be paid, and I was determined not to stay a moment longer in that theatre. In a white-hot anger I ran to Tillie Leblang, then one of the leading ticket brokers, and pleaded with her to lend me ten thousand dollars so that I could pay the cast and move the production to the George M. Cohan, which I knew was available. I signed a note for the money. On Monday I went to the Erlanger office and told them what had happened. Saul Baron and Marc Heiman listened with mild interest. When I suggested that the Erlanger firm ought to join me in the note to Tillie Leblang, Baron bluntly and with what amounted to tacit agreement from Heiman, refused. From Kern, at least, I gained praise. He called me his hero and blessed me over and over again.

Thus, Kern's action in regard to his new show was a bitter blow. The continuing slide in the nation's economy and the unsatisfactory rehearsals of *Flying Colors* did not help my state of mind. I had not been a sound sleeper for years. Now I began to suffer from insomnia and nerves. The slightest noise made me jump. I became increasingly irritable, and found myself screaming at Millie over minor incidents, something I had never done before.

Instead of matters improving for *Flying Colors*, they seemed to grow worse. Agnes de Mille, who was to distinguish herself so brilliantly in musical comedy choreography time and again, was unused to the pressures of preparing a Broadway show. Insecure in her handling of Broadway-type dancers, she was unable to organize rehearsals satisfactorily. Bel Geddes, overbearing and unsympathetic, insisted that some of the dances be made to fit what Miss de Mille regarded as unsafe sets. There were bitter arguments. Dietz tried to maintain the peace—fortifying himself with the help of a flask. Schwartz frequently lost his temper. Webb and Tamara, refusing to be caught up in the uncertainties of what was going on, proceeded to take care of their own numbers.

I was helpless. I shouted. But matters had gotten to the point where no one was paying any attention to me. "What's going to happen to me?" I wailed as visions of my indebtedness rose before my eyes. I began to worry about what would happen to Millie, to my mother, to Millie's mother and father, all of whom were dependent upon me for support. Fantasies leaped into my fevered brain. I saw myself working as a stage doorman, while Millie slaved in some department store—Millie, whose career I had clipped short out of my own selfishness.

Sleep now left me almost entirely. One day as I sat in the back of the theatre watching rehearsals, I began to sob. I knew that I was in deep mental trouble. In the succeeding days nothing anyone would say or do could calm me. Millie begged me to see a doctor. I refused. I was terrified at what the doctor might say. The crying continued. In the midde of ordinary conversations the merest hint of disagreement caused tears.

The night of the run-through was unbearably hot. It

did not help me either to see what was in progress on the stage. I felt myself being pushed to the edge of panic. More than ever now a sense of impending disaster began to rise within me, like a swollen river fed by flooded mountain streams. Friends assured me that the show would be in shape by opening night—"it always is" are among the more famous words in the theatre.

Tormented mercilessly in my mind, unable to sit still, unable to stand still, I headed for Philadelphia and the beginning of the tryout period.

The dress rehearsal in Philadelphia was my Inferno. I sat between Millie and Ben Boyar, my general manager. Nothing seemed ready—the dances, costumes, lighting—everything was out of joint. The rehearsal went on for hours. It was almost three o'clock in the morning. All that I had built and striven for in the last two and a half years was being washed away.

The Forrest Theatre, where the rehearsal took place, has a curving marble staircase. I happened to turn around, and it caught my eye. A thought flashed through my mind —at least Millie would have the insurance. I jumped from my seat and ran toward the staircase. Up the steps, up and around I ran until I had gained the top. Behind me came Millie and Boyar. They were calling me back. I began to climb the balustrade. I remember nothing else. Boyar told me later that I was threatening to jump. I hesitated. Boyar grabbed me.

When I regained a semblance of sanity, Millie and he persuaded me to return to my suite at the Ritz-Carlton. They thought it would be a good idea if we walked. They clutched me lest I break away. All the way back I cried, berated those associated with me, repeated mournfully that I was bankrupt, dishonored, that life was useless and no longer worth living. I wished I were dead.

As we entered the room, I found myself free and made a dash for the window. Boyar caught me again. He held me while Millie called a doctor. I was put under sedation. The next day they brought me back to New York, to the Leroy Sanitarium—behind bars. My lawyer and lifelong friend Abe Berman took over the management of my affairs and my interests in *Flying Colors.* My old and trusted friend Owen Davis protected my securities with his own funds. I was engulfed in what the doctors called a nervous breakdown.

Those first weeks in Leroy Sanitarium were one long, tormented nightmare. I made little progress. Actually, from a physical standpoint there is not much that doctors can do for a person whose nerve signals have become so jangled that they resemble the lights on a telephone switchboard gone wild. Sedation, warm packs, rest. That is all.

Suggestions that I submit to psychiatry seemed to upset me. In the end each case is individual, and recovery depends to a considerable degree on the complexity of the disturbance and the patient's own will to recover and live. For what seemed like an eternity to those near me, I did not care. There was no use in telling myself that after a series of hits I was entitled to one failure. All reason, all sense of proportion had fled.

Millie kept her vigil at my bedside, devoted, loyal, understanding. I dared not look at her. When I did, I could only think of the predicament to which I had brought her, and tears would fill my eyes. I needed her there by my bed. Yet there were moments when the anguish of these nightmarish visions made me wish she would go away.

Through the long hours of the night, as the tears streamed onto my pillow, I would try to review what had happened, how I had come to this pass from which there seemed to be no return. Occasionally there cut through the hopelessness the recollection that I was to produce Noël Coward's play. But that did not help me either. Suppose I was found out? Suppose Coward was to know that the man to whom he had entrusted his play was nearly out of his mind, a bundle of uncontrolled, jangled nerves, that this man was deep in debt? What would he do? Would I lose the play? Was there to be no relief from these burdens that had overwhelmed me?

The weeks passed. Rest and treatment had their effects. Raw nerves healed and quieted. My brain cleared. My body regained its strength, the crying became less frequent, less acute. Bleak despair gave way to cautious hope and gradually to determination.

Friends helped—those who would let few days pass without calling, without trying to give some word of cheer; those who wrote encouraging notes, who tried to say what I needed to hear. Wonderful Sime Silverman, that great man who founded *Variety*, would take me for drives to Long Island; Bernie Hart, Moss Hart's brother, George Kaufman, Sam H. Harris, Bobby North, Ben Boyar, Eddie Sobel and Bob Milford were among the many others who rallied round me.

There was a visit to the hospital by Harpo Marx that has been one of the more warming memories of my life. Harpo spent an hour with me, humoring me, showing me the promise of the future. As he arose to leave, he reached into his pocket and withdrew a roll of bills, threw it across the bed, and ran for the door. Four thousand dollars were strewn around—needed, helpful, reassuring. The following day Groucho called to tell me he knew what Harpo had done. "I want you to know," Groucho said, "that I've got fifty per cent and there is more where that came from."

I cried. But these were not the bitter tears. They were

the warming, heartening, cleansing tears—in their own way now helping me back to reality and new life.

Flying Colors had opened, not the shambles I had dreaded, nor the disgrace. Agnes de Mille had been relieved of her assignment and Albertina Rasch called to the rescue. The reviews were mild, the comparison with *The Band Wagon* inevitable. There was praise for three of the songs: "Louisiana Hayride," "Alone Together," and "A Shine on Your Shoes." The company was hailed and yet there was a pallor and a kind of languor over it all.

Happily, as time passed, I succeeded in accepting *Flying Colors* for what it was, a chapter among the darker pages of my chronicle. Now, I told myself, I must look forward only. I must completely regain my health and work as hard as I could to repay the friends who placed faith and funds in me and my career. I prayed that *Design for Living* would be my lifeline, and was daily encouraged by the excitement it appeared to be generating. Coward helped stoke the simmering hubbub by letting it be known that he had deliberately written the play for the Lunts and himself.

As *Flying Colors* neared the end of its engagement—188 performances at a cost of $125,000, none of which it regained—I received a call from John C. Wilson, Coward's American representative and business associate. Coward, Wilson announced, would shortly be on his way from England. I was to make arrangements for a theatre and an opening date, and set the time for rehearsals. Wilson added that the twenty thousand dollars Coward and the Lunts were investing had already been placed in the bank. A most fastidious businessman, Wilson also said it was highly desirable—he actually meant mandatory—that I have my ten thousand dollars in the bank by morning.

We had formed a corporation for the production, but

I had given little thought to my share of the deal, either before or since my illness. All along I think I had assumed that with two-thirds of the money available I would be able to get credit for my share. The call rattled me. For a few moments after hanging up, I thought I would faint. But I managed to pull my wits together and began to think. I dared not uncover my hand. Although Broadway knew that I had not been well, only a few knew how seriously ill I had been or, for that matter, how broke. To those not on the inside, I was one of the time's most successful producers.

I summoned Ben Boyar, told him what had happened, and asked that he give me whatever he could. He gave me three thousand dollars. Louis Lotito gave me thirty-five hundred dollars, and my sister Mary gave a similar amount. At that moment, in the eyes of those who mattered most, I was solvent.

Coward had said that *Design for Living* would be a lark. Actually it was hard, hard work. Its story line was somewhat on the thin side as Coward himself admitted. Otto, an artist (Alfred), and Leo, a playwright (Noël), have been fast friends for years and both are deeply in love with Gilda (Lynn), also an artist. She in turn loves both of them. But, harried by the dilemma and to escape the triangle, she marries a sober merchant from New York and crosses the Atlantic to Manhattan. In due course Otto and Leo turn up in her New York penthouse and proceed to disarm her with affection and impudent gaiety. There is only one avenue open. Gilda has a stormy showdown with her husband, who, being a gentleman, knows what he must do. As the final curtain nears, Gilda is bound back to the life she knows and on which she really thrives.

Design for Living, in short, was the sort of bizarre nonsense, the kind of breezy fandango, that required the most expert playing to bring off its artificial comedy, its bris-

tling wit, its delightful whimsey. Virtually all actors will
tell you that comedy is more difficult to play than straight
drama and tragedy. Anyone, they say, endowed with a
minimum well of emotion can turn on the tears. But
comedy, as Lynn herself has said, requires that an actor
possess "an outer ear and an outer eye," the one to hear
his manner of speech, the other to view his manner of
movement.

Needed also is an alertness, an awareness, a sense of
split-second timing. An actor must know how to feed
lines so that his fellow-actor can make the most of the
laugh required of a rejoinder, and he must know how to
go on even if the laugh does not come, and how to cut it
off when it does, lest it waste itself and subtly destroy the
play's pace. It is something many veteran actors say cannot be learned.

Rehearsals for *Design for Living,* carried on in a most
amiable atmosphere under Noël's direction, were nevertheless terribly exhausting for the stars, each a dedicated
professional, each given to perfecting every nuance and
gesture. Between giving guidance and acting his own role,
Noël had his hands full. Anyone who knows the Lunts,
who has seen them work or who has worked with them,
knows that they never spare themselves either during rehearsals or afterwards, or indeed even after the opening
of the play. They return to their apartment, parse everything they did during rehearsal, and work on scenes over
and over again. Alfred has said that he is never good
enough. I have heard that during the run of *Reunion in
Vienna* Lynn had a line whose comedic effect for some
mysterious reason eluded her. But she did not give up.
She kept working on it, working on it, until finally on the
very last night of the run she said it exactly right and
got the laugh she had been seeking.

To them, the foremost acting couple of our century,

every night carries the implicit challenge of a première. "It's a new audience every night, isn't it?" they will ask defiantly, these two who have forgotten more about acting than most actors ever learn. To laments of boredom in long-running hits, Alfred will say, "I don't understand it. I am never bored. There's always something new to learn about a part. The only time I am bored is when I'm shaving or washing my teeth before going to bed."

We opened in Cleveland and went from there to Pittsburgh, where old memories stirred and came to life. Almost a quarter of a century had passed since I first visited that city—the time when I had arrived for an appointment with Jack Singer to discuss being advance man for his burlesque show. I looked for the old theatre where the Behman Show had played, where Singer had given me my first instructions. The theatre had passed on. The young policeman on the corner did not even know where it had stood.

Meanwhile, in New York excitement over *Design for Living* continued to mount. Even before we announced that we would open on January 24 in the Ethel Barrymore Theatre, certified checks, money orders, telegraph orders and even cash had been pouring into my office. Everyone wanted to go to that opening night, what with Noël's army of friends and the Lunts' legion of followers.

Yet my own close circle of friends was so small that on the afternoon of the opening I still carried six pairs of tickets in my pocket. It was four o'clock when I received a desperate call from Sam Katz, who had arrived from Hollywood. His frenzied voice called over the telephone, "I need twelve tickets. Where can I get them without going into hock?"

"I'm glad you called," I said. "I've got them in my pocket. I didn't know what to do with them."

Design for Living was indeed my lifeline. Brooks Atkinson wrote in the *Times:* "It is one of the paradoxes of the theatre that the most trifling things are the most priceless. Skill, art, clairvoyance about the stage, even erudition of a sort have gone into this gay bit of drollery. It is highly diverting for the evening thereof."

In the midst of the Depression *Design for Living* proved to be exactly the sort of light entertainment the upper-middle-class theatregoers wanted. The twelve-week limit Noël had put on the engagement was extended to fifteen, then to seventeen. The first three months were played to a succession of sold-out houses. In spite of the stiff terms Noël had set, I made money. I had reached a favorable contract with Lee Shubert for the Ethel Barrymore in a season when half the theatres were dark. *Design for Living* netted $130,000, of which forty-two thousand precious dollars were mine.

In my office hangs a portrait of Noël on which is inscribed in his handwriting the following: "In memory of a long future association." I mention this not only because it is a funny line but also because it is indicative of the strange ways of the theatre and its children. I was never to have a future association with Noël. Never again was I to produce one of his plays. One day, some time after the closing of *Design for Living,* I received a letter from him saying that he had formed a partnership with Wilson and that wherever feasible I was to have an interest in any of his shows that they produced in the United States. As a consequence, I had a twenty-five-per-cent interest in *Tonight at 8:30* and also in *Blithe Spirit,* both great hits.

Our friendship has lasted through the years. On occasion Noël has asked for my advice. One such instance took place not too many years ago in connection with a play he had written, originally called *Home and Colonial,* but later retitled *South Sea Bubble.* He had written it for

Gertrude Lawrence, he told me later, but she became involved with *The King and I*. Noël never intended the play for Broadway, its subject being strictly British in interest, full of jabs at the Labour party and the problems of colonialism. But Wilson liked the play and prodded Noël into having it tested under Wilson's direction at the Westport Country Playhouse in Connecticut. When Noël indicated that he wished to fly over for the opening, Wilson, for undisclosed reasons, pleaded with him not to come. A confidential cable from Noël requested that I see the play and report to him my opinion of its content, direction and performance. "I know," Noël concluded, "I can trust both your critical capacity and your friendship."

Coward's instinct about his play was sound. Although the direction was satisfactory and Claudette Colbert, making her first stage appearance in many years, was utterly charming as the governor-general's wife, the play was not for Broadway. I cabled Noël and then wrote an elaboration of my reactions in no equivocal terms. The play was subsequently seen in London, where it was not an outstanding success.

Naturally, I was disappointed when he wrote that he was forming a partnership with Wilson. But, no matter. In my heart I have always been and will continue to be grateful to Noël and his *Design for Living*.

14

Hit, Hit, Hit, Hit

ONE OF THE humorous bits of theatrical lore tells of the time George M. Cohan had an argument with an actor. After ordering him from his office, he turned to Sam Harris and said, "Don't ever hire that guy—unless we need him."

I cite the story because it provides a key to the paradox of many relationships on Broadway and because, in particular, it helps explain the renewal of my alliance with Jerome Kern in the months that followed the closing of *Design for Living*. Truly, the people of the theatre are members of one big family, beset with the characteristic problems and traits of all families—quarrels, intrigues, sentimentalities, loyalties; but above all, the need for each other, their undeniable interdependence. Few feuds can long endure, and reconciliations are part of daily life. Producers need playwrights, playwrights need actors, actors need producers, producers need theatre owners, and the circle, like the music, goes round and round. Not infrequently it is wise for the lion to lie down with the lamb because the lamb someday may turn into a lion, too.

The reconciliation with Kern took place accidentally at a party. We had not seen each other since *The Cat and the Fiddle,* though Kern had made some calls while I was ill. He had no idea, he said, that I was upset over his having given *Music in the Air* to another producer. After all, he asked blandly, hadn't I announced that I would be doing *Flying Colors?* He thought I would not be able to handle both. To my remonstrance that he at least could have given me a chance, he shrugged a shoulder, saying that had not occurred to him.

We talked for a while the usual shoptalk of the theatre. Then he mentioned that he and Otto Harbach were together again and that they were doing a musical comedy based on Alice Duer Miller's *Gowns by Roberta.* Nothing especially adventurous this time, he said, but it did offer a chance for an effective and colorful production. As casually as I could, I asked him who would produce it, knowing that he had not been especially happy with the outcome of *Music in the Air.* It had been one of the major hits of the season, running 395 performances, only fifty-three fewer than *The Cat and the Fiddle.* Yet, as a result of poor management, Kern had not made the money he was hoping for or thought he had a right to expect. To my question, however, he responded only with a mysterious smile. I gathered later that he was simply playing the old game of hard-to-get. Otto, with whom I had gotten along most cordially before and who regarded me as an able manager, was on my side. After a bit of fence-straddling, Kern made up his mind. Whatever hard feelings he may have had toward me were brushed under the carpet.

The libretto for *Gowns by Roberta,* the title under which we opened in Philadelphia, was simple. An all-

American fullback named John Kent goes to Paris to visit his Aunt Minnie, who is better known as Roberta, the owner of a fashionable dress shop. He takes over the place as manager, and of course there is Stephanie, the chief designer, who ultimately turns out to be a true Russian princess, which is great for John because he loves her and she loves him.

For the title role we cast Fay Templeton, in what was to be her last stage appearance after a half century of stardom. Harbach developed the script so that it was logical for her to be seated throughout her performance. Miss Templeton, at that point in her career, could not get around very easily—she weighed 250 pounds. The role of the fullback went to Ray Middleton. Tamara, discovered in The Kretchma, an erstwhile Russian restaurant on Fourteenth Street near Second Avenue, stepped into her first major role as Stephanie. Clementina was played by Lyda Roberti.

If I had any illusions that my chagrin over his past behavior might have softened Kern in his attitude toward me, they were quickly put to rest when it came to selecting a comedian. We needed a comic to portray Huckleberry Haines, leader of an American orchestra, who knew how to handle the patter of an M.C. We were having some difficulty finding one. I went to the Palace. It was no longer, to be sure, the Palace of bygone days, but from time to time it was possible to see some fresh talent on its stage. This day there was on the bill a young comic, a monologist, who made a strong impression on me. His name was Bob Hope. He had a remarkably winning personality, and as I said of him not long ago, "Bob Hope never improved. He was always great."

I hurried back to Kern. "The problem is solved," I said.

In a voice as acid as it ever had been during the rehearsal days of *The Cat and the Fiddle,* he asked, "What are you trying to do, palm off one of your old vaudevillians on me?"

I did not react with anger. I said, with enough edge in my voice to jolt him a bit, "O.K. You don't have anyone now. Why don't you go over and look at him?" We signed Bob Hope and later Hollywood took him away from the theatre.

Kern received another setback in Philadelphia. He had decided to be the over-all supervisor, and when the show opened, it was in pretty poor shape. I pointed out to him that besides his score a major asset of the show had to be the clothes and the settings. "This show," I said, "takes place in a high-class fashion salon. We've got to knock their eyes out." I ordered sets and costumes redone. When business failed to develop after the mild reviews, I told Kern that it would be in the best interests of the show to call in Hassard Short and let him take over. At first Kern balked. But when the box-office receipts continued going down, he surrendered.

As a favor to me, Short agreed to come to Philadelphia and restage the production. On his arrival at the theatre one of the first things he did was to line up the girls on stage and begin experimenting with spotlights. He hit one of the girls with a pink spot. It so enhanced her features that Kern could not contain his pleasure. He turned to me and yelled, "The man is a genius."

We changed the name of the musical to *Roberta* before bringing it to the New Amsterdam in New York, lest the public be misled and think it was only a fashion show. In a way it was, of course, and in a way it helped, after the bumpy beginning, to put it over. The other asset was the delicious score, one of Kern's best, containing "Yesterdays," "The Touch of Your Hand," "You're Devastating," "Something Had to Happen," "An Armful of Trouble" and, need it be mentioned, "Smoke Gets in Your Eyes."

Once that song was heard on the radio and the country grew increasingly familiar with it, *Roberta* became a smash hit. Each night "Smoke Gets in Your Eyes" stopped the show, with Tamara singing it in her caressing, brooding way. It became one of the greatest hits ever written by Kern, a standard that as late as 1958, when it was revived by The Platters, sold over a million copies and for a few weeks in 1959 actually led "The Hit Parade."

There is a sidelight to "Smoke Gets in Your Eyes." Originally, Kern had written the melody as a signature for a radio series that never materialized. When it was decided that a song was needed for Stephanie in the second act, Kern offered it to Harbach to write the lyrics. In its original straight march rhythm it appealed to none of us. Kern was ready to give up on the melody when he was seized by inspiration. He tried it in the more leisurely tempo and sentimental style that gave it immortality.

Those months after *Design for Living,* including the time spent in preparation and production of *Roberta,* are among the most intense and satisfying of my life. They include a trip to California to discuss the possibility of a film which, though aborted, enabled me to bring back Clare Kummer's new comedy, *Her Master's Voice;* also the importation of Keith Winter's lovely drama *The Shining Hour,* which I presented before London saw it; and the picking up of the option on Sidney Howard's dramatization of Sinclair Lewis' *Dodsworth.*

All three, like *Roberta,* were major hits. All three made the list of the season's ten best plays, compiled annually in book form by Burns Mantle, then drama critic for the New York *Daily News.* When the final accounting was checked, I was able to repay all my creditors, with something to spare; to feel both newborn and free.

What happened to me happened also to the theatre. The

1933–34 season, without doubt, rates with the most thrilling in Broadway history. At the beginning, in June, even the theatre's fondest and most ardent supporters appeared to have lost heart. The Depression was still deep and unremitting. The pall that had hung over the theatre for the last five years gave no sign of disappearing. Many of the old dependable producers, their money lost, had crept away to live on memories. The backers had run for cover, theatres were in the hands of banks holding the mortgages. Actors, those who were not getting free meals or having their bills met by the Stage Relief Fund, had hurried to filmdom, along with the playwrights. The gloomy picture persisted through August. Yet within two months the theatre was going through an unmistakable rebirth. Hits came in rapid succession. By the end of October thousands of theatregoers, who either had lost contact with or interest in the theatre, were back at the box office seeking seats for the earliest possible date.

Her Master's Voice opened during the last week of October and immediately became one of the leading comedy successes. Besides serving to brighten the horizon with Mrs. Kummer's many graceful twists of dialogue and revealing bits of characterization, the play also served to bring back from Hollywood three popular performers who had stayed away too long—Roland Young, Mrs. Kummer's gifted son-in-law, whom I had known from vaudeville days when he performed in a sketch for Lewis and Gordon; Laura Hope Crews; and Elizabeth Patterson. It was Young who, on my meeting him in Hollywood, had put me on the trail of the play.

Her Master's Voice was produced not without some of the usual travail. For a while it was in rehearsal concurrently with *Roberta,* and I was shuttling back and forth trying to keep an eye on both, with Kern periodically wondering how I did it. The story of *Her Master's Voice* cannot be concluded without noting that it witnessed my one and only effort as a director.

Young and Worthington Miner, the director, had not gotten along almost from the start of rehearsals. In Washington, Young took me aside and told me that he could not and would not continue under Miner's guidance. As a result, Miner withdrew, saying that he really did not like the play anyway. I took over. We agreed on some changes of "business" in the performance and headed for New York. At the theatre, on the morning of the première, there was a note from Miner saying that he did not wish to be listed as director—would I please release his letter to the press and the critics.

He had done ninety-five per cent of the work. I saw no point in agreeing to his request. The next day when the reviews heaped praise on Miner's direction, I called him to the office. "Well," I greeted him, "how would you like it if I released that letter to *The New York Times?* That would look fine, wouldn't it? You getting all the great notices, and this letter saying you had nothing to do with it!" He gave me a rubelike grin. "Well," I concluded, "don't worry," and I tore up the letter in front of him.

Less than a month later *Roberta* opened. In February, within a fortnight, I presented *The Shining Hour* and *Dodsworth.* A newspaper columnist wrote, "Consider the astounding Max Gordon. At 9 P.M. Saturday night he will have four shows in town: *Her Master's Voice, Roberta, The Shining Hour,* and *Dodsworth.*"

I doubt that he knew how astounding it all was. Only a year or so before I had tried to jump off a balustrade in a Philadelphia theatre, and out of a hotel window in that same city.

Producing *The Shining Hour* had been easy. The play had been sent to me from England, and when I agreed to do it, the cast was assembled in London. It included the lovely Gladys Cooper, who, after a quarter of a century of stardom in England, would make her first appearance in the United States; Raymond Massey, the Canadian actor, who had made his New York debut in 1931 in Norman Bel Geddes' version of *Hamlet;* and Adrianne Allen, Mr. Massey's attractive wife, who had previously appeared on Broadway as the shop girl in *Cynara.* We opened in Toronto, where the enthusiasm was restrained. In New York the play, dealing with the love of two women for the same man, was an unquestioned success.

For a variety of reasons the triumph of *Dodsworth* remains a source of some of my greatest satisfaction in the theatre. Raising money for it had been extremely difficult. I had been compelled to borrow $35,000 with interest at one per cent a month. The remaining funds I got on credit from the scene designer and costume people. Also, I had produced the play against the advice of well-meaning friends. George S. Kaufman was one of several leading directors who turned it down. "Who's interested," the consensus seemed to be, "in a play about a middle-class fellow with a nagging, socially ambitious wife?"

I did not see it that way. I was convinced that there was a large body of Americans who would find identification with the problems the play projected. After all, had there not been a strong call for the novel itself? Also, Howard in my opinion had done a masterful and craftsmanlike job in translating the book to the stage, succeeding in retaining the vigor and honesty of the characterizations. Moreover, he had endowed the play with a frank theatricalism that I was sure would play beautifully. It was George Jessel who spurred me on at a moment when I was, if not dejected, then surely perplexed over the general professional reaction to the play.

Jessel, whose friendship I had continued to enjoy since

our association in *The Jazz Singer,* happened to visit my office one day, and I poured out my problems to him. Besides, I insisted that he sit in his chair and listen to me read the play. I read it from beginning to end, putting special emotion into the big scenes. When I was finished, George said, "Wonderful, it's going to be great." Whether or not he said that to make me feel good never crossed my mind. Such is the power of words, the need for reassurance in the human heart and mind, that I believed what he said. It helped. And then it occurred to me that if I could get Walter Huston to play Dodsworth, the play really could be "wonderful" and "great."

For almost fifteen years, starting in 1909, Walter had been in vaudeville, where I had seen him first. For years he toured both the Keith and Orpheum Circuits with his second wife, Bayonne Whipple, in an act called Whipple and Huston. In 1924 he gained his first Broadway glory in the title role of *Mr. Pitt* and subsequently appeared in such plays as *Desire Under the Elms, Kongo, The Barker,* and *Elmer the Great.* In 1929 he followed the crowd to Hollywood with further personal success.

I was in Washington with *Her Master's Voice* when, after many futile phone calls and letters trying to trace him, I discovered that he was in Fort Myer, only a few minutes away, making a film. I grabbed a copy of Howard's manuscript, hailed a taxi, and raced to Fort Myer. There was Huston, astride a horse. I rushed over to him, almost scaring the horse, and said, "Walter, I've got a great role for you. Here is the script." The next day he called me to say he was definitely interested. He did not stipulate that his current wife, Nan Sunderland, play the role of Edith Cartwright, but he said it would be nice if she could—they would like being together. I agreed, with mixed emotions. I could have spared myself—she was fine. Walter, his humorous hazel eyes twinkling, said to me later in his quiet soft-spoken way, "Max, I bet you thought I was trying to put something over on you."

What a treasure he was, Walter Huston, never to be forgotten for his Peter Stuyvesant in *Knickerbocker Holiday*, in which he sang Kurt Weill's haunting, poignant, wistful "September Song." Six feet tall, rugged and plain featured, there was something about Huston beyond his seriousness as an artist that made me comfortable in his presence—a quiet, genial, gentle manner, a lack of ostentation that put me at my ease. Millie and I had many pleasant evenings together with Walter and Nan before his death, the day after his sixty-sixth birthday.

For the role of Fran Dodsworth I wanted Fay Bainter. Fay read the script and vowed that she would work for anything in order to play this role. I told her she could have the part. When I asked her how much salary she wanted, she said, "I will leave that to you." She left New York to do a film. I drew up a contract for $750 a week, which I offered her on her return. It was not enough, she said. I reminded her that she had said she would take anything and pointed out that the salary I had named was quite liberal (this was during the Depression). Her lovely face wreathed itself in a smile suggesting that I had been incredibly naïve. We were only a short time from rehearsals, a week or so, and I did not wish to start searching for anyone else, although a threat to do so might have been wise. Fay settled for $750 a week against seven and one-half per cent of the gross. It would be gallant to say she was worth it. She was.

Under the direction of a newcomer named Robert Sinclair, whose work had come to my attention in a tiny theatre on Fourteenth Street, we went into rehearsal shortly after the opening of *Roberta*. I was taking a chance. But I was confident that Sinclair, on the basis of what I had seen, along with his understanding of the script, would make the grade.

In Philadelphia there was an ovation at the final curtain, and Huston had to respond with a curtain speech. In New York the acclaim was equally vigorous. From the night of its première *Dodsworth* became the most consistently popular box-office attraction on the dramatic list. And that was the season of the theatre's magical rejuvenation, in which there appeared on the boards Helen Hayes and Helen Menken in Maxwell Anderson's *Mary of Scotland;* George M. Cohan in O'Neill's *Ah, Wilderness!;* the Group Theatre's thrilling presentation of Sidney Kingsley's *Men in White,* with Luther Adler, Alexander Kirkland, Phoebe Brand, Sanford Meisner and Margaret Barker; John Wexley's *They Shall Not Die,* with Ruth Gordon and Claude Rains; James Dale and Laurence Olivier in Mordaunt Shairp's *The Green Bay Tree;* Melvyn Douglas, Lucile Watson and Ruth Weston in A. E. Thomas' *No More Ladies;* and Leopold Atlas' *Wednesday's Child.*

15

※※

"The Great Waltz"

I was back on top, in need of a rest, feeling like some traveler who, lost in a thick forest, has succeeded through luck, instinct and ability in finding his way back to the main road, lights, houses and friends. I had come back from overwhelming debt and despair to solvency and health. I should have relished the glow of triumphant achievement. To a considerable extent I did. But even as I did, there hung over me, hovering always on the perimeter of my mind, waking and sometimes sleeping, the theatre's perennially gnawing question—what now?

What now?—as much a part of the theatre's litany as Irving Berlin's "There's No Business Like Show Business." That defiantly exultant, sentimental ode conceived in a moment of exuberance may be true, but the brain that spawned the phrase "show business is no business" was, perhaps, closer to the truth. Certainly it was more realistic. In another time, before talking pictures, radio and television, a producer could have a sense of continuity and, precarious though it sometimes was, a sense also of permanency. Not infrequently he owned a theatre, or managed one, had stars under contract, playwrights from whom he could expect a fairly steady stream of material. He produced shows, sent them on the road, one after the other, maintained offices, held together an organization, was, though somewhat unorthodox in his working methods, at least a businessman.

In the modern American theatre this condition hardly exists. There are only a handful of regular producers with offices. Most are here one day, gone the next. Staffs are assembled for a single venture—one throw of the dice—and then disbanded. For those dedicated ones who seek their livelihood in the theatre because the theatre is in their blood and there is nothing else they wish to do, there is always the uncertainty of what now? A year, two years, sometimes more, are spent in planning a production—advising a playwright on changes in the script, raising money, assembling the company, getting a theatre. Then, hit or failure, ultimately the final curtain falls and the whole process must be started over again. Meanwhile, expenses continue—the office rent, the electricity, the secretary's wages. If the play failed to please, the problem of going on is compounded.

If I had not known before how much of a gamble the theatre really was, I certainly knew now. I had produced, on my own, three straight hits, and in spite of this, there had barely been sufficient money for me to carry on. My fourth production, a fiasco, threw me into deep debt and black panic. Plain, unalloyed chance had given me a new start. My meeting with Noël Coward had helped put me back on the road. Once again I produced a series of hits, and this time fate had been kinder.

What now?

The answer came shortly after the opening of *Dodsworth*. I was in the hospital recovering from a long-needed hernia operation when a letter arrived from Hassard Short. Did I not think, he was asking, that the time had come for me to produce the American version of *Waltzes from Vienna,* a continental triumph he had staged in London in August of 1931? Actually, the production had receded in memory. I had not given it any thought at all. I had attended the London opening at the Alhambra, and remembered that although intoxicated with the lovely Viennese music, I felt that the story treatment of the conflict between the Strausses, father and son, had been somewhat tepidly handled.

Now Short was suggesting that the libretto could be revamped entirely and that the show ought to be done on a lavish scale and presented in the smaller of the two theatres that had been built in Rockefeller Center. It was a wild idea and yet it had an inherent appeal. A new libretto, a big sumptuous production of a show that could appeal to the entire family—these were possibilities.

The world was drunk with the idea of pure size when the architects were drawing their plans for what became Rockefeller Center or Radio City. They designed two theatres for the area, a block away from each other, facing on the Avenue of the Americas. One of these the world knows as the Radio City Music Hall, a cavern that can hold 6,200 persons at a single sitting. The Music Hall originally had been thought of as a variety house. But after about ten days of futility it dawned on the guiding powers that variety was dead. Even were it alive, it would get lost in that gigantic hole. The policy was altered to a combination of stage and screen shows, and as such, with its famous Rockettes and the spectacles designed by Leon Leonidoff, the theatre became one of the imperative sights for every visitor to the metropolis.

The smaller theatre was the Center, no longer in exist-

ence, a victim like the dinosaur of its own size. But at the
time of which I write, it existed in all its majestic glory,
designed to be a home for Broadway musicals. It could
seat 3,822 persons, its orchestra floor alone capable of
engulfing the entire seating capacity of the New Amsterdam Theatre with two hundred seats left over. It was a
beautiful theatre, outfitted with the latest equipment, and
yet it found no takers.

Broadway knew from history that the place was too
large, that size is not what a theatre needs so much as a
soul. A theatre needs to have an atmosphere of friendli-
ness, it must be a place where nothing interferes with the
rapport between the audience and the stage. It needs the
warmth of intimacy. Live productions tend to be swallowed up in oversized theatres. The jokes and merriment
that delight audiences in small theatres can emerge as
cheerless, humorless nothings in larger houses. I have
seen top-flight comedians, who could turn a night club
into one mass of rocking, laughing humanity, appear like
wooden puppets in inhospitable hotel ballrooms. I remember Arthur Miller's magnificent play *The Crucible*
failing to get through to its audience when it was produced on Broadway. Nevertheless, revived in a small off-
Broadway playhouse, with the audience on four sides, it
swept everyone along with it—as if actor and spectator
alike were participants in the terrible ordeal of the
Salem witch hunts and trials with which the play dealt.

Unable to meet Broadway's requirements, the unfortu-
nate Center Theatre was being operated by RKO on a
straight film policy. But two theatres so close to each other
and competing for a limited supply of satisfactory Hollywood product was not only silly but also economically
unsound. The Rockefellers had been wondering for some
time whether there was an entrepreneur who would bring
it a vehicle that would enable the Center to perform its

original function. In conversations on Broadway it had been conceded that perhaps some giant-sized production could overcome the barrier. But who dared in those Depression days to even consider risking the needed investment?

Still, the more I thought about it, the more I was drawn to the notion. There was something in the idea that caught my penchant for a gamble, something of a challenge that kept bringing me back to the possibility—a huge spectacle, scores of waltzing figures on the stage, the most elegant of Viennese costumes, bubbling, melodious romantic music reaching out caressingly, affectionately, liltingly, filling a theatre with memories and the savor of a time gone by. I sank deeper into reverie.

Surely the elements of drama were present in the story for a thrilling, bittersweet operetta. How strange and odd a story it really was, this conflict between the Strausses, this paternal effort to frustrate a child's love of music, this plot that was, to our good fortune, thwarted and nullified. Music idol of a music-loving city, his melodies hummed and played in all the cafés of Vienna, an international celebrity making tours of the continent, the elder Strauss had honor after honor bestowed upon him—*Kapellmeister* to the first Burger regiment, provider of music for those gay balls at the court of the Hapsburgs, summoned to perform at the coronation of Queen Victoria, once escorted down the Thames, following a farewell concert, by a fleet of boats with a band playing his compositions. And yet if he had had his way, there would not have been such memorable waltzes as "Artist's Life," "Wine, Women and Song," "Tales from the Vienna Woods," "Die Fledermaus," "Wienerblut," and loveliest of all, the one to which the feet of the world have twinkled and hearts have quivered for almost a century, "On the Beautiful Blue Danube." He insisted that music was too difficult a mistress, the public too fickle, and financial rewards too uncertain. He wished, he asserted, to spare his children the hardships he had known before fame had kissed his brow. He opposed all musical training for his children, forbade their playing his piano, and once punished the young Johann when he found him practicing on a violin.

But the strictures had been foiled. His wife, whom he neglected and despised, circumvented edicts. Herr Amon, the first violinist in the elder Strauss' orchestra, joined in the conspiracy, giving the younger Johann his first lessons on the violin. Later there were lessons in composition with Deschler, the famous Viennese teacher, and then in time there was the younger Strauss himself writing waltzes and openly challenging his father's supremacy, a struggle that ended only with the father's death.

What more could be asked of drama than the deathbed reconciliation between father and son, the son summoned by the father to be told, "I wanted you to come here not only to hear you say you forgive me but to tell you that you are the greatest musician in the world. You have surpassed my every achievement. You won't forget me, will you, Schani?" To which the younger Strauss is said to have replied, "I can never forget the father who has been my inspiration."

It is one of the sadder footnotes of musical history that Strauss, Sr., did not live to hear "On the Beautiful Blue Danube."

The more I thought of the music and the story, the more irresistible Short's proposal became. I called Marcus Heiman, who had continued to invest in my productions. I told him what was whirling around in my head and suggested that he do me a big favor by sounding out the Rockefellers. I also took Moss Hart into my confidence when he visited me in the hospital. He gazed at me with tolerant amusement in his eyes and said he thought the whole enterprise sounded just a little mad. But after we got to talking about the Strausses and I had a chance to expand on my ideas, Moss's interest rose. He said he had considerable respect for Short's judgment and my instincts. Perhaps the idea was worth investigating. If I decided to go ahead with the project, he said, he might be persuaded to expand the libretto along lines recommended by Short.

By mid-April the foundations were set. Hart consented to overhaul the libretto, and the Rockefellers, although refusing to make a direct investment in the production, agreed to assist with up to fifty thousand dollars for the costumes. They would also help pay for the reconstruction of the stage and for the new machinery required to realize Short's notions for the spectacular.

Broadway skeptics had a field day. What I was about to undertake was regarded as sheer folly. The fact that the Rockefellers considered the project sufficiently worthwhile to help seemed to make no great impression. No matter how you looked at it, the skeptics said, the production was bound to cost $250,000 or more (actually it was $246,000). It was plainly ridiculous to expect that such an investment could be recouped at a three-dollar top when, as one wag quipped, "Everyone knows that not even Mae West playing *Little Lord Fauntleroy* could fill that theatre."

I took no heed. I continued to believe in *The Great Waltz*, the title suggested by Short to replace that of the London edition. If we had the show I was hoping for, I was convinced there would be enough New Yorkers and tourists who would welcome a family entertainment. I instructed my press agent to emphasize that we were producing the most stupendous operetta in Broadway history, that we were bringing old Vienna back to life. I also told him to place special stress on the fact that it would be "clean."

I might not, as the skeptics said, be able to fill the theatre, but I could certainly fill the stage—front and back. Determined to go all the way, I hired a singing chorus of one hundred, forty-two principals and supporting players, forty dancers for Albertina Rasch, and fifty-three musicians under the direction of Frank Tours. Backstage, handling the estimated ten tons of scenery designed by Albert Johnson, was a stage crew of ninety running up in that department alone a weekly wage bill of five thousand dollars. Doris Zinkeisen and Irene Sharaff had more than a score of seamstresses and tailors toiling over some five hundred costumes, including all the dress parade uniforms of the Austrian Army.

In an enterprise of this size there are bound to be problems, and we had our share—some serious ones, most on the ludicrous side, and none irreparable, including the one most unanticipated. This turned up the first day of rehearsal. We had assembled what we believed to be a first-rate company. For the role of the elder Strauss there was H. Reeves-Smith, a thoroughly seasoned veteran; we brought Marie Burke from England to play the Russian countess invented by Moss to help further the younger Strauss's career; Marion Claire, former soprano of the Chicago Civic Opera, was signed for the feminine love interest of the younger Strauss, while for that pivotal role itself we engaged a youngster from Minneapolis whose name I have mercifully forgotten.

He came to his audition highly recommended by Short. I, too, thought well of him during the trial. He could sing, and he seemed to have something of the quality needed for the role. But on the initial day of rehearsal it became painfully evident that we had made a mistake. As an actor, the youngster was totally inadequate. We held a hasty conference and summoned Guy Robertson, who, some seasons before, had won the hearts of matinee audiences by his singing of Rudolf Friml's "Indian Love Call" in *Rose Marie.*

Aside from the question of what the critics would say, only one problem remained—one terrifying uncertainty— as the curtain rose on opening night, September 22, 1934. Short's revolving and cantilever stages had been designed to shift and move scenery in full view of the audience, to transform in a moment verdant gardens into stately interior sets with clinking chandeliers, an attractive pastry shop into a concert hall and back to verdant gardens. At one point the ballet rose from the nether depths, and in the final scene the orchestra was to be lifted from the pit and moved to the rear wall while a huge ballroom formed in front. At rehearsals the machinery performed smoothly except during the big final maneuver involving the orchestra, when the platform would either stick completely or be delayed and ruin the whole effect.

On opening night I stood with Moss in the rear of the theatre, both of us praying that the gremlins would depart, that the spectacular finale would come through according to plan. Neither of us spoke. The military brass band marched across the stage, the richly dressed peasant girls filled the stage with lively movement, the fireworks went off on schedule and the audience held its breath or gasped in excitement. And then the dreaded moment approached—that moment that could turn the whole evening into a hideous nightmare.

Like two frightened children, Moss and I turned our backs to the stage and held hands. We could tell from the exclamations we heard that the orchestra had risen and was moving backward. Slowly we counted, and then, underneath the music, we could hear the meshing of the platform, a clicking as sweet as the music itself. Moss hugged me, kissed me and whisked me around. There it was, just as we had planned—the platform firmly set against the rear wall, in front of it thirty smiling, wonderfully graceful couples, radiant with joy and buoyancy, whirling and dipping to the strains of that immortal Strauss waltz.

There were critics, hard-bitten and austere, who still insisted that the hugeness of the theatre had not been and could not be conquered. One derisively called our production "The Great Waste." But others were with us. Percy Hammond of the *Herald Tribune* called it "the biggest, the most beautiful, the most tasteful and the most extravagant" show of its kind. Burns Mantle awarded us four stars in the *Daily News*. The public trooped to the box office, young and old alike. *The Great Waltz* became a family show.

We played through June 10, closed for a vacation, and reopened August 5. I had made plans to send the show on the road, somehow underestimating its staying powers. The final curtain fell on September 14 with the box-office demand still strong. But there was no turning back. The bookings had been made, the arrangements set, and another production, encouraged by our success, was being groomed for the rejuvenated Center Theatre.

We had given 269 performances before one million persons. No other New York theatrical production had ever been seen by that many people in the same span of time. Financially, we did better than break even, a considerable feat considering that our weekly operating cost was thirty-five thousand dollars and the maximum gross was fifty-five thousand dollars. The gamble had worked.

There has been nothing quite like *The Great Waltz* since, and it is a safe prophecy that there never will be again. Aside from the fact that the Center Theatre no longer exists, both the cost of mounting the show and the weekly operating expenses would make even consideration foolhardy. A duplication of *The Great Waltz* would actually cost more than a million dollars today. No contemporary ticket scale could balance that figure and show a profit. When I produced *The Great Waltz*, I took a gamble. A gamble implies a chance to win. No one would have that chance today, and more's the pity.

But, if the size and grandeur of *The Great Waltz* belong to an irrevocable past, one enduring truth remains—in which I put my faith, as others have on occasion since—that there are always those who will flock to the wholesome, romantic, beautifully designed musical. Even in these days, when standards of all kinds are in turmoil, *My Fair Lady, Camelot* and *The Sound of Music* offer supporting evidence. It is pertinent perhaps to remark that both *Camelot* and *The Sound of Music* failed to win the full approbation of the critics. They became, nevertheless, outstanding family attractions.

Actually, I never did understand the surprise expressed in some quarters over the success of *The Great Waltz*. That it was framed in one of the most beautiful theatres in the country, that it was large, spectacular and exciting in its mechanical magic undoubtedly had something to do with its magnetism. But what really counted was what took place on the stage—another of the eternal verities. Audiences do not come to sit in a theatre because of its plush seats, or to look at the hand-painted murals on the wall. They generally have perfectly good plush seats and attractive pictures in their own homes. They come to the theatre because of what intelligence, taste and talent have been able to place upon a stage.

16

Sam H. Harris

FOLLOWING the production of *The Great Waltz*, I did two other plays during the 1934–35 season: *Spring Song*, by Bella and Samuel Spewack, in which Garson Kanin appeared for twenty-five dollars a week, and *The Farmer Takes a Wife*, adapted by Frank B. Elser and Marc Connelly from Walter D. Edmonds' novel *Rome Haul*. The first appealed to me, I think, because its East Side setting let loose a nostalgia for the days of my childhood. But there is no sentiment at the box office, and the play survived a scant forty performances. The other, in which a young Henry Fonda played Dan Harrow, told of the days when the railroads began pushing out the men who made their living on the Erie Canal. It was received with enthusiasm by New Yorkers interested in early Americana. Unfortunately, there were not enough of them, and I had to close the production after 104 showings.

Two factors helped offset these disappointments. One was the continuing success of *The Great Waltz*. The other, a meeting between Moss Hart and Cole Porter. Cole and

I had been friends for years. We had been introduced by
Raymond Hitchcock, for whom Cole had written a dozen
songs for the *Hitchy-Koo* revue of 1919. Cole and I had
talked on occasion of doing a show together, but in the
brief time that I had been on my own as a producer, such
opportunity had not arisen. Now Cole had a musical
running, *Anything Goes,* in which, incidentally, he had in
his own humorous way with lyrics commented on my partnership with the Rockefellers. The show was a hit,
and the meeting with Moss called for celebration and
mutual compliments. Before the meeting was over, Moss
was suggesting, and Cole agreeing, that they ought to
take a trip around the world and write a musical together.

The celebrants ran into one hitch. Cole thought this
could be the show for me. Moss, proclaiming undying affection for me, said unhappily that this was impossible.
Since Sam Harris had brought him together with George
Kaufman for what became Moss' first Broadway hit, *Once
in a Lifetime,* he, like Kaufman, had an agreement giving
Harris first call on his services. Both, in fact, were Harris'
advisers and silent partners. Moss also explained that it
was only because of Harris' friendship with me that he
had been able to work on *The Great Waltz.*

"No," Moss wound up regretfully, "I'm afraid I can't
expect Sam to let me out again."

"How about the two of them getting together to do the
show?" Cole suggested. Moss perked up.

When the idea was broached to Harris, he agreed immediately. I could not be more delighted. We had been
partners before, in the days of Lewis and Gordon, and
fast friends since. Despite his being twenty years my senior, we were drawn together by a common background,
a mutual love of the theatre, and a shared affection for
"the sport of kings." We spent many happy afternoons
together at the race track, winning and losing, always

having fun. Hardly a morning passed that Sam did not call with his cheerful, "Hello, Maxie, what are we doing today?" We did not do something together every day, but the call was symptomatic of our regard for each other and the pleasure we found in each other's company. No man was kinder, more human, more understanding.

Quiet, soft-spoken, with big ears, a long nose, and black hair parted and combed straight back, Sam Harris was one of the most successful producers in Broadway history. He was not especially well known to the public as a personality, but the public came to know well the significance of his name above the title of a play or a musical. They learned that it stood for impeccable taste, shrewd showmanship, and something called, for lack of a better word, "class." More often than not the public knew that his name on a production meant a hit. Three productions he sponsored won Pulitzer Prizes: *Icebound,* in 1923; *Of Thee I Sing,* in 1932; and *You Can't Take It with You,* in 1937. *Of Mice and Men* won the New York Drama Critics' Circle Award in 1938.

Sam was a tireless individual who seemed to have a permanent claim on youth. In later years, when I thought that he could afford to take things easier, he would arrive every morning at his office, work all day, handle four telephones, and wind up as unflustered and cheerful as when he started. He was treasured by all who worked for and with him. They loved him for his exuberance, his zest for life, his enthusiasm for young people. "I like young people," he would say. "I like to work with young people. I have no intention of growing old."

Sam was not the most articulate of men. He was not a theoretician either. He could not discuss a play in the academic jargon of structure, climaxes and denouement, conflict and motivation. But he could feel when things were wrong—or right. He might not be able to tell a writer how to correct a fault. But I have heard that there are many editors who cannot tell writers what is wrong with their articles or stories either. They just know. Only the truly great ones can do both. Sam would say, "I don't believe it" of some piece of business. Or, "What this play needs is a dress suit," meaning that it lacked "class."

Although he was what you would call a materialistic man with little formal education, and I doubt that he ever opened a book of poetry or the plays of Shakespeare, Sam was a man of great sensitivity, with a feeling of kinship for his fellow men—a man with a heart. Intuitively, he knew the torments of uncertainty, confusion and quavering nerves that beset the greatest and most successful artists. No one could testify to this humanity and empathy better than Moss, whose account of Sam's solicitude for him in the final hours before the curtain rose on *Once in a Lifetime* is to me one of the theatre's great stories. I wonder how many of the current crop of producers possess the capacity to extend to a young writer the consideration Sam extended to Moss in those last hours before what turned out to be the most exciting and tumultuous night in Moss's professional life.

Once in a Lifetime had gone through its final dress rehearsal before the New York première. It had not, according to Moss, played with full conviction. Tired, disgusted and discouraged after endless days and nights of toil and sweat, he stood alone in the aisle as Kaufman and Sam carried on a brief but intense conversation. Kaufman started for the rear of the house. Sam was about to follow when he noticed Moss in the shadows. Instead of following George, he walked over to Moss, took a long look at him and said, "I think you need a drink, kid. Come on up to the office." For the next four hours, Sam, obviously in need of a few drinks himself, sought to distract Moss from his woes. He spoke of how the great George M.

Cohan had felt just before the opening of his first play, how George had overcome his fears, how George and he had met and formed their partnership. Then, suddenly, he stopped and confessed: "All of this stuff I've been telling you was just to take your mind off things so you could listen to what I really wanted to say."

Sam cleared his throat and continued, "Now I'm going to tell you why you shouldn't worry too much about this play, kid," and he proceeded to act out before Moss's eyes the entire script. As Moss has told the story, he found himself dozing off from time to time, being brought back from drowsiness by Sam's histrionics. When he finished, Sam put his hat and coat on and said, "Go on home and get a good night's sleep, kid. I think you'll sleep better now."

Standing on the street, as the first rays of dawn shot through the sky over Broadway, it occurred to Sam that there was no point in Moss's going home to Brooklyn. A final line rehearsal had been scheduled for eleven. Then, through Moss's protestations that he would rather go home than sleep in a hotel, Sam divined the true reason. As a cab pulled over to the curb, he put out his hand in the farewell gesture, got into the cab, and was off. In Moss's hand was a hundred-dollar bill, a passport to the Astor Hotel, a suite, a short sleep, a massage and breakfast in bed.

That was Sam. That was my friend, with a pearl stickpin in his tie, a ring on his right little finger—a gentleman, nay a prince, one of the theatre's true aristocrats.

There was still a touch of winter in the air when Moss and Cole embarked on their world-circling journey. Neither had done a bit of work on the proposed musical. Full of the *bon vivant*'s insouciance, they assured Sam and me that they would have a completed show on their return.

I shall never forget Moss standing at the *Franconia's* rail, watching Cole arrive at the pier with his personal entourage. There was, of course, Mrs. Porter, and there were, in addition, three of the Porters' friends going along as guests, also a valet and a maid. Watching them mount the gangplank, Moss's face became longer and longer. "We'll never get a thing done," he observed sourly. "It will be just fun, fun, fun."

Superficially there was, indeed, reason for concern. Cole had won an international reputation as a playboy. He was regarded as one of the most lavish and gracious of hosts both in Europe and at home. His parties filled the gossip columns of the press and the magazines of the *haut monde*. Once, in Paris, when he was maintaining a sumptuous apartment in rue Monsieur, he hired the entire Monte Carlo Ballet to perform at one of his parties. In 1923, living in the Rezzonico Palace in Venice, he had built in front of it a floating night club capable of accommodating a hundred guests and a Negro jazz band. At his behest, Elsa Maxwell staged treasure hunts through the canals, fabulous soirees and masquerades at the Lido.

Moss need not have fretted. Cole could be all business and a hard worker. With a task at hand he could not be distracted by idle diversions. The two met daily for intense conferences about the plot. By the time the ship passed through the Panama Canal, the story was under control. By the time they reached Cape Town, the entire show was written. They were in the South Atlantic when they got the idea for the title. The *Franconia* was a British ship, and on the night of the twenty-fifth anniversary of the coronation of George V there were grand doings in the dining salon—toasts to "Their Majesties," emotional tributes to "This blessed plot, this earth, this realm, this England." When the partying was over, Moss and Cole cabled, "The title is *Jubilee*. We'll tell you all about it when we get home." That was sufficient signal for us to talk to Hassard Short about the staging, alert Albertina Rasch to stand by for the dances, and to approach Jo Miel-ziner about the sets.

In late May the *Franconia* steamed into port. Three days later, in Sam's office in the Music Box Theatre, we listened to the plot and the score. We were satisfied. Moss's story told how a ruling family in a mythical kingdom, tired of the folderol and restrictions of the court, had dis-appeared into private life to follow their personal in-clinations: the king to perfect his skill with parlor tricks; the queen to indulge and amuse herself with a brawny swimming champion, known in the movies as Mowgli the Apeman; the prince to find a beautiful night club per-former; and the princess to sing duets with a precociously brilliant young playwright. There were sly suggestions and veiled resemblances to the British royal family, and who could deny that the swimming champion really was Johnny Weissmuller, who had become Tarzan in filmdom, or that the precocious young playwright was Noël Cow-ard? There was also a character in the cast who bore a striking resemblance to Elsa Maxwell. Cole's lyrics were original, as expected, and his music was tuneful, including the immortal "Begin the Beguine." We were confident that we had the foundation of a highly amusing musical comedy—a mixture of satire, sentiment and humor.

Moss and Cole flew to Hollywood to cast the show. They took a suite in the Beverly-Wilshire Hotel and spent nine days giving personal renditions of the script for every movie celebrity who could be induced to visit them. For six days, so the reports went, they remained in their apartment, never even getting out of their pajamas or dressing gowns.

Cole played the piano. He also sang all the solos and chorus numbers. Moss read the dialogue. The duets they sang together. By the time they left, they had persuaded Mary Boland to play the queen; Melville Cooper, the king; June Knight, the beautiful night club singer; and May Boley, the Elsa Maxwell portrait. The other principals we cast in the East: Mark Plant for Mowgli, Derek Williams for the precocious playwright, and lovely Margaret Adams for the princess.

Our early optimism, however, was not long sustained. Too soon it was evident to Sam and me that considerable revisions would have to be made, particularly in the second act which seemed to consist of too many short, choppy scenes. Boston, allowing for out-of-town crudities, gave us a hearty welcome. But we knew the flaws would not be overlooked in New York. During the three weeks in Boston we continued to work almost around the clock. Some of the original songs were dropped. Cole wrote new ones seemingly overnight. One number was completed at six o'clock the morning of the final dress rehearsal, sent to the orchestra at breakfast time, rehearsed that afternoon, and performed that night.

We opened *Jubilee* on October 12 at the Imperial Theatre. The reception was good, and we played to crowded houses for several months, until Mary Boland took sick. Laura Hope Crews agreed to take over. But *Jubilee* was not the same. Laura, as Burns Mantle observed, was more the queen than the comedienne. *Jubilee,* born in gaiety and laughter, had reached the end of the dance. In the record book it is credited with 169 performances, a sufficiently rewarding success at a time when shows running one hundred performances were regarded as being hits.

17

Abe Lincoln in Hollywood

FORTUNATELY, no man knows his destiny. *Jubilee* was less than a month old when I began a series of moves that was to lead me to my personal Gethsemane.

It is true that I had not run with the pack to Hollywood, knowing that I would never be completely content away from Broadway. But I certainly was not beyond the golden blandishments of that incredible city. Stories of fabulous wealth reaped in the western fairyland formed a staple of gossip among show people, particularly those of the legitimate theatre. On someone like me, in whom there has remained through the years—including my best ones—a constant subconscious concern for financial security, these stories acted like an evil deliriant.

I could, it dawned on me, continue to produce on Broadway, but an occasional coup in filmdom would provide a cushion against the arid years that every Broadway producer must be prepared to endure. Until *Jubilee*, however, my experiences with Hollywood had been inconsequential or abortive. My initial excursion there took place in 1932, the result of a suggestion from Groucho Marx that it would please him and his brothers if I would assist them in the making of two of their zanier enterprises, *Monkey Business* and *Horse Feathers.*

Jesse Lasky, then head of Paramount, for whom the films were made, paid me $250 a week for my services and included me in the deal for the pictures' profits. According to the contract, the Marxes would receive fifty per cent of the net profits over four hundred thousand dollars on each picture, of which I would get the first ten thousand dollars.

Eighteen years later, these terms obliterated from memory, Gummo Marx notified me that *Horse Feathers* was just one thousand dollars short and that it would not be long before I began collecting the money owed me. Suspicious that Gummo was participating in a practical joke, I asked my attorney to look up the contract. Gummo was not fooling. I mention this partly because I wish to pay tribute to such honesty and partly because it provides a clue to one of the many reasons for my deep regard and affection for those beloved Marx brothers.

My ventures with the Marxes on the Coast whetted my appetite considerably. When, after *Horse Feathers,* Paramount offered me a position as consultant, I grabbed it. As matters turned out, I never worked under this contract. Just about the same time I became involved with *Flying Colors,* which, as I have related, came near ruining me. In 1933, while *Design for Living* was helping me to rehabilitate myself, Sam Katz (who with a man named Barney Balaban had built a chain of movie houses), Marc Heiman, Sam Harris and I began talking about the possibility of forming our own film company. The Marx brothers, good friends also of Harris, said that they would be willing to appear in a movie if we formed such a company. One of the first prospects we approached was

Duncan Holmes, a banker, who Katz had heard was look-ing for attractive investments. Katz said Holmes was a friend of Bernard Baruch and that I might try arranging a meeting through Baruch. I had never met Baruch, but we had corresponded before the opening of *The Band Wagon,* when he had written to me to purchase opening-night tickets.

For me there was a certain awe in the Baruch name itself, aside from its prominence as a result of the mani-fold public services with which it has been linked. I was still a barefoot youngster on the Lower East Side when the city, with money donated by him, built a public shower house on the corner of Rivington and Lewis Streets.

I called Baruch, as Katz suggested, and told him of my wish to meet Duncan Holmes. He was most gracious. It happened, he said, that Holmes and he were going to Washington in a few days. If Katz and I would meet them at Pennsylvania Station, we could ride with them to Newark, during which time we would be able to ex-plain our proposition. We did, but Holmes was not in-terested. Nevertheless, that ride from Manhattan to New-ark was not wasted. Baruch and I became good friends. He was to help me in the years to come by his advice and encouragement, his example and his precepts. Some of the happiest days of my life have been spent in his company, either in New York or on his plantation in South Carolina.

Undismayed by Holmes' refusal, we persisted. But everywhere the Depression had left its mark. The whole thing evaporated when Nicholas Schenck, one of the powers in the Metro-Goldwyn-Mayer organization, per-suaded Katz that he would be foolish to set up an inde-pendent company when he could align himself with Metro. The offer was irresistible. I could not blame Katz for accepting.

Two years later, while I awaited the return of Moss and Cole from their trip with *Jubilee,* Katz asked me to the Coast to serve in an advisory capacity on several films being made by his studio. I worked there for fourteen weeks. My services ended, I returned to New York convinced that I could never make Hollywood a permanent home. There was an insularity among its inhabitants, a remoteness from the realities of life, an overindulgence in luxury that I knew I could not tolerate for an extended period of time. I knew irrevocably that I could not do without the excitement of Broadway life—or New York life—of opening nights in the theatre, the stimulation to be derived from theatre people—writers, actors, directors— who are among the most vital and volatile of all human beings. Living in the midst of one of the world's great crossroads, they are everlastingly aglow with ideas. Their commitments to living, their intellectual awareness are among the pleasures of their company.

But I returned to New York convinced also that I must have some stake in the making of films. It had become increasingly clear to me that the more successful plays made the more successful films. Since Broadway producers were the ones who found these plays, raised the money—or risked their own—to put them on, there hardly seemed any valid reason why they should not bring them to the screen as well. At least, that is the way I was determined to have it. The main thing in the theatre was and always will be the script. Once that has been found, the rest is, in a manner of speaking, a matter of mechanics.

I could hardly wait to discuss my ideas with Sam Harris. When he agreed that I made sense, I was encouraged. But, he added, he had lost interest in film production. Marcus Heiman, however, stood ready to invest in a company, and he thought that Harry Goetz, whom both of us had known for some years, might be persuaded to join us. Goetz was involved with his own film unit, Reliance Pictures, a small company distributing its products through United Artists. Heiman had heard that Goetz was not especially happy with his situation. Goetz would be valuable. Money was available to him and, of no little importance, he appeared to have the experience necessary to take over the business side of the venture. Heiman arranged a meeting. By the time *Jubilee* neared the end of its run, we had worked out most of the preliminary details. By July the rumor factory was at work reporting that Goetz and I were in daily huddles and that Goetz would disband Reliance Pictures as soon as shooting on *The Last of the Mohicans* was completed. The rumors had solid foundations. In December we made them official, announcing the formation of Max Gordon's Plays and Pictures. At last I was to be a motion-picture producer. The Golden Fleece of which I had dreamed was now within my grasp.

That winter our first Broadway production was Clare Boothe Luce's *The Women,* which included in its all-feminine company such excellent performers as Ilka Chase, Margalo Gillmore, Betty Lawford, Phyllis Povah, Arlene Francis and Jane Seymour. The play itself was a somewhat daring and biting satirical comedy about a group of women "native to the Park Avenues of America," as Mrs. Luce phrased it. The script had come to me from Bernard Baruch, long-time friend of Mrs. Luce. Once before he had sent me a play by her, which I had rejected. But I had said then that I was sufficiently impressed with the writing to want to see whatever she wrote next. *The Women* was it.

Actually, opening night in New York stirred mixed reactions. There was interest in the play but no marked enthusiasm. Some said the critics blushed, that men in general were uncomfortable at being let in on some of the more secret manifestations of the opposite sex. Indeed,

Mrs. Luce pulled few punches as she removed not only the stage's so-called fourth wall but also the partitions that hide bathrooms, powder rooms and maternity wards. Women, on the other hand, relished the merciless exposure of their kind. Word-of-mouth, that most potential of all advertising, was good. Three weeks after the opening the matinees were jammed to capacity. Soon the evening performances were doing as well—gentlemen friends, sweethearts and husbands having been persuaded to submerge their inhibitions. *The Women* built itself into a major triumph, giving 657 performances on Broadway, while a road company was formed to appease the demand across the country.

But irony, I found, has many faces. With the opening of *The Women* my luck ran out. As a producer I became a helmsman in a chartless sea. It was as if the guiding stars had disappeared from their accustomed places and I had lost my way. I was still the same man with the same talents and abilities, the same tastes and standards. Yet I produced only failures: *Othello,* starring Walter Huston in a production designed and staged by the great Robert Edmond Jones (21 performances); *Save Me the Waltz,* a comedy presented in association with Sam Harris (8 performances); *Spring Thaw,* a comedy by Clare Kummer, who earlier had given me the hit *Her Master's Voice* (8 performances); *Missouri Legend,* produced with and directed by the late Guthrie McClintic, husband of Katharine Cornell (48 performances); *Sing Out the News,* a revue by Harold Rome and Charles Friedman, produced in association with George Kaufman and Moss Hart (105 performances).

Under the circumstances, my dreams of Hollywood gold and grandeur receded. Although we had, in accordance with my original plan, purchased the film rights to *The Women,* we never made the picture. Metro-Goldwyn-

Mayer offered us $200,000 for our rights, for which we had paid only $125,000, in that period before anyone suspected the magnitude of the play's popularity. It offered us, besides, $50,000 if the film's gross went to $2,500,000. We sold. The profit helped offset our subsequent failures.

Disappointed and depressed, trying hard to fight off panic, I consoled myself with the thought that he who retreats lives to fight another day. That other day came during the 1938–39 season. Robert E. Sherwood, lean giant of a man, who later was to help President Roosevelt write some of his most eloquent speeches, had created his stirring *Abe Lincoln in Illinois*. The first production of the newly formed Playwrights Company, the play opened in October and immediately gave Broadway a luster that was to light the remaining months and bring a touch of immortality to Raymond Massey in the title role. In January, 1939, in association with Harris, we sponsored *The American Way*, by Kaufman and Hart, in which the stars were Fredric March and his wife, Florence Eldridge. Both plays were conceived by men of good will who, worried by freedom's retreat and the rattling of Hitler's ominous saber, believed that the time had come to restate the American heritage and American ideals.

Sherwood drew an inspiring portrait of Lincoln during the prairie years, the years when he was being shaped and molded for the great trust to come. *The American Way* tried to evoke the greatness of America through her history and evolution, and testified to the momentous validity of the democratic process. For me, whose eyes never fail to fill when a band strikes up "America the Beautiful" or someone recalls the ringing lines from Emma Lazarus' "The New Colossus," inscribed on the Statue of Liberty, the productions of *Abe Lincoln in Illinois* and *The American Way* were deeply emotional experiences. I watched audiences witnessing the plays and became imbued with the idea that both needed to be heard by Americans everywhere. The shrinking theatre, wonderful though it was, could not provide such dissemination. I made up my mind that both plays should be filmed. Goetz agreed with me. However, since we were not in a position to finance such a two-way venture, we decided to approach RKO Radio Pictures, which had indicated interest in *The American Way*. In March we concluded a deal for the purchase of *Abe Lincoln* and a few weeks later completed the deal for *The American Way*, signing notes for our share of the needed capital.

March turned out to be my month to remember. The ink was not long dry on our film contracts when there was new excitement. During the weeks of negotiations with the Playwrights Company and RKO, when matters were still in the balance, I received a call from John F. Royal, for years one of the key men in the Keith vaudeville circuit and once manager of its Cleveland Hippodrome. A colorful, resourceful and efficient showman, trained under Keith, Royal had moved into radio in Cleveland and in time attracted attention for his running of Station WTAM. As a result, he had been invited to take charge of network programing for N.B.C.

"They've given me a helluva job," he complained when I visited his office. "They've placed me in charge of television, and I guess I've got just about the toughest assignment in show business. I'm supposed to find out how television, which has an income of nothing a year, can compete with the movie industry, which you and I know has a box-office take of a billion annually."

I was not sure what I could do about it and said so.

"Oh, you can help," Royal replied. "How would you like to join us in a general advisory capacity and assist in the production of television programs? You know all the people in the theatre, the top ones, and I think it would be great if we could obtain the rights to some of the best plays they've done and put them on. Last year, in June, we put on some scenes with Gertrude Lawrence from *Susan and God,* and the program was a big hit. Now, the World's Fair will be opening in April, and we think the time has come to go to town."

"How much are you offering?" I asked.

"We'll give you twenty-five thousand dollars a year."

I did not wish to appear too eager. "How much are you offering for material?" I asked.

"Well, Max," Royal replied, "as I have said, we don't have too much of a budget. My notion here is that the playwrights really will be helping to feather their nests. Television is a great new medium, and too few of them realize that in time it's going to hit the movies hard. Tell them that they're really investing in their future."

Royal's enthusiasm for the future of television was no secret. He had been on the bandwagon from the early days when the main part of the television apparatus was a steel mill-wheel that revolved at a rapid pace and produced pictures that, as Alva Johnston once reported, "looked like soapy, funny-pier mirrors." Royal would inveigle hapless actors and paint them with gorgon's blood and jungle-green make-up, which was then the only way to register facial images on television.

"John," I said, "I'm with you. I also think that television has a future and I'm willing to do anything I can to help you. But I just cannot go to Kaufman or Sherwood or Sidney Howard and ask them for their plays for nothing. There's a principle that a professional believes in. Even a token payment will be something."

"All right," Royal replied, "offer them fifty dollars. The

point is that there is no work for them to do on the plays. They keep the rights. When the big day comes for television, they will have money in the bank."

That night I did not sleep. For days, even after we had bought *Abe Lincoln in Illinois* and *The American Way*, I hesitated over Royal's offer. I wondered whether in taking the job, even though it was comparatively simple, I might be spreading myself thin. Hammerstein and Kern were working on an operetta that I wanted to produce; I had the film project under way. Yet the temptation was strong. Here was an opportunity to lay the groundwork for a future in a medium that could give me the additional insurance I craved, a craving that had impelled me toward Hollywood. Also, there was that challenge so hard to deny, the challenge of pushing to new frontiers. Royal's assignment was, after all, something I felt I could and wanted to do. The real deterrent was whether or not I could hold my nerves in check, withstand the pressures and tensions of additional work. I did not mention these fears to my wife, but as Royal continued to press, I knew that I would yield. Temptation, greed, the need for kudos, fear of financial insecurity—I don't know how to unravel these factors, or which to charge most with my final decision.

On March 23 N.B.C. announced that I had signed a contract. In a statement made at the time, I said, "By furthering and developing TV right from the start, I hope to prove to theatrical people that television is the greatest supplementary medium for their activities. TV provides a new field for the showman to apply his knowledge of the public's likes and dislikes. It will be my task to bring more of this knowledge to sound-and-sight broadcasting."

Meanwhile, there were plans to be made for the *Lincoln* project, which, at the request of the Playwrights Company, would go before the cameras during the summer. Raymond Massey had agreed to re-create his role, and it was deemed best that the movie be completed before the play went on tour. In the interim a replacement would be found for Massey on Broadway.

I hurried to the Coast, spoke to John Cromwell, who had been designated to direct, and returned to New York. We decided to aim for a July 25 shooting date, and I planned to be in Hollywood the third week of May and remain there for the duration. Nothing was to interfere; everything possible was to be done to ensure the making of a great film. Few projects have been as dear to me.

During the negotiations for film rights Sherwood and I reached complete understanding about our aims. There would be absolute fidelity to the spirit of Lincoln; nothing that might suggest "going Hollywood" would be tolerated; every line spoken from the screen would be written by Sherwood himself.

Such was the rapport between us that only once, in the earliest stages, was there a marring incident, and then Sherwood apologized. Sherwood, going to England for a spring visit, was to turn in a script before he left. I was told by Cromwell that if he had the time, he and a script girl could put the script into shooting form. As it turned out, Cromwell was delayed by a previous commitment and suggested that we call in a writer to do the work for him so that we would be reasonably sure of making our shooting date. When Sherwood heard of my approval, he lost his temper, fearful that our agreement would be jeopardized and that in his absence we would have another writer make the adaptation.

I tried to placate him by explaining that the writer we had called, Grover Jones, understood our position; it had been strongly emphasized to him that every line spoken was to be Sherwood's. In fact, Jones was not even interested in receiving screen credit if there were any objection.

But Sherwood, incensed also by the information that Cromwell had not yet been able to give the script a careful reading, would not listen. He had expected that Cromwell would read the script and make recommendations for revisions. He went into a testy dissertation on continuity writers. He said he was certain now that the spirit of our project would be violated. I tried to allay his suspicions. Naïvely I remarked that perhaps I did not know what was going on or what continuity really meant. That touched the fuse.

"If that's true," Sherwood barked, "then what the hell are you doing in the picture business?"

Sherwood's rage notwithstanding, we went ahead with Jones. I was convinced this was sound procedure; in fact, imperative, considering the circumstances. Furthermore, subsequent conversations persuaded me that concern was groundless. Jones had seen the play several times, was in love with it, respected its sincerity and beauty. He reiterated that he sought no personal glory from this particular assignment.

In a letter to Sherwood, now resting in Surrey, I reported that we had signed Gene Lockhart to portray Stephen Douglas. I recalled his acerbate taunt, noted that it still rankled, and in a moment of premature cockiness, added, "I will stay in the picture business and make money at it because I know something about a play and actors. The boys who know all about the continuity and have no feeling for a good play or good actors are going broke. In other words, the same old movie stuff is finished, and I believe our time has come."

A week later, right after the announcement that *Abe Lincoln in Illinois* had been awarded the Pulitzer Prize as the best American play of the season, I received a letter from Sherwood. He wrote that he would like to "dispose of the subject of the intemperate crack." He went on to explain:

I was very upset, as you doubtless gathered, at the suggestion that someone else was to be brought in on the script even before I had been given a chance to hear John's views and do a second version. That action smelt of the ancient movie practice of turning a writer's work over to one of the many hacks who infect the studios just so that the director could be relieved of responsibility which should rightfully be his. I felt that you, of all people, going into the picture business, would be the one to stop such practices, and when you said you didn't understand what was going on, I burst out—for which I apologize. I have complete confidence in you to do a magnificent job of this picture and to start something that will be of enormous value to all of us and to the movie industry as well.

Our rapport re-established, there was no further friction. Nor did anything arise of any consequence to halt our progress. We did have a few disquieting days when we discovered that Darryl Zanuck was rushing into production with a film called *Young Mr. Lincoln,* seemingly inspired by Sherwood's Broadway success. But Sherwood succeeded in getting a copy of the script, which proved so inferior as to be hardly worth our attention. We put the matter out of mind. I told Sherwood that the best thing we could do was to watch our own business and not the other fellow's. The clear task ahead was to concentrate on getting our picture right and forget theirs.

May flew. I cleared my desk of various bits of unfinished business. Oscar Hammerstein told me excitedly that the musical on which he and Kern were working was going well. I said I would listen to the score when I saw Jerry on the Coast. I continued my missionary work for N.B.C., selling playwrights the vision of television's future and, on the whole, earning my money. One major coup, worth practically my year's salary, was my delivering Noël Coward's plays. Somehow, the Columbia Broadcasting System had been under the impression that it had the inside line. "Here is the body," I said to Royal triumphantly when I had won the rights. I continued in constant touch with Jones and Cromwell on the Coast and with Sherwood in England, to whom I made a variety of suggestions on how I thought certain transitions could be made for the screen.

On May 17 Sam Harris gave me a going-away party in the Tenderloin Room of Billy's Gay Nineties Restaurant. There were sixty guests, instructed by Harris to come dressed in costumes appropriate to the Civil War period. I went as a slaveowner. I remember Kaufman arriving as the mustachioed villain Simon Legree. The food was plentiful; wine and whiskey flowed; toasts were made in honor of my new undertaking; there were the usual quips about how I would become a Hollywood potentate with a swimming pool, *palazzo* and Cadillacs a block long. It was all gay, convivial, hearty. The next day I boarded the Twentieth Century Limited.

In Hollywood the auguries continued good. The studio promised the fullest co-operation. *Abe Lincoln in Illinois* would be one of the year's major enterprises. I was treated royally. Slowly but surely, with Cromwell's expert help, a strong and reliable cast was assembled. Ruth Gordon agreed to appear as Mary Todd Lincoln. Mary Howard was chosen to play Ann Rutledge. Jones, true to his word, was producing a script that had fluency as well as honesty. In between all the preparations I found time to listen to Kern's score for what was to be *Very Warm for May* and loved it.

Clearly, there was a jackpot in my future. I was as

buoyant as a soap bubble on a summer breeze. Not even
Baruch's warning that I was undertaking too much made
any impression. "Max," Baruch had written, "you're
doing too many things. You will not be good at any of
them, and if you don't watch out, you are going to wind
up broke."

Baruch just did not understand. I had the energy, the
drive, the know-how. Besides, I had it worked out. According to our schedule, the filming of the play would be over
no later than the first week in October. Then I could turn
my thoughts to casting the musical, open it in Hollywood
around Christmas, and tour it eastward to Broadway.
Simple. Only it did not work out that way.

Kern decided he preferred a fall production on Broadway, when the theatre season was getting under way. I was
agreeable, though it meant that any casting done in the
East would have to be done without me. Still, this did not
appear to be too much cause for concern. There was the
telephone for consultation. In an emergency I could always fly. I knew all the actors of any quality on Broadway
and, certainly, I had the utmost respect for Hammerstein's
good sense, perspective and experience. Besides, we were
supposed to complete shooting in September. This would
allow me time to be present at rehearsals prior to the
November opening in New York.

Again my calculations were knocked out. We did not
begin work on *Abe Lincoln* until August 7, two weeks
late. The shooting did not go as smoothly as we had
anticipated. There were no particular problems, but I
discovered that I had been foolish to count on anything
resembling a split-second timetable. Consequently, I did
not catch up with *Very Warm for May* until shortly before
Wilmington, first stop on the pre-Broadway tour. When I
did, I knew we were in trouble, and George Kaufman's
letter rose up to haunt me. He had written in a caustic

vein while I was in California that he found it odd for a producer to be producing a show in New York while that producer was in Hollywood.

The company itself was fine. So were Albertina Rasch's dances. The score, with which I had fallen in love immediately, had lost none of its beauty or inventiveness. One song was as beautiful as any of the melodic jewels Kern had ever fashioned—"All the Things You Are." The problem was in the libretto, which on a first reading seemed to have a certain affecting charm. It was a delusion. On the stage the story was tame and thin as it told of a young girl wanting to run away from school to go into the theatre. The opening in Wilmington confirmed my fears. When the pattern of impending failure again was drawn in Washington, I decided to call my old reliable, Hassard Short. Guided by Short, Hammerstein made various revisions in the script. In Boston, where we played next, there was a surge of interest. Our confidence returned and everyone had the feeling that we might be on the way to a hit after all.

We were wrong. So was Boston.

Writing in *The New York Times* the morning after the opening at the Alvin, Brooks Atkinson reported, "The book is a singularly haphazard invention that throws the whole show out of focus and makes an appreciation of Mr. Kern's music almost a challenge." Richard Watts, then of the New York *Herald Tribune,* found the book "excessively tedious and humorless," and Richard Lockridge of *The Sun* considered the plot thoroughly exasperating.

I was flabbergasted. To have been so wrong seemed impossible. The book was not a masterpiece, but it could not be that bad. I stuck my head in the sand. Certainly, the public would love the score. Hammerstein urged me to close the show. I refused.

My gesture of defiance was as foolish as it was futile.

The public believed the critics and did not come. The few who did were not sufficiently enchanted to send their friends. What had happened in the case of such productions as *Roberta* and *The Women* was not to be repeated this time. I surrendered after fifty-nine performances.

Aside from the financial setback—no mean consideration in the light of the long string of failures that preceded it— there was the pang of self-recrimination to be endured, Baruch's warning to be recalled, Kaufman's taunt, the sense of guilt for not having been on the scene from the start. There is no way of knowing how much help I could have given had I been a participant in the early story conferences. But that does not cancel the thought that I might have helped, that I might have detected weaknesses earlier. Then there would have been more time for remedies. No matter what my personal feelings toward Kern may have been, I could not help being sorry also for his sake. This was his first show since *Roberta,* six years before. He had wanted a triumphant return to Broadway. I had let him down. He never did anything for Broadway again, and it has always grieved me that his career in the theatre, begun so gloriously many years before, should have ended with a show deemed unworthy of his talents. He was a puckish, sometimes unbearably superior man, but he, more than most, helped to design and give shape, significance and integrity to the American musical theatre.

One way to sublimate disappointment is to plunge into new activity. For me that was at hand. The final editing and cutting on *Abe Lincoln* had been made. Now arrangements were being worked out for its bookings. In Hollywood there was a sort of buzz-buzz of excitement. Columnists and newspaper and magazine correspondents who had seen private screenings were predicting all sorts of prizes. One jarring note came from Charles Skouras, the Greek movie magnate. We were spending an afternoon together when he remarked in his broken English, "Max, the people don't want no Lincoln pictures."

I paid him no heed. *Abe Lincoln in Illinois* had, as far as I was concerned, taken on a new meaning for our country. Hitler's Wehrmacht was on the march. Europe had entered its long night. We needed Lincoln's words now as never before.

It occurred to me that a Washington première would be appropriate, with the first showing taking place in the White House in deference to President Roosevelt's physical disability, which would have made it awkward for him to attend the theatre. Calling the White House entailed no special problem for me. I had met the President some time before.

I had been in Washington with a play when, one morning, I received a call from Marvin McIntyre, secretary to the President. McIntyre informed me that the President wished to see me. Thrilled, I arrived at the White House at eleven o'clock and found myself locked up with Mr. Roosevelt in his office for an hour and a half. The President, it seemed, was interested in my career, show business, films and other matters. We talked while others waited outside the door. One of the President's aides then walked in and whispered in his ear. What he'd said was that Bernard Baruch was in town. The President told his aide to drop everything and find Baruch because he wanted to have lunch with him. I said good-bye and on my way out ran into Baruch coming up the walk. "B.M.," I greeted him excitedly, "the President is looking all over for you."

Baruch replied, "Don't get excited; I have been here before."

That afternoon I left Washington on the Congressional with Baruch. On the train someone introduced me to

Harry Bridges, the labor leader. We exchanged pleasantries and began discussing show business. In a few minutes I excused myself, telling Bridges that I had to rejoin Mr. Baruch. At the mention of Baruch's name, Bridges shouted, "That's one man I want to meet." I took him into the drawing room, introduced him to B.M., and left them together.

When I called the White House to suggest the première of *Abe Lincoln in Illinois*, I found Mrs. Roosevelt most receptive. Indeed, she suggested that if it was agreeable all around, she would arrange for us to have dinner with the President the night of the show. We set the date for January 21, the public première in the capital scheduled for the following night in the RKO Theater.

The dinner in the White House was a thrilling event for us—Millie, Ruth Gordon, Sherwood and myself. During the dinner my wife sat at the President's right, exchanging humorous and affectionate stories about Baruch. Roosevelt remarked at one point, "How I love that Bernie." After dinner we adjourned to the East Room, where I arranged for Sherwood to sit next to the President. Following the projection of the picture, there were warm compliments from the President and Mrs. Roosevelt. The President remarked to Sherwood how amazing it was that so much of what Lincoln had said in those turbulent days was applicable at the present time. He wondered whether Sherwood would do him a favor. Would he look through Lincoln's public addresses for such observations and send them to him? Sherwood did, beginning the fruitful relationship between them in which he was to be so effective in helping to frame many of Roosevelt's great speeches in the grim years that began with Pearl Harbor.

The première in Washington the next night was a complete triumph. The audience was as enthusiastic as it was brilliant. The following morning in a letter to Baruch I wrote: "I think it's a good thing, and we will probably make some money with it." I spoke too soon. The general Washington public seemed disinterested. The cold terror of Charles Skouras' remark ripped through my heart.

The New York première took place, oddly enough, on Washington's Birthday in the Radio City Music Hall. A man would have had to be a god not to have his head turned by the reviews the following day. Frank Nugent, then film critic for *The New York Times* and now an important screen writer himself, turned cartwheels in print. Moved as he had not been for some time, he reported that the picture "was better than the play," that Raymond Massey's performance was superior to the one he had given on the stage; he called it "a grand picture and a memorable biography of the greatest American of them all." In the *Daily News* there were four stars. I received a letter from Sam Goldwyn congratulating me and telling me that I was needed in Hollywood. Our London distributor cabled, *"Lincoln* one of the most soul-stirring pictures has been our privilege to see." Sherwood was overjoyed. "I am more than encouraged," he wrote shortly before the film's release, "to go ahead with some big schemes, and I certainly want you to be in on them."

Four weeks after the opening at Radio City Music Hall I stared stark disaster in the face. The picture was a failure. It was a failure in New York, a failure wherever it was shown. Bookings dried up. There was no interest. Whether, and how much, Zanuck's earlier film hurt us is hard to say. As far as I know, it did not make any money. Skouras had been a valid prophet of doom. The people did not care for pictures about Lincoln. The people somehow never really seem to care much about pictures dealing with the great men of this country. Is it part of our democratic tradition that refuses to acknowledge the stature of other men? Are we too prosaic to respond to the inspiring examples of our true leaders? I do not know the explanation. But I do know that you can search the records and you will find that films based upon the lives of our national heroes have been mostly failures. Such was even the destiny of Dore Schary's *Sunrise at Campobello,* that stimulating and uplifting account of how a man conquered poliomyelitis and went on to become President of the United States. One of the major successes on Broadway, it was refused by the country at large.

RKO decided to postpone the filming of *The American Way.* If the country was not interested in Lincoln, it was not likely to be interested in the patriotic propaganda incorporated in the Kaufman-Hart tract. Instead, studio officials suggested that Harry Goetz and I return to the Coast and find another property to offset the debacle building up around *Abe Lincoln.*

We went to California. We found nothing.

18

Moss Hart

MY WORLD was slowly but surely blowing up again. I did not need an accountant to tell me that I was heading toward the worst financial crisis of my life. My name was on various notes in behalf of Max Gordon's Plays and Pictures. These would have to be met. I was still in California when a friend of mine—a betting companion at the horse races—informed me that I owed him five thousand dollars. He had been, at my request, allotting me ten per cent of his bets. He had run into a bad streak, and we had continued the arrangement in the hope that he could square my losses. He failed.

The nights grew longer. I tossed on my bed, got up, paced, smoked, slept little. Once more I could feel panic reaching my throat. Recollections returned to haunt me, memories of that other time in Leroy Sanitarium. Desperately I fought to maintain balance, to quell the simmering anxiety. The threat of insolvency was not to be put aside by reason alone. One day there was a call from N.B.C. informing me that the war made it necessary to put television on the shelf for the duration. My services had been deeply appreciated. I was no longer needed.

What little resistance was left, now crumbled. The years of ill-starred Broadway productions, the unexpected failure of *Very Warm for May,* plus the guilt it left, the collapse of *Abe Lincoln in Illinois* had drained my strength. And now this. The tears would no longer be contained. They came and there was no stanching them. I was again an irrational human, useless to myself and to everyone else.

Millie came West and took me home. On the advice of Dr. Henry C. Fleming, I was taken to Regent Hospital. There began the not unfamiliar treatments—the hot-water bags, the hot blankets, the sedatives, the unending hours of enforced rest. This went on for two months. On the bad days I cried until it seemed there could be no more tears. Somehow there were. A look, a word on a wrong note, a wisp of sad thought was enough to set me off. On bad days, too, I tore at my hair, berated myself as a failure, accused myself of ineptitude, mocked my achievements, screamed that they were due to luck and not ability. In the silence of the night I sometimes prayed for death, though this time, unlike the last, I made no overt effort to end my life. One day, amid the tears, I told Millie of the other money I owed—the five-thousand-dollar betting loss. She bent over me and kissed me, her way of saying that she understood, that all she wanted now was for me to regain my health. Even her fortitude was enough to upset me.

During the long nights I took inventory. Thirty years in show business and what had I gained? I had less than when I began. Hope, money—gone. Also my dreams. Worse, I was in debt. Millie sat beside my bed and tried to comfort me. Instead she made me cry. I looked at her and visions of her struggling to support herself and her aged mother and father brought on the tears.

Friends came when they were permitted, bringing with them what solace they could. Someone suggested that I ought to consider leaving show business for something less risky. Yet what else could I do? Someone suggested I go into bankruptcy, and my nerves went off again. Being forced into bankruptcy by others is understandable. But to seek it—I could not tolerate the idea. My name was too dear to me, pride too strong. When Bernard Baruch came and offered me fifty thousand dollars to get started again, I thanked him but refused. I would make my own way back, I said.

Oscar Hammerstein reiterated his confidence in me, told me what an important man I was in the theatre, assured me that he had always respected my judgment. "Nothing is going to stop you," he would say. "All you need is your health, and nothing is going to stop you."

Moss Hart sat with me often, encouraged me, tried to make me laugh. "Max," he would say in dead earnest, "please stop worrying. I'm going to find you a play. I don't know where I'm going to find it, or whether it will be a hit, but I'll find it." As if plays, good ones, are that easily found.

And then some time later he walked in with one of those thirteen-by-ten envelopes, from which he took a conventional-looking manuscript. He handed it to me with a flourish of mock grandeur. "Here is the play I promised," he said in his beautifully modulated, urbane voice. "I think it's a hit." The script was *My Sister Eileen*.

The play was based on the now famous Ruth McKenney stories that originally appeared in *The New Yorker* magazine. It had been sent to Moss by the authors, Joseph Fields and Jerome Chodorov, at the suggestion of Jerome's brother Eddie, Moss's friend from their apprentice days.

Moss had read the play and, like the true theatre man he was, sensed its possibilities. He called the playwrights in California. "You must let Max Gordon have this play," he said.

Moss left the script of *My Sister Eileen* on the table next to my bed, but some time passed before I brought myself to pick it up. The extent of Moss's concern for me was unsettling. I looked at the script, knowing how easy it was to be disappointed. Nor dared I hope. I might not agree with Moss's judgment. Still, in my condition I could not be sure of my own.

At last I summoned the nerve. I started to read. As I did, all my qualms subsided. I laughed for the first time in months. I never had read Ruth McKenney's stories, in which partly in fact and partly in fiction she told how she and her sister had come to New York from Ohio to make careers for themselves, told of the adventures they had in their respective quests, the comic perils they endured living in that perennial outpost of bohemia, Greenwich Village. The play was a distillation of those stories, and I had not proceeded much beyond the first act when I knew that Moss was right.

The essentials were there, what George M. Cohan called "the good premise." *My Sister Eileen* was a potential hit. What it needed was some work, but more than anything, a promise from George Kaufman that he would direct it. George liked the play but was contemplating another collaboration with Edna Ferber, with whom he had written such scripts as *Minick* in 1924, *The Royal Family* in 1927, and *Dinner at Eight* in 1932. He was willing to make suggestions, he said, and if his own plans did not materialize, he would direct *My Sister Eileen*.

Jerome Chodorov came to the hospital with Moss. He said that Fields and he were delighted to have George make suggestions. They also hoped that George would

decide to direct their play. I had the feeling that Jerome
had come to see for himself what my condition was, to see
whether or not I could fulfill my intentions. Happily, the
turn had come and Moss was able to assure him that I
would be fine.

Moss's action was typical. He was without doubt the best
foul-weather friend any man ever had. Close associates
knew that when they were well they might not hear from
him for days, even weeks. But they also knew that when
difficulties arose, or illness, he would be there, appearing
as if out of the clouds, anxious to help, to cheer, to comfort. He was never too busy to read a friend's play, or
that of a friend's friend. He might be deep in rehearsal
of his own play, yet he would not forget to call a fellow
playwright to inquire how his second act was progressing.
How many trips he made to out-of-town tryout cities—
Philadelphia, Boston, Washington—to sit up into the early-
morning hours giving of his wisdom, his experience, his
wit, to help make a colleague's play a success!

I have a letter from Moss that I cherish as much as any
material thing in my life. Written by hand from the Coast,
where he was working on a film for Judy Garland, it came
to me at a time when I was low in spirits and depressed
over my failure to secure a musical in which I had been
interested. It reads:

Dear Max:

Forgive the notepaper—I have stopped in the middle of
work to send you a word of cheer—I talked to George this
morning and he said you had been feeling poorly—and though
I know how very little it means to have merely a letter from
someone this far away—still it may help a little to know that
I am concerned for you and thinking about you. Dear Max,
I know all about the kind of pain you are going through—and
because I know so much about it I can say little. Is it at all
possible for you to go and see someone—not to talk about

yourself, but just *this particular thing?* Don't you think it would help? I know too well that words of sympathy from me or anybody else are fairly meaningless, but for what they are worth, you have all of mine. I can also tell you that people out here speak of you with respect and affection, and I think you know how much you mean to your friends. Small comfort, I know, in the middle of the night, but sometimes these things need re-stating, and so I say them to you again. But more than that, Max, if you continue to feel badly, won't you try to see someone? I hate to think of you living out the days and nights in torment. I am *not* suggesting an analysis for you—just see a good therapist and spill out all the business about the musical and see if it doesn't lighten the load a bit. Do discuss this with Millie and see if she might not agree—she loves you and it must cost her a great deal to see you this unhappy. Not that I could help much, but I wish I were there to let you talk it out with me—but I know, unfortunately, that this is not the answer. One of the truly sad things about human beings is how very alone they are—friends and loved ones are sometimes not enough—and it is our own pain we must face out for ourselves.

I'm afraid all this is not much use to you, Max, but at least it tells you that I am thinking of you and deeply wish I could help. And if it helps just a small amount, then I have wasted Judy Garland's time to good purpose.

Forgive the haste and the scrawl—I must get back to work; I am working against time these days. And our love to you both always.

Moss

A few months later when I was able to write and tell him that I had snapped back from my difficulties, he wrote immediately:

This is just the hastiest of notes to tell you that your letter containing the news that you were up again and about and feeling well again was the most cheery news you could possibly have written. I have thought about you and, as a matter of fact, tried to phone you once, but there was no answer. This is just an excuse for a letter, and I will write you another one in place of it, but I want to tell you how wonderful it is that you are back in harness.

Kitty joins me in sending all love.

Moss's thoughtfulness extended even to those he had never met. During the Second World War, he wrote and produced that classic tribute to the United States Air Force, *Winged Victory,* all the proceeds of which went to Army Emergency Relief. Moss then conceived the idea of writing a letter to the mother and father of each American flyer who received the Distinguished Flying Cross. With each letter he sent a silver Winged Victory pin, accompanied by two tickets to the show.

After the publication by Random House of his autobiography, *Act One,* he was deluged by letters of praise and appreciation. Because he enjoyed reading them, and because he felt simple courtesy required that he do so, he insisted on sending a personal reply to every letter. Not perfunctory polite notes, but each with some comment, some revelation of himself, of the deep springs of his humanity. He wrote to a man named Max Lewis:

One of the rewards of the aloneness that is so necessary a part of the profession of being a writer is the thought and ultimately the sound, if one is successful, of applause that comes with success in the theatre. I have been hearing audiences applaud, not always, but most of the time, for thirty years now. But it is an anonymous sound, and though extremely pleasant to a playwright's ears, it lacks the warmth and touch of the truly personal.

Act One is the first piece of prose I have ever written, and perhaps its greatest reward, apart from its critical reception, is a letter like yours.

I was immensely pleased, of course, with your liking the book, but more than that, I was touched by what you said and by your thoughtfulness in taking the time and the trouble to write to me.

Act One has given me a far deeper sense of personal satisfaction and pleasure than any play I have ever written, and your letter is one of the things that has made it so. Thank you indeed.

I first met Moss Hart in the fall of 1930. His initial triumph, *Once in a Lifetime,* was running at the Music Box. My own successful production of *Three's a Crowd* was at the Selwyn. We were introduced by George Kaufman. When I met Moss, his hair had not yet begun to recede into that unusual shape which, with his long, narrow face and high cheekbones, was to give him a remarkable resemblance to Mephistopheles, albeit a benign one. Six feet tall, with gaiety in his eyes, he already had about him the beginnings of that air of elegance that was to become a marked characteristic during subsequent years, enabling Walter Kerr, drama critic for the New York *Herald Tribune,* to describe him without thought of contradiction as "a natural aristocrat."

Moss, in that fall of 1930, was for the first time in his life free of financial insecurity, free of what he called the unrelieved taste of poverty forever in his mouth and "the grim smell of actual want always at the end of my nose." Free, he was, as the saying goes, to live it up. Under the guidance of Kaufman's wife, Beatrice, he was finding his way into the drawing rooms and parties of the elite, making friends with the literary and social world of New York, already busily creating a legend as a playboy and profligate spender. It was not only a conscious but also a determined effort to make up for so much that he had missed as a boy, for the stabbing pain of wanting and not being able to have even the cheapest toy. The legend of his extravagances began the morning following the opening night of *Once in a Lifetime.* After reading the ecstatic notices, he literally thumbed his nose at the subway, which he never was to ride again, took a taxi back to Brooklyn, ordered his mother, father and brother to leave their apartment without so much as a toothbrush, ushered them into another taxi, and rode them back to Manhattan.

He rented an apartment in the Ansonia Hotel. With the help of interior decorators he turned the place into a plushy haven of velvet, gilt and carved Spanish furniture. For each of the windows in his bedroom he ordered four sets of curtains—net, chiffon, satin and velvet.

"I never had any curtains," he would explain when telling the story, "and I thought it would be nice to have plenty."

This was the beginning of what became known among Moss's friends as his "gold-garter period." He became a steady customer at Cartier's, headquarters for gold garters and such emblems of affluence as gold suspender buckles, gold pencils, gold pens, gold and platinum cigarette cases— items which he bought not only for himself but also as gifts for friends. He bought a dog, the first he ever had, fell in love with it and bought seven more. He was a frequent visitor to such exclusive men's furnishings establishments as Sulka's, Charvet's, and Brooks Brothers', where he indulged himself in monogrammed accoutrements of all sorts and descriptions.

Edna Ferber, who took him to her heart "as the son I never had," once described him as being monogrammed in the most improbable places. It was said that after Moss spent an hour at Sulka's, Charvet's or Brooks' "they could pull the shades down and call it a day." Moss bought by the dozens—monogrammed dressing gowns, monogrammed shirts, monogrammed underwear. In wonder I questioned him about these indulgences.

"Max," he replied, "I don't think you understand. I simply love the feel of silk next to my *derrière*."

None of these splurges, however, compared with his purchase of a farm in Bucks County, Pennsylvania. He had spent a weekend with the Kaufmans at their New Hope place and was riding home when he caught a glimpse of an old stone farmhouse on the top of a hill. He liked it—one of those whim-of-the-moment adventures. The next day he arranged for the purchase by long-distance telephone. The purchase price was nothing compared to the investment he made to fit it to his taste. He added wings and ells to the old stone house, converted the tool shed into a library, and refurbished the old beams with oak casings. The single well on the eighty-seven acres went dry during the hot spells of July, August and September, and seventeen other wells were drilled until one delivered sufficient water for regular purposes and the swimming pool that Moss built.

He wanted a forest on the hilltop and overnight there was one—3,500 pine trees transplanted. He did not have the patience to wait for saplings to grow and provide the place with shade, so he had 139 elms planted, each at least twenty years old; he also had set in the lawns copper beeches, larches and willows of equal age. A visitor, whether it was Kaufman or Alexander Woollcott has never been settled, took a look at the place and remarked, "Oh well, it just goes to show you what God could do if he had a little money."

Moss catered to his pixieish whims all through his life, once he achieved prosperity. I have a letter from him written two days before he died in Palm Springs, California, in which he reported: "All my life I've wanted a monkey, just the way a Latin Quarter chorus girl longs for her first mink coat. Well, at last, I have one and he is glorious. We breakfast together on the terrace and he chatters away, making more sense than many of my social —or what you consider my social—friends. I discovered yesterday that he was also one of us. He adores matzos and smoked salmon."

Still, no one can say that wealth, fame and position softened Moss or made him lazy. His energy would not permit; nor would his vanity let him rest. He was an indefatigable worker when he had an idea, a great craftsman blessed with one of the sharpest wits of our time.

Those who worked with him came to love him for his decency and his patience. The destructive, malice-laden jests and jibes he saved for the stage. To his colleagues at work, he was gentle and understanding, eager always to bolster self-confidence and ego. When news came to Julie Andrews minutes before the matinee of *Camelot* that Moss was dead, the only thing she wanted to remember was the forty-eight hour ordeal she had gone through with him—they called it "The Terror"—while preparing for *My Fair Lady,* which Moss had directed. It was the second week of rehearsals and, as Moss said later, he was getting "really terrified" because Julie did not seem to have a clue to her role of Eliza Doolittle. He called off rehearsals. For two full days, alone in the theatre, he worked with her on the part, went over it line for line, scolded gently, pleaded, cajoled, encouraged. When the session was over, he had succeeded in putting her on the road to the performance that was to send her star high into the theatrical heaven.

Writers do not generally relish working with directors who themselves are creative men. Too often in those instances the directors are like editors who can only see a script in terms of how they would have written it. Moss was not that kind of director. He never tried to impose his ideas on a writer. Alan Jay Lerner, author of *My Fair Lady,* has said, "If he felt that in places you were becoming myopic or astigmatic, he became your glasses to enable you to see your own work clearer. Were there ever a disagreement, you won. If you were proven right, he was the first person to admit it. If you were proven wrong, he was the easiest person to be wrong with. In either case, it was accomplished with warmth and humor. *My Fair Lady* ran long in New Haven. Condensation, not cutting, was required. Moss came to me with a solution. I went to work on it and, in so doing, found what I thought was a better one, entirely different. I read it to him. He listened, thought, then rose and said, 'You dirty dog. How dare you give me an inferiority complex?' On another occasion we disagreed totally about how a number should be staged. We agreed that we should try it his way first. It was perfect, and I went over to him in the back of the theatre to eat my crow. Paraphrasing Gershwin to Levant, he looked down at me with mock lordliness and said, 'Well, my boy, that's the difference between talent and genius.' "

And yet this gracious man had his own private demons, his own secret suffering and unspoken torments. He knew, as I knew, all the self-doubts, the uncertainties, the long sleepless nights. He distrusted his own talents and harried himself with the superstition that every success was a combination of luck and a modicum of skill, that with each new play the luck would run out. He lived always with the fear that time would pass him by and he would, to use Ben Hecht's words, "rot on the vine in full view."

Under the glossy veneer of his sophistication he was a shy man, sensitive and vulnerable to what people said and thought of him. He never achieved, as some do, that position of impregnability against the critics' barbs and shafts. He read every word of the reviews, gulping praise with an addict's avidity, suffering deeply over adverse criticism and failure. The unfriendly reception given *The Climate of Eden* left him shattered and actually resulted in his writing *Act One*. The play had lasted twenty performances on Broadway and Moss, in order to regain his equilibrium, went off on a trip with S. N. Behrman.

Morose and full of despair, he did not know what to do. He knew that he did not want to go to Hollywood, and he knew that it would not be right for him in that mood to try another play. It was Behrman who said to him, "You're a professional writer. You must write. Go to your desk and write every day, even if it's only a diary." Which is what he did for a year. At the end of the year he destroyed the diary and began what ultimately was to become his autobiography.

Even success could trouble him. He once said, "It's interesting that the great mystery of unhappiness is not the story of the failure. A man who is a failure complains about fate, about bad breaks, and you can understand it. But when you're completely successful and you're unhappy, it becomes a mystery. Most of the successful people I know are unhappy. Success is like anesthesia. You can increase the dosage and increase it and finally it doesn't work." In the years when he was enjoying repeated successes with other writers, he tortured himself with the thought that he might not be any good writing alone. He worried himself to the borders of breakdown. At a time when he had three plays running on Broadway, had received with Kaufman the Pulitzer Prize for *You Can't Take It with You,* he was, as he put it, "carried feet first to the analyst's couch." For almost seven years he underwent treatment in his effort to exorcise the doubts and distrust. It undoubtedly convinced him that he could write plays alone, because he did, but it did not bring him total peace. Yet, after more than a quarter of a century in the theatre he was able to say and believe that "in the theatre you get more than you deserve and sometimes you get less than you deserve—and there is no use being bitter about it."

Moss, as director, and everyone else connected with the production of *Camelot* knew that they were in for a typical Broadway torture test. Broadway is full of sentiment and sentimentality. But underneath it also is full of bitterness, cynicism and jealousy. As the same team that had created *My Fair Lady*, Alan Jay Lerner, Frederick Loewe and Moss knew that everyone was expecting them to either surpass or at least equal that achievement. Anything less would be regarded as failure.

As veterans tempered in Broadway ovens, Alan, Fritz and Moss had seen similar situations before—the gloating satisfaction that followed the mild reception accorded *Allegro,* by Richard Rodgers and Oscar Hammerstein 2nd, after the successes of *Oklahoma!* and *Carousel.* That they ever went through with *Camelot* is in a measure tribute to their gallantry. I have no doubt that the pressure contributed to Moss's coronary and, ultimately, the shortening of his life, as well as to Lerner's severe case of bleeding ulcers.

When the show opened on Broadway, following all the dire forebodings and advance reports from the tryout cities, its reception could be foretold. Only a miracle could win for it judgment on its own merits. There was no miracle. Yet Moss, taking everything into consideration, was able to say to me, "Well, at least we aspired." Time, to be sure, justified the effort. *Camelot* surmounted the Broadway professionals' verdict and won its praises from the general public.

It was Edna Ferber who, for me at least, said it best at Moss's memorial tribute on the stage of the Music Box, where he had won his first fame:

"Nothing," she said, "that exists, nothing that exhilarates and exalts the dignity of man, ceases to exist. Moss never will pass into nothingness. Human beings like Moss are forever and ever."

19

George S. Kaufman

How much of my recovery could be attributed to the prospect of producing *My Sister Eileen* is, of course, hard to know. The treatments, the medication, the rest, the encouragement from my friends—all had their effects. But I am certain the play had an important share. Shortly after I had read it, the periods between crying spells lengthened. One day the crying stopped. Then came the night I slept six hours without taking a sleeping pill.

I went home. It was May. There was balm in the air and new hope. Sam Harris called for me and we went for long rides in his car. The countryside was magnificent: the young, tender green grass vibrant and dancing in the sun; the graceful, slender new leaves bursting forth on the oaks, elms and maples; the azalea bushes in the suburbs radiant in splashes of reds and pinks. It was good, I knew, to be alive.

I went for walks again with Oscar Hammerstein in Central Park. We talked long and earnestly about the theatre, about my future in the theatre. There were days when all did not go well, when there were hints of old fears, old doubts. Oscar, quick and sensitive to these moods, would talk about the new triumphs he foresaw for me, would urge me to realize that what I had accomplished could not be marked down to luck. Ability and judgment, he said, played their parts. I had not lost these, and I would come back "bigger and better than ever."

For a while I tried going to a psychiatrist. Up to now I had fought such suggestions. I had little faith in the procedure whereby I was to probe the subconscious and let a stranger know what went on in my mind. I believed that my problems were my own, that no one could understand them as I did. Too many persons I knew, once they started treatment, seemed unable to break away. My convictions were regarded as old-fashioned. I let myself be persuaded, though I remembered a doctor in California saying to me, "Mr. Gordon, I could give you all the money you need to pay off your debts, but it would not help. You will go on having these collapses from time to time." I lasted about eight visits with the psychiatrist. I was an unco-operative patient. Perhaps I was too old. I decided I must fight in my own way.

One day I met Bob Sherwood, who said to me, "Max, I've got the answer for you. Hang a sign in your bathroom with all the hits printed on it to remind yourself of your own worth." I rejected that, too.

Slowly the nightmare receded into the shadows. In its place there grew within me a determination to vindicate Oscar, Moss, Baruch, and all those wonderful friends who believed in me, who had stood by me. I reached that day when my accountant could sit down and explain my financial situation—that I had signed notes with Harry Goetz to the extent of three hundred thousand dollars in behalf of Max Gordon's Plays and Pictures, that my personal debts, accumulated through my illness combined with what I owed the Federal Government in taxes, came to an additional one hundred thousand dollars. I listened and I did not flinch. That was the mark of my recovery.

I resolved that I would pay back every cent, knowing that I could not expect any help from Goetz, who himself was in difficulties, and certainly nothing from Heiman, who had refused to sign the notes at all. I resolved also that as soon as Max Gordon's Plays and Pictures was in the clear, I would get out. The dream was over. I had had enough of movie-making. Nor had either of my partners contributed creatively to our enterprise on Broadway. What I did henceforth would be strictly on my own. This was the lesson I had paid for at a heartbreaking price.

Meanwhile, rewriting on *My Sister Eileen* went well. Fields and Chodorov, deeply appreciative of the suggestions George Kaufman had made, were doing everything he wished. Then, it was fall. George's plans for his play with Edna Ferber did not jell. One day he came to my office and said, "I will direct the play for you."

George was not the one to say so, nor the one to even hint at the idea that he was doing this for my sake, to help me out. But I knew. I knew because he could have chosen any one of a dozen other projects that were constantly being presented to him.

Although I had no money of my own to invest, financing *My Sister Eileen* was no problem. Costs were lower in those days, and for a play such as this there was no need for an extravagant budget. Fields and Chodorov, confident of their work, each invested $2,500. Mrs. Kaufman put in $1,500, Sam Harris $1,000, and Moss $750. Other friends chipped in $6,000. My share of the gamble was notes I signed with the scene builders and costume people, for which I received a fifteen-per-cent interest in the production.

In the fall of 1940 George assembled the company for its first rehearsal. Plans had been made for an opening at the Biltmore Theatre the day after Christmas. George decided that it was not necessary to go out of town. Aside from the obvious savings, he was confident that the play was in sound shape and that we could open "cold," giving a few previews before the première. At the outset there seemed to be little anticipation of the play on Broadway. Perhaps it was because Shirley Booth, cast as Ruth, had not yet attained her full stature and popularity, and Eileen was to be played by a newcomer, Jo Ann Sayers. Perhaps it was because the playwrights themselves were comparatively unknown. Actually, there was benefit to be derived from the apathy. Better to come in a "sleeper" and become a surprise hit than the other way around.

With George in charge and Moss hovering closely on the sidelines, I attended rehearsals infrequently, keeping busy with the other details involved in preparing a production. Determined also to guard my health, I arranged each day to go to my club where I spent time in the steam room, the swimming pool and on the massage table.

One event marred the rehearsals. Four days before our opening word came that the real-life Eileen and her husband, the novelist and screen writer Nathanael West, had been killed in an auto accident. The news was appalling. For a while consideration was given to postponing the opening. It was George who decided to go ahead, saying that a delay could hardly do any good. The gloom did not lift. Fields and Chodorov, trying to brighten a sagging point in the third act, found it difficult to be funny. The mood affected the first previews, and one theatre veteran left the Biltmore saying, "It ain't there. It just ain't there."

By opening night, however, the ancient show-business tradition gained control. The challenge of the première revitalized the company. The somber mood was replaced, it seemed, by a desire to make the debut worthy of Eileen's memory.

Up until opening night I had restrained my anxieties. But as curtain time neared, my heart beat faster. Millie noticed a flush in my cheeks. I could not stand still. If this were "it," if this turned into a smash hit, I could begin to extricate myself from the mess into which I had fallen.

I grabbed Jerry Chodorov by the arm and pulled him out to the sidewalk. Up and down Forty-seventh Street we paced. Once we stopped briefly to talk with Richard Rodgers, whose *Pal Joey* was running at the Barrymore. The clock in the corner store moved on.

Toward the end of the third act we returned to the theatre. The audience was laughing—riotously. The curtain came down. The applause boomed forth. In the excitement I heard someone say that the whole thing had been wonderful. The comedy, we were told, had built steadily through the first act and the turning point had come in the middle of the second. Even Robert Benchley, the humorist and critic, was laughing out loud.

I went backstage with Millie. Congratulations were exchanged on all sides. I told Fields and Chodorov I would call them at their hotel as soon as I read the reviews. At about 3:30 A.M. I called Jerry at the St. Moritz.

"We're in," I screamed. "Listen!" And I proceeded to relay the content of each of the reviews while he relayed them to Fields standing next to him. In the morning there were lines at the box office, lines that never seemed to stop. The afternoon papers followed the morning leads. *My Sister Eileen* ran 865 performances on Broadway; there were road companies across the country. Ultimately,

I sold the picture rights for $225,000 and signed a separate contract with Columbia for $50,000 to produce the film and act in a general advisory capacity for six months of each of two years.

What a season that was for all of us. *My Sister Eileen* made Burns Mantle's list of ten best plays. So did *George Washington Slept Here,* by George and Moss. So did *Lady in the Dark,* written by Moss alone.

What a season it was, indeed—and yet not without its sadness. In March Sam Harris underwent an emergency appendectomy, in Florida, from which he never recovered his strength. He returned North and developed pneumonia. On July 2, at the age of sixty-nine, he died in his apartment in the Ritz Tower Hotel—Sam, who would not grow old, who once had boasted, "I have no intention of growing old despite the fact that my birthdays pile up," Sam, who had loved youth, life and the world.

Sam's death brought to an end his unofficial partnership with Moss and George, a partnership that had given the theatre some of its richest and happiest moments. For me it was the end of a precious friendship. Sam, like my brother Cliff, occupies a place deep inside my heart.

Not long after the funeral Moss and I spoke of our future relationship. I suggested that I would be happy to serve him as Sam had. But even as I made the offer, I knew that the chance of its being accepted was slim. Moss said he would think it over. When he made up his mind to cast his lot with Joseph Hyman, it was a gesture of friendship and loyalty that needed no explanation. Hyman was a businessman with a passion for the theatre, a man who had befriended Moss when he was the social director at a hotel in the Catskills. Hyman had unhesitatingly given him two hundred dollars at the end of that summer when the hotel owner disappeared without paying the staff. Through all the years that followed, Hyman remained one of Moss's dearest friends and counselors.

When Moss told me of his decision, he was careful to assure me that he would always be at my service. He also expressed his wish to be considered a potential investor in future productions of mine. And that is the way it was.

With George it was different. After directing *My Sister Eileen,* he returned to collaborating with Edna Ferber. They had just about completed *The Land Is Bright,* a serious play about a wealthy American family, which Sam Harris was to have produced in the fall. I hinted to George that I wanted to reach an agreement with him.

"Max," he announced one day, "Edna and I have completed *The Land Is Bright,* and we would like to have you produce it. Edna and I have eighty per cent between us, and you can have the remainder. It will mean a great deal of prestige for you—doing a play by Edna and me—even if it isn't a hit."

It was gratuitous and irritating advice. But I did not have the nerve to say, "George, it seems to me I already have prestige. What about my productions of *Three's a Crowd, The Band Wagon, Dodsworth, Design for Living* and all the others? What about Coward, what about Jerome Kern? George, don't you think my successes have far outweighed my failures?"

I dared not say these things. Nor did I dare reject what he must have thought was a magnanimous offer. I was on the first leg of a comeback from disaster. I may not have expected an alliance with Moss, but with George I felt that I had earned preference. As far as I knew, there was no one like a Joe Hyman in his life, no one to whom he owed prior consideration. We had, indeed, worked together on and off ever since *The Band Wagon.* I had been with him, as with everyone else, a loyal and fastidious manager. If I did not produce his plays now, others certainly would, regardless of terms. Moreover, if I did not, it would appear, however untrue, to be an unfavorable reflection on me. I knew that George would be difficult. But I also knew that he was George S. Kaufman—writer, director, synonym for genius in the field of American stage comedy.

Aligned with him and having, in addition, Moss's assurance of co-operation, I would have as good a hedge against insecurity in the theatre as any man could wish. And, heaven knows, I was hungry—hungry for solvency, security and stability.

The Land Is Bright was short-lived. But it was not without its compensation. When the production had been wrapped and stored away, parts of it, perhaps, to be used another time, I received a call from George. The outcome was a loose arrangement between us to work together. He received half of my interest in any show he wrote or brought to me for which there was outside financing. When I put up money, so did he. We had no contract, George not being interested in such formalities. And that is the way it was for the twenty or so remaining years of his life.

By all normal standards ours was an ideal relationship. I did everything possible, always, to please him, to guess his needs, to understand his whims. I can remember only one instance during our relationship when he reproached me for something I did as a producer, but not a single instance when he whined or whimpered over failure or money lost. And yet, what a strange man he was, one of the strangest I have ever met in more than half a century in show business. In the years of our association I don't think I really ever learned, as I had feared I would not, how to relax in his presence.

Tall, lean, with a long, bony face, his head was topped by a bushy pompadour. He had a large nose, large ears, and he never seemed quite certain that he was holding his six-foot frame together, there being a looseness about him that suggested a perpetual disjointedness. Most striking, however, were his eyes, shielded by glasses. Above the eyes there were two heavy black brows, generally arched in plaintive inquiry. The eyes themselves could be piercingly sharp, disconcerting as they reflected what would appear to be an internal sneer, a sort of derision. Generally, though, they suggested funereal mournfulness, the look of a lonely, troubled, harried man, remote and beyond the crowd. It was a look that earned him the sobriquet "The Gloomy Dean of Humor." But the eyes alone did not always repel. What put most persons off, what actually frightened them, was his impatient brusqueness, a cantankerousness that caused strangers and ordinary acquaintances to shy away and avoid his company, which I'm sure was just what he wished in most instances.

So unlike Moss he was, Moss who had the knack of making every man think he was his friend. George deliberately shut people out. And if he did not succeed with his eyes or his manner, he did so with his rapier wit, which he used so effectively on stage and off. He had, as everyone knows, a great gift for satire, a gift for making fun of both people and the mores of the time. But constant derision is not pleasant. Indeed, it has been said that a "satirist is too often a sadist, very thinly disguised."

George had additional weapons with which to scare people. He could be the most impatient and irritable of men—as taxi drivers, office boys, barbers, waiters and telephone girls learned to their discomfort. There once was considerable jubilation among those who had felt George's sting when word passed around the Broadway district of a courageous taxi driver's rebellion. The driver had been hailed by George to take some of his relatives to a midnight sailing from a North River pier. About halfway between Tenth and Eleventh Avenues the driver, weary of the caustic comments George had been making about his driving, suddenly pulled over to the curb and refused to move a wheel's turn farther. He ordered George and the other passengers from the car and roared off, leaving them on the wind-and-rain-swept sidewalk to trudge the remaining distance on foot, carrying their own baggage.

It still nettles me to recall George's begrudging attitude following the opening of *The Late George Apley,* one of the finest pieces of work he ever did as a writer and director. I had read J. P. Marquand's Pulitzer Prize-winning novel about upper-strata life in Boston, and it had occurred to me that it would make an excellent play. I urged George to read it with that in mind. Before he finished, he said he would like to do it. I called Harold Freedman, Marquand's representative. A meeting was arranged at which it was agreed that Marquand would collaborate with George on the play. It opened in the fall of 1944, was recognized as superior work, and played 385 performances on Broadway. Looking for a little kudos, I remarked to George about what a good idea it had been to make him read the book.

"I can't understand," I said, "why no one else ever thought of doing this play."

"Oh," he said dryly, "someone would have."

Nothing, I think, epitomized George's reputation more tellingly than a suggestion made by the late S. Jay Kaufman. An erstwhile journalist and Broadway press agent, Jay was concerned over the tendency of the uninformed to confuse him with George because of the similarity of their surnames. He would say that he could be identified as the *kind* Kaufman.

But, paradoxically, those who knew George, those who had survived his slings and arrows and had succeeded in breaking through the outer ring of his defenses, knew that *this* Kaufman could be kind, too. I had only to remember his reply when, after the crash in '29, I told him I was broke. "I have twenty-five hundred dollars in the bank," he said. "You can have fifteen hundred."

There were, as Moss once pointed out, many Georges. There was George the misanthrope, the harsh, metallic, poison-tongued George who, like some ogre out of an old-fashioned fairy tale, could scare people off, the "wintry and distant George, sad, lonely, remote from his fellow men." But there was also a loving George, a man who, beneath that jaundiced, craggy façade he presented to the world, could care deeply, could be a determinedly devoted friend, who could be, and was, thoughtful of the needs of others. When he heard that an actress was having difficulty making ends meet, he could write to me and say, "I don't know how much she's getting. But I hear she's got a little boy and other problems. Can we afford to give her a little more?" Or, "Dear Max, I keep thinking about those Christmas bonuses for the box-office boys and wish they could have been larger. Am I crazy? We expect, and I think we get, complete honesty from them in a tempting job. Any chance of giving them something extra, or are you against it?"

Years after S. Jay Kaufman had basked in the smiles of those who sympathized with his wish to be identified as the *kind* Kaufman—a quip that hardly endeared him to George—he lay in a London hospital, alone and miserable, victim of a stroke. George also happened to be in London and Jay, knowing this, and in trouble, swallowed his pride. He asked George to visit him. George went. Later he wrote:

Well, yesterday I did a Good Deed, and I should learn that it is out of character. I went to visit (at his request) S. Jay Kaufman, whom I never could stand, but he had had a stroke, is paralyzed on the left side, leg and arm, and is in the ward in

Paddington Hospital. You can imagine how I transferred all this to myself and spent a splendid night in a cold sweat. The poor fellow will be taken home in the hospital of the *Queen Elizabeth* this week, and there is a nephew there who will put him in a home somewhere in Jersey. How it depressed me, even a fellow whom I never have liked. I even offered him money if he needed it. . . .

How revealing that remark about his good deed being out of character. How he tried to cover up the sweeter aspects of his nature. Although he was incapable of praising me to my face for *The Late George Apley,* he could, in letters, tell me what he truly thought of me. During one of my recurring periods of self-doubt, he wrote:

The main thing is that you know your judgment is still good—in fact, better than ever. If you have not produced a lot of hits in recent years, it is because there were not a lot of hits written. You also did not produce a lot of failures, remember—and remember that *hard.* Most producers temporarily down on their luck would lose their sense of balance and do the stinkers. You didn't. Nobody but you and I notice that you have not been active, and you and I know that you are waiting for the good one. . . .

And, in the same vein later:

I wish there were some way that I could restore your faith in your theatrical judgment, which has always been close to one hundred per cent sound and I am certain still is. Despite your present low estate, you had no trouble detecting that *Men of Distinction* was not a masterpiece. . . . And why do you think Lee Shubert sent you that script to appraise? Obviously, because he valued your opinion above anyone else's, or he would have sent it to someone else.

On higher ground, there was *Camino Real,* a difficult play to assess. Your judgment coincided, almost to the word, with that of Ruth and Gus Goetz, who are terrifically good judges—some beautiful scenes they said, but some bad ones. Which was what you said . . . you are miles above the run of them. I am not handing you therapeutic guff when I say this—why the hell am I so insistent on having you for a producer if I don't believe it? I am not *that* crazy.

It was the same—this face-to-face reticence—with Moss. Once when Moss was leaving on a long and difficult journey, he chose to spend the night before his departure with George because, as he said, "George in many ways was more father to me than my own father." They dined together and talked through the evening. Not once did George say a word about the impending journey or the reason for Moss's going. When it came time for Moss to leave, George walked him to the door, made a perfunctory farewell gesture, and that was all. Hurt and bitter, Moss walked home. When he arrived in his room, he found on his desk a three-page, single-spaced, typewritten letter from George, delivered while they had sat together. In it George had written all that he knew he would be unable to say to his friend that night.

What George could never conceal, however, was his love for the theatre, though, characteristically, there is nothing in his early history to indicate that he would make it his goal. Born in Pittsburgh, of middle-class parents, he had planned to be a lawyer. But the profession proved inhospitable and he withdrew. There followed a variety of jobs: member of a surveying team, window clerk in a tax office, secretary to the comptroller of a Pittsburgh coal company, and wholesale agent for hatbands and ribbons for women's shoes.

It was during this time that he began contributing bits of humor to the well-known column "Always in Good Humor," conducted by Franklin P. Adams for the New York *Evening Mail*. So good and so frequent were George's contributions that F.P.A., as Adams was popularly known, invited him to lunch. Thus began a long and happy friendship. When the *Washington Times* sought a bright, inexpensive humorist to conduct a column, Adams recommended George, who held the post for a year or so, until he ran afoul of the paper's owner, the late Frank A. Munsey. Rushing through the composing room with some corrected proofs of his column, George bumped into the ill-tempered Munsey, who promptly fired him.

When F.P.A. moved to the *Tribune* and the *Evening Mail* was casting about for a replacement, the management, at Adams' suggestion, settled on George. Eventually, George and the management did not see eye-to-eye on some matter and George was out again. Adams got him a job writing drama notes for the *Tribune* under the late Heywood Broun. In 1917 George went to *The New York Times* as a drama reporter, subsequently becoming its drama editor. There he began testing himself as a playwright. He wrote thirty-five drafts of a play called *Going Up,* which no one would buy. But, in making the rounds, its humor caught the attention of George C. Tyler, one of the important producers of that period. When Tyler needed a writer to brighten a script he was planning to produce, *Someone in the House,* by Larry Evans and Walter Percival, he sent for George. That was in 1918.

Someone in the House was a failure. George's next try, *Jacques Duval,* an adaptation he did alone, opened and closed in Chicago. But in 1921 came *Dulcy* and fame. I did not yet know George. But Marc Connelly, who collaborated on *Dulcy,* has spoken glowingly of those years, of how George loved to work, of his energy and his drive. Marc and George collaborated until 1924, turning out *To the Ladies; The '49ers; Merton of the Movies; Helen of Troy, New York; The Deep Tangled Wildwood; Beggar on Horseback;* and *Be Yourself.*

George left the *Times* in 1930. He left, I think, for two reasons. One was his concern that his growing involvement in the theatre might be considered prejudicial to his objectivity as a newspaperman, though heaven knows, he was ultrascrupulous about the shows in which he figured. Indicative of this is one frustrated press agent's complaint: "Kaufman says if I want space for his show in the *Times*, I'll have to shoot the star." The other reason was George's realization that, for him, writing plays and working in the theatre were the most fascinating activities in the world.

Those who worked with George found themselves infected by his love for the theatre. He was an indefatigable worker who enjoyed the process of creating a play so much that he wanted to work on it as long as he could stay awake. Characteristically, he derived an extra bit of pleasure from working on plays on holidays. He and Edna Ferber found enormous satisfaction in writing plays on New Year's Eve. "We used to thumb our noses at the world," he once said. "There was no need to go out and get drunk."

Just as he regarded many of the formalities of life a bother and a bore (he once wrote to me from Hollywood that he had attended a formal dinner party in a blue suit—"I figure they're lucky to get me even without a shirt"), so he constantly frowned on the pomposities behind which so many theatre people hide. He had pride but no vanity. He would be astonished and disbelieving if he were told how great a debt the theatre owed him, how many playwrights, including Moss himself, were obligated to him for guidance.

To George, a play was not a message or a moral or an opinion. What interested him above all else was simple: Is it first a play, a good idea—something that will work on a stage and draw an audience? He saw little point in talking about art in the theatre since he felt there was little of it in evidence. What he sought, and what he believed there was evident in the theatre, was good workmanship. It was his conviction that making dialogue sound natural on the stage was a knack, a trick of the ear, and not an art in itself. A really great writer of novels, he would point out, might lack that instinct and fail when he turned to the theatre, as many have. George considered himself "merely one who happened to have the knack."

That "knack"—others have called it genius—accounted for one of the greatest records ever made in the contemporary American theatre. In the more than forty years of George's labors he was associated in the authorship of forty-three plays and musicals, many of them containing the most trenchantly funny lines ever written for the Broadway stage. A score of his works were purchased by Hollywood, eighteen of them ran for longer than two hundred performances in New York. He shared in the winning of two Pulitzer prizes, for the musical *Of Thee I Sing,* on which he collaborated with Morrie Ryskind, and the hilarious *You Can't Take It with You,* written with Moss, which Groucho Marx estimates is probably the most produced stock and little-theatre vehicle written in this country.

But it was not only as a writer that George gained his fame. He also excelled as a "play doctor" and director. Let a farce, a comedy, a musical flounder in its pre-Broadway trials on the road, and the first thought would be, "Can we get Kaufman to fix it?" At least forty-three productions of his own authorship and those of others were put on the stage under his direction. No one knows how many others, desperate for help, received his ministrations.

George's approach as a director was simple and straight-forward. Just as he had little use for idle talk about art in the theatre, so he refrained from the ritualistic hocus-pocus common to many contemporary directors. He did not regard himself as a combined psychoanalyst, father confessor and high priest. Nor did he conduct extensive excursions into the motivations of each character in a play, his or her psychological background, or the deep, hidden intentions of the playwright. In contrast to some of the present lot of directors, George never considered himself the stage's all-around actor—a genius who could portray every role better than any member of his company. He had the old-fashioned notion that the actors he had chosen possessed intelligence, taste and talent—otherwise they would not have been selected. Given a chance and some guidance, he believed they could gradually work out their roles and problems in their own way.

Equally old-fashioned was George's theorem that the best directed play was the one in which there did not seem to have been a director at all, in which what truly counted was the over-all effect, not the highlights of showy pyrotechnics. Nevertheless, there was something about the plays that George directed that had his special touch no matter how much in the background he kept himself. There was a neat, unified pace to those plays. The comedy always seemed sharper and wittier under his guidance. The lines and situations seemed always to have been heightened by his own unerring ear and eye.

Unlike other directors who require considerable advance study of their designer's sets before arriving at the first rehearsal, George asked only that the windows, doors and stairways, if any, be chalked out on the floor. Then, with a few chairs or a sofa for props, he would proceed to guide the players so expertly through the rehearsals that when the time came for them to work in the actual sets and with the real furniture, the transition was made with the greatest of ease.

It must, of course, be conceded that watching George direct a play in a dark theatre on a bare stage could be among the most tranquilizing of experiences. I cannot remember that I ever heard George shout or saw him lose his temper—though I am sure he did once in a while. Mostly, when I was in the theatre, he spoke in even tones and was extremely considerate of his players. He rarely used on them the vitriol that tipped his tongue. There was a modesty about his general demeanor, a reticence that sometimes left a viewer wondering whether the play would ever be ready. Holding a script in his hand, George could be seen on the stage at the beginning of a sequence talking in hushed tones to an actor, as if he himself were asking advice. At the end of the conversation, in which plans for the playing of a scene had been discussed, George would return to his seat, slouch down, and peer intently at the stage. When the scene was over, he would again haul his lanky frame to the stage. There would be more conversations with individual members of the cast. He may have detected a flaw that needed correcting; he may have detected a piece of business he wished retained for the future. Gradually, the actors seemed to find the pattern they were seeking. Nothing had been imposed upon them. What they accomplished came from their own inner consciousness. As the rehearsals progressed, they gained in poise and naturalness, achieving more in a week than others do in twice the time.

George's easy manner, seemingly so laissez-faire, concealed a firm determination to get what he wanted, a devotion to detail, a dedication to discipline. Once he achieved the performance he visualized, he tolerated no deviation. Those who strayed into new inventions, either through a desire for bigger laughs or out of boredom with a long run, would be sharply reprimanded. George was not a director to permit a production to run down or become seedy. To do so, he felt, was unjust to the public and poor business to boot.

From time to time George would visit a theatre where one of his productions was playing. No one ever knew when such visitations would take place. When he spotted carelessness or casualness, he was uncompromising in his reactions. Once, after he had been away for a month's vacation, he slipped into the standing-room section of a theatre to watch a musical in which he had been involved. It soon was evident that the male star's performance had deteriorated considerably. George left the theatre, went to the Western Union office in the Hotel Astor, and sent the following message to the actor: "Dear ———: I am watching your performance from the last row. Wish you were here. George." Another time he discovered that the star of a play had made some changes in the lines—a not unheard of predilection on the part of actors. The wire to the offender read, "Your performance magnificent and improving every day. Sorry I can't say same about lines."

There are hundreds of stories such as these illustrating his talent for cutting men down, illustrating his wit: George saying "Satire is what closes on Saturday night," and George saying "One man's Mede is another man's Persian." There are bound to be those like the late George Jean Nathan, drama critic and possessor of no little venom himself, who will tend to regard George as a "gag man, a slick contriver of stage comedies, a skillful director"—an estimate perhaps induced by George's own attitude toward himself and Broadway. But to those like the late humorist James Thurber, George was *comedy*, as the late Robert Benchley was *humor*. Thurber wrote after George's death:

"The legend of George Kaufman will grow; the truth about the man himself will probably stay just where it is, but time will brighten the light he brought to American

humor, comedy and wit. If the theatre is to have a re-
nascence of comedy, it will need another Kaufman, and
the need is extremely great in the present period of
decadence, in which we do not seem to be able to tell the
difference between *avant-garde* and *fin de siècle,* talent
and sickness, the giving up of taboos and the breaking
down of morals, the experimental and the expiring
theatre."

20

∾ᴄ᳐

Musical Merry-Go-Round

A MONTH after the opening of *The Land Is Bright* I presented my second comedy by Fields and Chodorov. It was *Junior Miss,* derived again from some stories in *The New Yorker,* these by Sally Benson, in which she described with great insight and fun the assorted crises that beset a fourteen-year-old subdeb and her friend. To everyone's delight Moss had decided that he wished to direct. As soon as the script was ready, we began a search for the two young actresses who could play the main roles.

It is common knowledge in the theatre that adolescent heroines are not easy to cast. If an actress is young enough to look the part, she is likely to lack the required authority on stage. If she is old enough to have acquired that authority, then more than likely she is unable to convincingly suggest an adolescent's shifting moods and reactions.

While Moss and the rest of us searched high and low, a sixteen-year-old, Patricia Peardon, whose father was Commander Rowell Peardon, U.S.N., turned up in my office to wait for a young actor who was applying for a part. She was sitting in the anteroom, wearing a sweater, skirt and saddle shoes, and as she told us later, she had no thought of looking for a role for herself. She had, however, done some work on the stage and in radio, so that when my stage manager happened to notice her and ask whether she was an actress, she said, "Yes." He suggested that there might be a role for her in the play. If she was interested, she should return at four o'clock.

Patricia, understandably excited by this unexpected de-velopment in her life, hurried home to change into clothes she thought would make her appear more grown-up. She rouged her cheeks, daubed on a good measure of lipstick, replaced her low shoes with high heels, and returned for her big chance. When the stage manager brought her onto the stage and introduced her, Moss studied her for a moment or so and decided that she seemed more suitable for the part of Lois, our subdeb's sister. Patricia gave only a fair reading. Moss was about to say the usual "Thank you," when he had a hunch. Beneath the camouflage he detected possibilities. She might suit Judy. He gave her the lines to read. The transformation was amazing. Patricia *was* Judy. The sought-for quality of the fourteen-year-old, along with that elusive authority, came through in spite of the high heels, the reddened lips and cheeks. Two days later, after Moss had looked over several other candidates just to convince himself, he gave her the assignment. The role of her friend Fuffy Adams went, incidentally, to a precocious youngster named Lenore Lonergan, daughter of Lester Lonergan and Amy Ricard, long-time favorites of the theatre of another day.

We opened *Junior Miss* at the Lyceum in November, 1941. Patricia and Lenore were superb. It was a moment when Broadway was desperately in need of a good comedy.

This one answered that need. Three weeks after our opening came Pearl Harbor. The lighthearted, innocent complications of *Junior Miss* were all the more desirable in the dark and troubled days that followed. On Broadway for more than two years the comedy provided an antidote. Road companies helped brighten playhouses across the country. The burden in my heart lifted along with the balance in my bank account.

Twentieth Century-Fox paid $450,000 for the screen rights. My fifteen-per-cent interest in *My Sister Eileen;* the thirty per cent that I owned of *Junior Miss;* plus the fifteen-per-cent interest Noël Coward had given me in *Blithe Spirit,* which had opened that same season; and the five-per-cent share of *The Man Who Came to Dinner,* a gift from Sam Harris, had at last wiped out my debts.

The day the last dollar was paid, I hastened to tell the good news to Bernard Baruch. I had in the past, out of admiration and respect for his greatness, for his courage and wisdom, often called him Mosher, the Hebrew word for Moses. Now as we walked down Fifth Avenue together, he suddenly threw his arms around me and said, "Max, you are a double Mosher."

With *My Sister Eileen* and *Junior Miss* running concurrently, the failure of my next production, the musical *Sunny River,* was not overly distressing. Besides, it was not long before Joe Fields was talking about a new comedy that he would write alone, Jerry having gone into the service. The idea resulted from a business trip to Washington. Unable to get hotel accommodations in the wartime capital, Fields had finally gone to Baltimore to get a room. The comedy would be set against this background, a satiric view of life among the overstuffed civilian wartime workers with and without service commissions in the overcrowded capital. To George, who said he would direct it, and to me, the idea appeared to be a natural—a comedy with a sound premise on a topical theme.

How much Joe missed the collaboration of his younger writing partner is hard to guess.

We went into rehearsal knowing there was still much work to be done on the script, unaware of the actual degree until we got the play in front of an audience. We opened in Bridgeport. The first act was good but the rest of the play seemed to go to pieces. A major effort was needed to get the script in shape for the New York opening. George's contribution to the rewriting must have been considerable, though he never conceded that he did more than make suggestions to any playwright.

Whatever it was that George did or advised was fine. My only objection was to the lines, "I had children at the drop of a hat. Suddenly my husband went to Australia and took the hat with him." The lines were erased before the curtain went up on Broadway. As had been the case with *Junior Miss,* this comedy was made to order. It had been preceded by a succession of rather serious plays with a war background, but none of them was sufficiently worthy to merit more than passing attention. The time was ripe, as one critic said, for a comedy that would reflect wartime conditions and also keep the audience's mind free of wartime miseries. *The Doughgirls* answered the requirement. It had, besides, an extra dash of sophistication and sex to titillate the customers. It was an instant success.

For the first time since my Hollywood disaster the money I was making was mine. Under Baruch's guidance I began a long-term investment program looking toward the future, toward the freedom from financial uncertainty that, like the old will o' the wisp, kept eluding me.

Truly, I was indebted to Jerry and Joe. *My Sister Eileen* had given me a new lease on life, had led to *Junior Miss* and now to Fields's *The Doughgirls*. I was, and still am, deeply grateful. And yet, *The Doughgirls* was to be our last association.

An old Broadway maxim maintains that there is nothing in the theatre like success to bind the bands of friendship. Even the tensions generated during rehearsals, the clashes of temperament, the bitter words, the hostilities fed by the intense familiarity which, of necessity, develops during the preparation of a show—all are supposed to be washed away, forgiven and forgotten in the flush of triumph.

For us, the maxim did not work. I had grown extremely fond of Jerry and, being twenty years his senior, had come to regard him with paternal affection. But my relationship with Joe, at best, never was more than cordial. Almost from the first we seemed never quite to coincide in our feelings or our attitudes. There was always about him, more marked as time went on, an edgy belligerence poised on the brink of explosion. When I had to discuss a matter of mutual interest—a business detail, for instance—I found myself trying desperately to find the right words, the right approach. Awkward and gauche as it may seem now in retrospect, I would begin such conversations with what I thought was a facetious approach, like "Now, Joe, don't put 'em up," or something equally inane.

The battles over lines in *The Doughgirls* were vehement—not unusual in the stress of preparation. What was wearing was that they seemed endless. Joe never gave up. Even after I succeeded in convincing Kaufman to eliminate the lines about having children at the drop of a hat, Joe persisted. After opening night he got George to reinsert the lines. I gave up. Technically, there was nothing I could do. According to the Dramatists Guild contract, it is virtually impossible to alter a comma without the play-wright's approval.

There is one more melancholy footnote to my relation-ship with Joe Fields. Even now in recollection it upsets and depresses me. Nevertheless, it should be told because it is part of my story, because it reveals an aspect of the often-not-so-glorious backstage theatre life. It is also a testament to at least one producer's foolhardiness, as well as to Broadway's mixture of sentimentality and realism.

Time is not the only agent that heals. In show business, rationalizations and necessity frequently take a hand. Five years had passed since *The Doughgirls* when it crossed my mind that *My Sister Eileen* would make a great and lively musical. Coincidentally, a few weeks later I met Dorothy Fields, Joe's sister, at a dinner party. She and another brother, Herbert, were relaxing in the glow of the success scored by Irving Berlin's *Annie Get Your Gun,* for which they had written the book. I mentioned my idea to her and suggested that she and Herbert consider doing the book for a musical version of *My Sister Eileen,* as I wanted very much to produce it. That is, I wanted to produce it provided Joe and Jerry had no objections and were willing to make the necessary financial arrangements. Dorothy thought the idea was every bit as good as I did. She wrote to Joe in Hollywood and received a quick reply saying that he would not stand in the way.

However, except for sporadic letters and telephone con-versations, the project remained dormant. Dorothy and Herbert had commitments requiring a year or so to com-plete. Finally, Joe and Jerry decided that they would like to do the book themselves. I felt this was a family affair among the Fieldses and left the matter to be settled by them. Meanwhile, I suggested to Joe that overtures be made to the late Harry Cohn, then president of Columbia Pictures, about a motion-picture deal.

When we first began to talk about the musical, Irving Berlin indicated that he might be interested. He was regarded as ideal and in Joe's words, "would be insurance for all of us." But, by the time we began thinking actively about a composer, Berlin was involved in another musical, *Call Me Madam,* in which Ethel Merman would appear as a counterpart of Washington's great hostess Perle Mesta. We were all deeply disappointed.

In the ensuing months we spent many hours discussing composers who might be acceptable. At one point I recommended Cole Porter, but Joe said Cole was a little too sophisticated and risqué for this sort of show. I reminded him that Cole did not write only sophisticated songs. "After all," I wrote in one letter, "he has written the score for *Jubilee,* simple songs like 'Old-Fashioned Garden,' and so many other lovely numbers." I made no headway. I suggested then that Dorothy could do the lyrics, and that we ask Harry Warren, one of the strong popular song writers of the period, to do the score. "The only thing I want to do," I wrote to Joe, "is to get into action. So the sooner we can put all these parts together, the better off we'll be."

Before long I began to feel that I was on a carrousel that had gone out of control. I am still not sure I ever actually grasped everything that was happening. There did not seem to be any sensible sequence to the unfolding chronicle. Suddenly, Jerry no longer was to be involved. Dorothy, Herbert and Joe would most likely work on the musical. Harry Warren was acceptable one day, doubtful the next. Then there was word that Dorothy and Herbert had become interested in doing a book for a posthumous score by Jerome Kern. And so it went, a crazy quilt of shifting minds and notions. Finally, during a weekend at

Dorothy's country home, I received a categorical decision. Herbert and she had decided not to do the adaptation. They preferred to concentrate on an original idea they had. That meant Jerry and Joe would be working on the book again. But the problem of finding a composer and a lyricist remained. I wrote to Joe urging that we ask Frank Loesser, who could do both the music and lyrics. I had just heard his work for *Guys and Dolls* and was enthralled. In fact, at Loesser's request I cabled Kaufman in London to stop equivocating and accept the invitation to direct *Guys and Dolls,* predicting that it would turn out to be one of the plums of his career, which it did.

My suggestion to Fields about Loesser failed to stir his enthusiasm. Although he regarded Frank as a superb composer, he did not think he was right for our show. "We need," he said, "the Vincent Youmans-type songs rather than the popular hot tunes that have been Frank's biggest hits."

I did not agree, but I did not argue. I still lived in the hope that somewhere, somehow, there existed a composer who would be satisfactory to all of us and free at the time we needed him. I assumed that Joe nourished a similar hope.

Consequently, I was stunned when I received a telephone call from him during which he disclosed that at least two producers on the Coast had talked to him about a musical version of *My Sister Eileen.* These conversations had been going on intermittently for six months and, Joe said, each of the producers was interested in making a deal. These producers, he added, could not understand why I had not made the deal myself. Would I, Joe wanted to know, be willing to make the deal now? Several moments passed before I regained my composure and grasped the full import of what he had said. It never occurred to me to make a deal, or contract, until we found a composer and lyricist. It always seemed a waste of time and energy to go through the motions and deliberations involved in the drawing up and signing of a contract until all the basic elements of a production were brought together. Simply having a piece of paper made little sense otherwise. Besides, I belonged to a school whose credo was that a handclasp can be as good as any contract.

What was happening, I surmised, was that Joe was trying to put me in a corner, applying, as they say, "the squeeze." He was demonstrating not so much his impatience as his lack of confidence in my intentions, in spite of the fact that I had continued to reiterate my belief that *My Sister Eileen* was the best musical property around and that the quicker we could do it, the better I would like it.

I knew for certain that the pressure was on when, a few days later, he indicated that he was expecting a fall production. Aside from the fact that neither a composer nor a lyricist was in sight, I already had other commitments. The best I could do, I said, was to plan for the spring. I suggested that he come East in September. Then we could thrash out the whole problem and the differences in understanding that appeared to be mushrooming. Instead, several weeks later, there was another call.

Did I, Joe asked testily, have the money for the production?

The question was like a gauntlet's sting across my face. My reliability was being doubted, my capability as a fundraiser investigated. My record spoke for itself through bad times and good. Never had I failed to produce a play or musical for lack of money. I lost my temper and began to shout.

In the fall I read in *The New York Times* that Rosalind Russell would appear in the musical version of *My Sister*

Eileen, with Leland Hayward possibly the producer. I wired Fields inquiring whether or not this was true, whether or not his promise to hold the comedy for me was still good. It was a futile and foolish gesture. I was out of the picture. That should have been obvious to me, but I had refused to see. I had lost, a victim of misunderstanding, procrastinations and confusion. What I had started, someone else would finish.

In the winter of the 1952–53 season *Wonderful Town,* the musical adaptation of *My Sister Eileen,* went into rehearsal. Joe and Jerry had written the book; Leonard Bernstein, the music; Betty Comden and Adolph Green, the lyrics. Rosalind Russell was Ruth and a lovely newcomer named Edith Adams had been selected for Eileen. George Abbott was the director, and Robert Fryer, who had been associated with Abbott in the production of *A Tree Grows in Brooklyn,* was making his debut as a full-fledged producer. I went to New Haven to see the tryout. The production and score, I thought, could have been better, but the book was so good and Rosalind Russell so magnificent that I wrote to Moss, "I don't see how it can stop from making a fortune."

For weeks after the New Haven opening I slept little. The play that helped save me in 1940, now, thirteen years later, had returned to torture me. Millie, fearing another breakdown, pleaded with me to control myself, to let the dead past bury its dead. Night after night, and during the days, I rehashed silently or to whomever would listen the bewildering chronicle of my frustrated efforts to produce a musical based on *My Sister Eileen.* I recited the episodes over and over again until they seemed to form a sort of litany. My feelings toward Joe Fields were indescribable.

There is a last word to be said of this strange account. I do not know whether it comes under the heading of poetic justice or destiny's practical joke. Shortly before the opening in New Haven I was leaving a building in downtown Manhattan when I encountered Robert Fryer. We discussed his plans for the production, and then, somewhat sheepishly, he confessed that he was still twenty-five thousand dollars short of his needed capitalization. I said that if it would help him, I would invest twenty-five hundred dollars. I never saw twenty-five hundred dollars received so rapturously.

Fate had laughingly allowed me a small share in what really had been my dream.

21

"Born Yesterday"

HAVING LAUNCHED *The Doughgirls,* which became one of my six most durable successes, I then ran into two failures: *Men in Shadow,* by Mary Hayley Bell, and *Those Endearing Young Charms,* by Edward Chodorov, Jerry's older brother. Both plays touched on the war in varying degrees, as did so many of the period. But, contrary to a still popular legend, not everything went, even in those boom days in the theatre.

The summer of 1943 saw me back in the hospital. But, for a change, the trouble was physical—prostate surgery. I had come through the operation nicely and was enjoying my convalescence when, one day, the telephone rang. The voice was unmistakably Ruth Gordon's, a little breathless, a little twangy, a little like a chirp.

"Max," she was saying, "this is Ruth Gordon."

"You don't have to tell me, Ruth," I said. "I'd know your voice anywhere. To what do I owe this honor?" I was completely mystified by a call from someone I had not seen for several years. Actually, the last time I had heard of her was when she married Garson Kanin the previous December.

"Max," Ruth went on, "I hope you are getting better. Max, are you strong enough to take a shock?" I assured her that I was feeling fine and ready for anything. "Well, Max," she ran on in characteristic fashion, "I've been down in Washington with Gar. You know he's in the army and we're stationed there. Now, Max, you know me. I can't waste a minute. That's my New England training. So, I've written a play. Gar thinks it's your kind of play, a comedy, and we want you to be the first to read it. Max, Gar is here with me and he wants to talk to you."

I had barely managed to say that I would be delighted to read the play when Gar was on the telephone.

"Listen, Max. I'm sure you're going to like Ruth's play. At least we hope you do. She's cooked it up from our experiences here and elsewhere. It's got a good topical slant. Max, it's the first one she's ever finished, the first one she's been willing to show me or anyone else. And listen, Max, if you like it, you get Ruth, too. She's written herself a big fat part."

"Send it right away," I said. "I'm ready for anything."

I hung up, lay back on my pillow, and closed my eyes. I knew that Ruth had writing ambitions. I also knew that what she wrote generally was charming, graceful and etched with her humorous view of life. But Ruth a playwright? That was something else again. Well, I told myself, I would know soon enough. If she was, what a dream package I was getting. Certainly she could act. Everybody on Broadway had known that since her first appearance on a New York stage in Maude Adams' revival of *Peter Pan*, when Alexander Woollcott said, "Ruth Gordon was ever so gay as Nibs."

She was nineteen then, a year out of Quincy High School in Wollaston, Massachusetts. She had come to New York

with that dream in her heart—to be a stage actress. Not even
the rebuff she received at the end of a term in the American Academy of Dramatic Arts could deter her. She did not
have what it took, she was told, and they dropped her.

With the courage that always has marked her life, she
remained undaunted. She persuaded her father to advance
her another fifty dollars and set out to prove true to her
dream. Every day she made the rounds of the theatrical
producers' offices—"What a lot of walking it takes to be
an actress," she once said, remembering those days.

She starved a little, cried a little, and compromised a
little by taking jobs as an extra in the films being made
across the Hudson in the studios at Fort Lee, New Jersey.
The five dollars here and there helped her continue the
quest until that day in December when, with the sicken-
ing feeling of disenchantment coming more often, she
went again to the Charles A. Frohman offices in the old
Empire Theatre. Her ears disbelieving, but her heart
pounding, she heard the man at the desk say, "Go see
Homer Saint Gaudens. He's casting for *Peter Pan*."

After that the climb was steady, and the gallery of her
stage portraits contains some of the greatest achievements
in our theatre: Lola Pratt in Tarkington's *Seventeen,*
Bobby in Maxwell Anderson's *Saturday's Children,* Na-
tasha in Chekhov's *The Three Sisters,* Natalia in Tur-
genev's *A Month in the Country,* Nora in Ibsen's *A Doll's
House,* Mrs. Pinchwife in Wycherly's *The Country Wife,*
the title role in *Serena Blandish,* Mrs. Levi in Thornton
Wilder's *The Matchmaker,* Lucy Wells in *They Shall
Not Die.*

For me she appeared first as Mattie Silver in *Ethan
Frome.* I have never erased from memory that afternoon
I dropped in on the rehearsals going along under Guthrie
McClintic's direction. Owen Davis and his son Donald,
who had done the adaptation based on Edith Wharton's

great novel, sat together watching Ruth in a scene with Pauline Lord and Raymond Massey. I moved across the rear of the darkened theatre's empty orchestra, quietly slid down the left center aisle, and let myself into a seat. I watched—for want of a better word—transfixed. Mattie Silver has always been one of my great tragic heroines of literature, a gay, ebullient, much-tormented young girl, described with deep compassion by Mrs. Wharton.

Ruth was playing the role like an actress inspired, adding details out of her own understanding. She gave the part all the dimensions it had in the book, with something more—an aliveness, an awkwardness, a simplicity and a gaiety that wrung my heart. When it was over, I could not contain myself. I blurted out in that quiet theatre, "Good God!" and my comment was heard right up on the stage. Ruth, misinterpreting the inflection in my voice, thinking that I had expressed disapproval, and full of tension from the emotion of the scene, burst into tears. It was some time before I succeeded in explaining that my reaction was one of amazement, that the impact of her performance had been so sharp, I could not contain myself.

Perhaps the finest compliment ever paid her talents came not so long ago from the great director Tyrone Guthrie, who guided her in *The Matchmaker*. "She is," he said, "the most original, least stereotyped actress I have ever known. Every part she plays is the creation in terms of herself of a vivid imagination, a brisk, satiric intelligence and a feeling heart."

I began reading Ruth's play *Over Twenty-One* at six o'clock in the morning. It was about the adventures of some Army Air Force officer-candidates and their wives. Mainly it was the story of a former newspaper editor, a man of thirty-nine, who had quit his job because he thought he could serve his country better by fighting; his discouragement and tendency to agree with the notion that a man over twenty-one cannot learn anything new. Ruth's role was that of his wife, a successful novelist and screen-writer who doesn't share the over-twenty-one idea at all.

The setting was a bungalow court in Miami, one of those jerry-built jobs where the architect forgot to place the sink in the kitchenette; where the bedroom light switch was in the living room, and the living room switch was outside on the porch; where the only way to get the case-ment windows open was to stamp on the floor and watch them fly apart. All of this was seen through Ruth's amused eyes, abetted by her flair for the whimsical and her knack for the funny line.

It was nine o'clock when I finished the third act. I grabbed the telephone. I had just completed giving Ruth's number to the operator when my doctor walked in. "Dr. Bandler," I shouted exultantly, "you are going to be the only human being who ever saw me buy a play." When I heard Ruth's voice on the other end of the connection, I continued to shout. "Damn it, Ruth, I'll never forgive you for what you've done to me," I said, enjoying my joke with mischievous pleasure. I heard her concerned voice asking what she had done to offend me.

"Offend me, hell!" I exclaimed. "You've done worse than that. Here I am lying in a hospital bed, my belly all swathed in bandages, and you write such a damned funny play, I came near bursting these bandages—and the stitches, too."

I heard her relieved laughter. I told her that I would send the option money immediately and that I wanted to get the play on as soon as possible. I sensed another hit coming up. I could hardly wait until I was discharged from the hospital. I showed the script to Kaufman who, I was certain, would share my enthusiasm and be ready to direct it. I was flabbergasted when, instead of congratulating me, he grunted something about not agreeing with me at all.

"I don't think it's a good play," George said.

"Well, George," I replied in utter disbelief, "I differ with you. I think it's one of the funniest plays I've read in a long time. With Ruth in it and you directing, I don't see how we can lose. What's the matter with you?"

"Nothing's the matter with me, Max. It's not a play, that's all. There's hardly a plot, and it depends almost entirely on its lines."

We argued this way, back and forth. Finally, I said I did not give a damn whether or not he directed it. Nor, I said, did I care whether or not he joined me in the production financially. "I'm going ahead with this play," I announced.

For a moment or so there was no response. Then he said, "I'll tell you what, Max. Let's ask Moss. If he agrees with you, I'll do the play."

Moss saw it my way. He agreed with George that the play was far from being a perfect farce and that it would need a lot of work. But, he said, he thought the work could be done and that the play should be produced. He would invest in it.

George, always a better loser than winner, kept his word. He plunged into work. He did a superb job. He made shrewd, incisive criticisms that sharpened scenes, made situations hilarious where they had been merely funny. Moss attended rehearsals from time to time and made suggestions. Ruth was most co-operative. Both as actress and playwright she behaved like the true professional she is. She followed direction, took advice with a minimum of fuss and a maximum of goodwill. She knew that what counted was the end result and not her vanity. As the play shaped up, George became hopeful. The script was not all it should be, he persisted, but, he conceded, it had something of the comic sense.

The only thing that went wrong on opening night at

the Music Box was the failure of the prop man to be in his appointed place to blow a bugle at the end of the first act. It did not matter. When the final curtain fell, there was no doubt at all in my mind that we had a hit. With the laughter and the applause making lovely sounds in my ears, I went backstage to Ruth's dressing room. Her eyes shone and her mouth was wide in a wonderfully glowing grin.

"It's Christmas, Max," she said. It was the expression her father used when something good happened to his family or to him.

Gar was still in uniform that last summer of the war when Ruth and he joined Millie and me for dinner in Manhattan's exclusive Colony restaurant. The war in Europe was over. Victory in the Pacific appeared imminent. We were a gay foursome. The chicken, washed down with champagne, was delectable, the camaraderie among us warm and buoyant. Ruth especially was in top form, drawing repeated peals of laughter with her witticisms and recollection of backstage experiences in *Over Twenty-One* and other productions in which she had appeared.

Gar's blue eyes bespoke his pleasure in the evening. With characteristic restraint he told of his trials as an officer attached to the Office of Strategic Services. Never for a moment did he give the faintest hint of the surprise he was saving for me when dinner was over. As we arose from the table, he handed me an envelope on which he had been sitting. "Max," he said, "here is a play I have written. It's a comedy. Please read it—you are the first. Tell me as soon as possible what you think of it."

I had noticed the envelope when we met, but it never occurred to me to ask what it contained or to guess that it was a play by Gar. As far as I knew, he had never written a play before. I knew only that he had started his career in show business as a saxophone player, appeared in burlesque and vaudeville with no great success, and that one of the first Broadway acting jobs he ever had was with me when I produced *Spring Song*. Subsequently, he had become an assistant to the veteran stage director George Abbott, was taught much by him, and staged a couple of Broadway plays before going to Hollywood as a director.

I took the envelope and muttered some inanity about his holding out on me, that I never knew he could write. We all laughed at my astonishment and awkwardness.

"You'll have to get to know this boy better," Ruth chirped. "He's got talent."

The next morning I rose before six and began reading Garson Kanin's *Born Yesterday*. If I was astonished the night before, my astonishment now knew no limits. My amazement was soon mixed with excitement. The story of Harry Brock, the salvage king, and his dumb girl friend, Billie Dawn, was not exactly fault-free. It was possible within a few pages to predict the outcome. But it was, nevertheless, thanks to Gar's inspired basic notion, a truly hilarious comedy. It was also a little more. Along with Billie Dawn's awakening to the fact that life was not confined to the boudoir and that her keeper was a threat to the national welfare, there was a serious underpinning. Gar was throwing a javelin at robber barons and crooked politicians. The villain got his in the end, the meek inherited the earth, and there was laughter all around.

The sweet smell of success again was in my nostrils as I made an appointment with Gar to meet him for lunch at The Lobster restaurant. "I'm ready to talk terms, Gar," I said. "We've got a great comedy."

By the time lunch was over, we had agreed that Gar would direct his play; that I would pay one thousand dollars for the option; that he would receive ten per cent of the weekly gross as the author, plus two and one-half per cent as the director; and that his good friend Bob Sherwood would be permitted to purchase a five-per-cent interest in the production.

I sent Gar my check for the option and instructed my lawyer to draw up and send him a contract. And then something happened for which I never received a really satisfactory explanation. Gar procrastinated. He did not cash my check. Nor did he return the contract with his signature. Weeks passed. I waited. Meanwhile, there was news that he had agreed to direct Sherwood's *The Rugged Path* and that for it Spencer Tracy had been persuaded to make his first appearance on Broadway in fifteen years. The play lasted less than three months.

At last, Gar said he was ready to go ahead. We began talking about casting. Gar said he wanted Jean Arthur for the role of Billie Dawn. He thought she would be ideal, and fortunately, she was willing to take the part. To do so, however, she was asking twenty-five hundred dollars a week and the right to purchase a twenty-five-per-cent interest in the venture. Both George and Moss, who were enthusiastic over *Born Yesterday* and were ready to invest in it, thought the terms a bit steep. But mindful of the fact that she was recognized as one of Hollywood's best comediennes, and mindful of her box-office potential, they advised me to make the deal. I did, but not without considerable reluctance.

It was not that I failed to appreciate her qualities as an actress, that I did not think she would bring to Billie Dawn the flair for comedy that had won her stardom, or that I thought her terms beyond reason. I have always operated under the rule that if a producer has a hit, there is enough pie for everyone.

What actually worried me was that this lovely, talented actress, possessed of a style and a voice that none could imitate—Sidney Fields, the newspaper columnist, has compared her voice to a "running brook that often stops on its way down the mountain and looks around surprised"—had become known as a woman of mystery, a woman whose behavior bordered on the eccentric. Worst of all, she was regarded by studio executives and members of the press as "difficult." She could be gay and effusive in front of a camera, but off a studio set she seemed to retire into a shell from which she emerged only for her closest friends and relatives. Next to her, it was said, Greta Garbo was both gregarious and positively garrulous. Many regarded Jean as a snob.

Gar assured me that her shyness was mistaken for aloofness. He urged me to disregard all that I had heard. He had come to know her on the Coast, where, in fact, he had helped write one of her hits, *The More the Merrier*. Gar insisted that Jean was nowhere near as troublesome as the stories made her out to be; she was frightened of strangers and consequently misunderstood by them. Furthermore, aside from respecting her dignity and her right to privacy as a human being, he felt he could handle any problem she might present professionally.

I tried to be hopeful, though my first meeting with her when she came East was not promising. She seemed hardly to acknowledge our introduction. She was either shy, as Gar said, or a first-class snob.

The rest of the casting went easily enough. For the role of Harry Brock we got Paul Douglas, who had gone from the stage into radio, where he had performed for years as a sports announcer. Gar, as I recall, mentioned to a friend that he needed someone like Paul Douglas, and the friend said, "Why not Paul Douglas?"

There is an old saying that two persons do not really get to know each other until their toothbrushes hang side by side. Gar did not really know Jean until he began working with her as playwright and director. There was trouble from the beginning, even from before the beginning. We had not yet gone into rehearsal when Gar, sitting in my office, complained that Jean was trying to rewrite the play. That was the cue I needed.

"O.K., Gar," I said, "now is the time to put a stop to this. I'll call her and tell her we're sorry, but she doesn't fit into the scheme of the play."

I reasoned that if she were as sensitive and shy as she was supposed to be, she would not wish to continue the arrangement. I reached for the telephone, but Gar laid a restraining hand on my arm. "No, Max," he pleaded, "please don't. It would hurt her too much. Let's wait. I'll manage."

Throughout the rehearsal period there was trouble. Nor was it our private secret. Items appeared in the press—all sorts of items, all with just a grain of truth, none with the whole story. Meanwhile, Jean complained that some of the words she had to say were too unsavory. She complained about lines. She wanted scenes changed. Gar, directing by day and trying to please her by rewriting at night, was near distraction. No one dared to tell her the plain truth—that her complaints were masks behind which she was trying to conceal her fears. As she admitted later, she was near panic at having to play farce. She had been accustomed to playing comedy and had failed to realize Gar's concept called for a stroke or two, on some occasions even more, of the farcical touch. Billie was Harry Brock's mistress, a former chorus girl, good in bed. She could not be portrayed as a lady.

Two weeks before the New Haven world première Gar asked me what to do. I could not resist recrimination. The play was too sound for these unnecessary headaches and aggravations. Bitterly I reminded him that I had doubted the wisdom of having her in the first place, and that he was the one who had insisted. With equal bitterness I recalled the day in my office when I was ready to get rid of her and he had held me back.

"Now," I said, "we are two weeks from opening in New Haven. What can I do? We're all set to go. You've got your head in a noose. You'll have to work out of it as best you can."

The opening in New Haven went well. During the first intermission I said jubilantly to Moss, "There's a helluva hit circling around here."

When the final curtain fell, it was clear that the first act was in good shape. So was the second. The principal problem was in the third. At our meeting, which also involved George and Moss, Gar reported that he was worried. "That girl's giving me trouble," he said. "Now she says she's not feeling well. She says her throat is bothering her. She's threatening to quit."

"Well, let her quit," I said.

In Boston, Jean's playing lacked lustre. The reviews were mild. Her doctor came up from New York. He said she did have a bad throat, but nothing was said about her having to quit. At one performance she seemed to black out, missed about sixteen of her lines and only by pumping her full of coffee and stimulants during the intermission was she able to continue. I went to her hotel room after the performance. There she was with pitchers of heavy cream on the table, and bananas. She said the doctor had ordered her to eat as much as possible. I asked her whether she intended to appear at the matinee the following day. She said, "Yes."

"Will you call me?" I said. "Say about ten o'clock. I'd like to know. If you don't, I'll call you." She assured me she would call. She had, she said, no intention of quitting.

The following morning I awoke in a cold sweat. It was

seven o'clock. I was horrified by the thought that Jean might not show up, and I immediately called Dave Pardoll, my stage manager. "Dave," I shouted, "I'm sorry if I've awakened you. But I can't help it. Dave, just in case Miss Arthur doesn't show up for the matinee, I think you had better get the understudy ready."

"We don't have an understudy, Mr. Gordon," I heard the sleepy voice saying. I could feel the blood rushing to my head.

"What do you mean we don't have an understudy?" I shouted. "Surely you've got a girl who can go through the role."

"Oh, we do, Mr. Gordon. But she can't act that part. She's the manicurist in the play. She just reads the part when we need her."

"I don't give a damn, Dave. You'd better get her over to the hairdresser right away. Get her fixed up. She can read. She can talk. Get her ready to go even if she has to read from the script."

At ten o'clock I called Jean's room, my heart in my throat. I asked her whether she was ready to play that afternoon. She said, "No."

"Well, that's just great, Miss Arthur," I jeered. "I'm putting your understudy in."

"You can't do that, Mr. Gordon," she whined. "You can't do that to me."

"I can't, can't I?" I said, more harshly than I intended. "We're giving a performance this afternoon."

At the theatre I watched the expectant members of the matinee audience arriving. I felt a twinge of conscience, like some big, rich uncle about to disappoint his poor nephews and nieces. As the lights dimmed, I stepped in front of the curtain and heard the pained "oh" of anticipated disappointment sweep through the theatre like the amplified groan of a wounded animal.

"Ladies and gentlemen," I began, "I regret to inform you that Miss Arthur will not be able to play the role of Billie Dawn this afternoon. She is suffering from a throat ailment. Her understudy, Miss Mary Laslo, who normally plays the part of the manicurist, will substitute for Miss Arthur. This is a fine comedy, one of the best I have ever produced. I am asking you to put your faith in my judgment. All I'm about to ask you is that you take a chance on me. If you don't like this play after the first act, go out to the box office and get your money back. Others may get their refunds now."

I made the same speech that night and the following night. For the matinee we returned sixty-five dollars, that night a little more than one hundred dollars, and the next night about ninety dollars. Friday night and both Saturday performances were sold out, bearing testimony to the strength of *Born Yesterday*. It could surmount even the loss of its star.

Meanwhile, I had begun to make plans for the future. We could not go on this way. If a replacement were needed, one had better be found in a hurry. Jerry Chodorov's sister Belle, a talent agent, suggested that I give consideration to a young actress named Judy Holliday. Daughter of a writer for a Jewish newspaper, Judy had been a member of a clever night club act called "The Revuers," which included Betty Comden and Adolph Green, now two of the theatre's leading librettists. Judy had appeared in a few films and the previous spring had made her debut on Broadway in *Kiss Them for Me*, by Luther Davis.

I had missed her performance, but everything I heard and read was praise. She had played the role of a dumb but sweet little tart who worked in a war plant and wished to contribute her all to the war effort. It was a portrait that could have been broad and vulgar. Instead, under Herman Shumlin's experienced guidance, she had made it

touching and endearing. Shortly after the play's opening
she won the Clarence Derwent Award, given annually for
the season's best supporting performance by a nonfeatured
player. On the face of the evidence I asked Belle to have
Judy in my office on Friday.

Gar and I left Boston Thursday night. In my office
Friday morning I waited for Judy Holliday. The minute
she walked in, I knew she was it. I listened to her talk—
even without giving her a script to read—and was certain
that she would make an ideal replacement if she were
needed. I asked her to leave the room so that I could call
Gar.

"Listen," I said, "she's absolutely right. I'm sending her
over to your hotel right away."

"Max," Gar demurred, "I've been thinking—"

"Thinking, hell!" I blasted into the mouthpiece. "If
we need her, she's going to be on the train to Philadelphia."

On Sunday, joining the company, Gar and I were greeted
with the news—Jean had collapsed, her doctors were advising hospitalization. Whatever it was that had invaded
her throat now had spread into her bloodstream. The
decision had been made for us.

Judy was told to rush to Philadelphia. After a quick
conference it was agreed that there would be no further
performances until we were sure she was ready. Gar prepared to have the company work day and night. The New
York opening was set back. On Tuesday Judy began rehearsing. By the end of the day we knew that we were
luckier than we had a right to dream we might be. By
Thursday I was able to announce that we would give
a performance on Saturday night at the Locust Street
Theatre.

For that first performance Judy was letter perfect and
hilariously funny. Gar's new third act worked. The week

opened in a blaze of glorious reviews and box-office excitement. In New York the grapevine was busy. News began percolating that we were coming in with one of the smash comedies of the year. I was Max the nonpareil, Gar said; Max *the* manager, Ruth said.

We raised the curtain on *Born Yesterday* February 4, 1946. The reception is part of theatrical lore. The critics, alert to both the comedy and the serious implications of the play, heaped their praises on it. Broadway found a new playwright-director and two magnificent performers. For Paul Douglas, the remaining years of his life were never the same. He went on to fame and Hollywood stardom. Of Judy, Louis Kronenberger wrote: "Miss Holliday is often quite wonderful—particularly before her education sets in, and she can make the most of her flat voice and high-styled floozie walk. Just watching her sort her cards at gin rummy is a treat." The headline over John Chapman's review in the *Daily News* read:

JUDY HOLLIDAY PERFECT

AS DUMB BROAD IN

VERY FUNNY PLAY

Born Yesterday became an immutable fixture on Broadway, more even than that—part of the American scene. By April the advance sale had risen to almost $125,000, this in the days before productions opened with huge advance sales sold through benefit parties and ticket clubs.

We had, each of us, hit the jackpot.

But, as Emerson so wisely wrote in his great essay on compensation, "Every sweet has its sour."

One night, about two months after the opening, I returned home in high spirits. The box-office figures for *Born Yesterday* were at capacity. I changed into lounging clothes and began reading the evening newspapers. Millie had given me her customary kiss, and I suspected nothing.

Suddenly I heard her saying, "Max, I have something important to tell you." I looked up. I felt my hands tremble and the blood rush to my head. She was unusually somber for Millie.

"What's wrong?" I stammered.

"Max, dear," she began, "I have not told you these recent months because I knew you were preoccupied with the show and I didn't want to upset you."

"What is it, Millie?" I rasped. "Is there any trouble?"

"Yes, Max, there is trouble. I have to undergo an abdominal operation. The doctor said it must be done immediately."

"What are you talking about? He must be crazy," I said stupidly.

"No, Max, dear, he's not crazy. I have been seeing him for a while now, and the medication hasn't helped. He says the tests have been inconclusive."

"You're not going to take his word, are you Millie? Let's see another man."

"Max, dear, you do not understand. There have been other consultations." She came over to where I sat, kissed me on the brow and said, "Max, the doctor is a good man. I'm in good hands. What we have to try to do is be calm and hope. We'll know soon enough."

"But, Millie . . ." I began, still disbelieving.

She cut me off. "Max, listen. I may not be able to say this to you later. I want to say it now. No matter what happens, I want you to know that I know we have had a wonderful life together. Whatever happens, I want you to know how happy you've made me through the years and that I have always loved you."

I couldn't talk. I couldn't do anything. Life seemed to have left my body.

In the morning I called the doctor. He repeated the urgency of the operation. The few remaining days were full of terror, foreboding—and memories. Memories of our courtship, of the night I had introduced her to my parents, how her sweetness and ease had won them to her side, triumphing over their prejudices. I remembered all the happy times together. I wept where none could see. Through the early years, when I looked after the vaudeville acts that Lewis and Gordon produced, Millie drove me wherever I had to go. We were constantly together. We played golf together, not very well but enjoying each other's company, enjoying being in the country together. We swam together, walked together, shared our interests in the theatre and politics, as well as mutual friends. She went to the races with me, always amusing me as she made her own selections, never betting more than two dollars on a race. Her love and understanding had helped me through crisis after crisis. I could still feel that kiss of forgiveness she had given me when I told her remorsefully of the racing debt I had accumulated years before. I remembered how she had offered her rings to me to help us through another financial debacle.

I could not live without Millie, I told myself over and over again.

On the day of the operation, shortly before she was to undergo surgery, the doctor came to offer me some words of encouragement. I remember little of the next three hours other than that about an hour after I had kissed Millie a nurse reported that the operation was under way, and about two hours after that our family doctor, who had insisted on being present at the operation, came down to say, "Everything will be all right."

When I got to my club, where I had moved, I wrote to George Kaufman, in whom I had confided. I said, "This is the biggest hit I ever had, and you will never hear a beef out of me again. . . . I am the happiest man alive."

Millie's recovery, of course, was slow. But the doctor assured me there was no need for further concern.

There were other difficulties now. Paul Douglas was drinking excessively, living his role backstage, and blatantly brushing aside all my pleading and threats. Judy and her agent, Dick Dorso, opened talks for a new contract and, fortified by the acclaim heaped on her, demanded a thousand dollars a week. That was almost double the amount she had been receiving. Also, they asked for a three-month notice clause. The negotiations developed the only real friction between George Kaufman and myself up to that time. In a letter from the Coast, where he was working, he implied that I lacked the will to bargain in the situation and I, forced to defend myself, wrote:

No one could be more frank or truthful with you than I am, so here goes. There isn't anything weak or yellow about me. If you think there is, try having two nervous breakdowns and paying off two fortunes. I gave Dorso a worse lacing than you could have given him. I also told Judy off, so there isn't any lack of guts in telling both what I think of the whole situation. . . . I can blow my top higher than you can, but I can cool off too when I look at the weekly statement. . . . You, on the other hand, would kick the bucket over, and I have to keep you and the bucket balanced. The record clearly shows that we have done all kinds of shows together, hits and flops, and this is the first time we ever had any trouble. I never annoyed you with the many petty things I have had to put up with because in most cases I knew you would flare up and do something that you would regret, and so the wise thing for me to do is straighten them out as I have in the past and keep the shows and the business running. . . .

I tried to keep the deal to seven hundred fifty dollars. We considered possible replacements, but none met all the requirements. I was trapped. I finally agreed to nine hundred dollars a week and a secondhand car, a sort of cockeyed compromise suggested by Ben Boyar, my general manager—but a genuine inspiration. Judy signed a run-of-the-play contract.

There were other headaches. In keeping with an old faith, I sent a script to Noël Coward, giving him the first opportunity for a London production. On May 1, I received his cable: "Absolutely delighted *Born Yesterday*. Definitely want produce London. Hope you can arrange Garson direct and of course bring American principals London. Love, Noël." Four days later there was a letter reiterating the contents of the cable and winding up with, "I am always touched by your loving fidelity to that brief handshake in the Waldorf-Astoria. My love to you and thank you a lot."

On receipt of the cable I told Gar the glad tidings only to be left stunned with embarrassment. Without giving me even a hint, he had committed the London rights to his friend Laurence Olivier. He apologized profusely for the humiliating circumstances in which he had placed me and protested that he was ignorant of the fact that he should have told me. Nevertheless, under the terms of the Dramatists Guild contract, I, as the American manager, had the right to make an English production. However, if I were to do this in association with anyone else or assign my rights, I would have to secure the consent of the author.

I decided to write Noël and explain the situation. His reply was characteristically gracious. The cable read: "So many thanks for your clear and concise letter. Completely understand situation. . . . As far as we are concerned, don't give it another thought, and thanks again for your usual generosity and consideration, and our very best wishes for the success of the play when it is done."

The embarrassment he had caused me did not stop Gar from occasionally interfering and criticizing my management of the play. I was not, he would complain, operating my end of the business as efficiently as he wished, though I never was sure that I understood what he meant. From time to time, consequently, there would be sharp words, these generally glossed over with dinner and the normal process of cooling off.

The final curtain in New York fell on *Born Yesterday* with the New Year's Eve performance, 1949, one month short of four years on Broadway. It had strung together 1,642 performances to become the eighth-longest-run production in the history of the Broadway theatre and the fifth-longest-run play, preceded only by *Life with Father* (3,224), *Tobacco Road* (3,182), *My Fair Lady* (2,717), *Abie's Irish Rose* (2,327), *Oklahoma!* (2,248), *South Pacific* (1,925) and *Harvey* (1,775).

The show made $722,625.49, plus $360,000 from its share of movie rights. Millie's and my personal shares came to over $250,000. In addition, there had been the satisfaction of writing to George Kaufman: "The deed is done. The picture is sold for one million dollars, spread over a period of ten years." For the first time in my life I knew—and much more important, believed it—that I was rich. Between *Born Yesterday* and my stock market securities I knew that I was rich beyond my wildest boyhood dreams. Never again, if I was careful, would the specter of financial instability haunt me.

During the 1946–47 season, following the opening of *Born Yesterday,* I presented Ruth Gordon's autobiographical play *Years Ago,* with Fredric March and Florence Eldridge playing Ruth's parents, and Patricia Kirkland impersonating Ruth. The play opened in December, 1946, and ran through the remainder of the season. With Ruth and Gar agreeing to do the screen treatment, the rights were sold to Hollywood and the film ultimately issued as *The Actress,* with Spencer Tracy as the father and Jean Simmons as Ruth.

Years Ago proved to be my final professional association with the Kanins. Neither Ruth nor Gar wrote another script to catch my fancy. Gar once ruefully wrote: "The record shows that you were offered every play I ever wrote—and I must say you proved to be a good picker. With Ruth and me you had only hits—and never had to share the agony of our flops."

My refusal to produce Gar's plays and a disagreement we had over the television rights to *Born Yesterday* chilled our friendship in later years. We did make up in time, as we always had in the past, and when Gar's musical *Do Re Mi* was trying out in the fall of 1960, I decided to surprise him. With Sam Schwartz, manager of the St. James Theatre, Millie and I went to Philadelphia to see the show. The stars were Phil Silvers and Nancy Walker, two of the funniest people in show business. Gar gave me a warm welcome. After the performance I made some suggestions that I thought would help. He had created two lovable characters for Silvers and Miss Walker, and I was convinced that he needed to concentrate more on them and soft-pedal the gangster characters who were part of the plot.

Following the New York opening, I received a telegram:

"Dear Max: I feel bound to tell you that your trenchant perspective and wise Philadelphia comments several weeks ago stayed in my mind and were of immeasurable help in turning a promising dream into fulfilling reality. You are what you always have been, a real theatre man, and I am grateful to you and for you. Old love from Ruth and new love from me. It's Christmas. Gar."

22

Television Tales

WHO KNOWS what awaits the opening or closing of a door, the rise or fall of a theatre curtain?

The Broadway blight that descended on the Kanins following *Years Ago* fell on me, too. I was unable to find a script worthy of production. I missed the 1947–48 season, the first since I had become an independent producer in 1930. Nor were succeeding seasons crowned with laurel and gold. In the fall of 1948 I presented Gertrude Tonkonogy's *Town House,* a three-act comedy adapted from the brilliant *New Yorker* stories by John Cheever. When I read it, I thought the play had a good chance provided George Kaufman injected a stronger story line and gave it the right directorial guidance. It turned out to be one of his poorer efforts and the play faded after a dozen showings.

Two months later, under protest, I produced *Bravo!,* the latest collaboration between Edna Ferber and George Kaufman. I had tried desperately to forestall the production, engaged in one violent argument with Miss Ferber in the dining room of the Hotel Plaza, and went ahead only because of George's insistence. *Bravo!* was about a displaced, once-great Hungarian playwright and his mistress, a faded stage star. It survived for forty-four performances.

The following seasons were repetitions of disaster: *Metropole,* by William Walden, in December of 1949, and *The Small Hours,* by Kaufman and his second wife, Leueen MacGrath, in February of 1951.

Goaded by failure and frustration, I had been watching with increasing restiveness the renewal of activity in television. The manufacture of sets, abandoned for the war effort and held up afterward by strikes, scarcity of materials and various Office of Price Administration rulings, had started up again and the public was buying. Men were speculating about the future of the medium, wondering whether or not the nation's business concerns could afford the cost of sponsoring television programs on a mass entertainment basis. It is curious to recall now how many skeptics there were, how primitive the thinking. I had no better crystal ball than the next man, but the economic intricacies did not trouble me. I was convinced that ways would be found to overcome them. More important, and not so easily hurdled, I felt, were the twin problems of talent and ideas. Never before in the history of show business had there been a medium so voracious in its appetites, so consuming in its needs. It was in this area that I was anxious to become involved.

As activity in the field grew increasingly frenetic, I looked forward with proportionate eagerness to a resumption of my relationships with N.B.C., certain that I possessed invaluable assets: long experience in show business, an eye for a script, ability to recognize talent. I believed that I could give writers and actors the benefit of my counsel, patience and understanding. With money no longer my prime motive, I wanted now ego satisfaction and a sense of participation in a new world.

The call did not come.

At first, preoccupied in the theatre, my disappointment was only an occasional twinge. Once in a while I disclosed my feelings to friends and wondered why I was being ignored by the television powers. When my stage activities began to diminish, my irritation increased. I wanted to be part of television. I had need for it. Certainly, it should have need for me, as it had before the war when John F. Royal had summoned me to use my influence with Broadway's leading playwrights so that N.B.C. could produce their plays on television for token fees.

In the spring of 1951 I lunched with David Sarnoff, chairman of the board of Radio Corporation of America, parent body of N.B.C. We had seen each other only intermittently since vaudeville days. During lunch I recalled my reaction many years earlier when he had boasted of the "great" board of directors he had set up for RKO.

"Yes, David," I had said, "but what I want to know is who's going to write the jokes?"

I reminded him that his great board of directors had not been able to save vaudeville and that I had been outspokenly critical of his selection of a leather man, Hiram Brown, to head the vaudeville circuit. I recalled how Brown, after pushing me out on the excuse that I could not get along with my colleagues in the organization, had himself come to me years later with an invitation to join him in making moving pictures on Long Island.

"That was ironical, wasn't it, David?" I asked and went on. "The point is that this television industry is something in which I am vitally interested. I look around at the inferior producing talents and I get mad. Then I think of my bankroll and my independence and I calm down. But the fact is, David, that like vaudeville and all other forms of entertainment, television needs showmen. Who's going to write the jokes has as much application here as it had in vaudeville. Television needs people who know what talent is, how much it is worth, how to work with it and develop it. You know what I have done in the theatre. You know the number of hits I have had. I must know something."

Sarnoff listened, nodding his head from time to time. I felt that I was scoring. Then he asked, "Why haven't you gotten in touch with Joe McConnell? He's president of N.B.C."

"I hardly think that's the answer, David," I replied. "I am not going to place myself in the position of begging for a job. Why can't McConnell get in touch with me?"

I got the impression that Sarnoff would look into the matter. But I did not hear from McConnell. I must have failed to make myself clear to Sarnoff, I told myself. I wanted nothing more than to be an adviser; I wanted to help. But perhaps I was not wanted, and Hiram Brown's edict still stood: "Gordon is not an organization man."

Meanwhile, at parties and elsewhere I had been meeting a young man named Hubbell Robinson. With a background in advertising and radio, Robinson had joined the Columbia Broadcasting System, in 1947, as vice-president and director of programs. That was the time when commercial television operations were really getting under way. A dapper young man with a lively mind and a pleasant personality, he had about him the air of a man going up. We seemed to get along. I told him what I thought of television, and we exchanged ideas on what was needed to ensure its success.

That summer, while waiting for McConnell's call, I received instead a call from Robinson, asking if I would take a crack at producing a show for which Frank Sinatra would be the master of ceremonies. Strictly speaking, it was not what I had in mind. I did not wish to produce so much as advise, ferret out, cultivate. Nevertheless, after all my talk I felt that I could not back out, not even when I discovered that the program was expected to buck the inordinately popular Milton Berle—an assignment which, as Jack Gould, the reviewer for *The New York Times*, remarked, was generally regarded "as an invitation to walk the last mile." When I agreed to do the show, signing for seven weeks at one thousand dollars a week, I quipped to Harpo Marx that I had finished up in show business trying to knock off Milton Berle.

The first program was set for October 9. It did not take long for me to get a good taste of what it was going to be like—producing in television.

Aside from what Robinson had said about the format of the program, I was given no further inkling of what to do. Nor had I met the writers by the end of the first week of September, a month before "opening night." I tried to remain calm even in mid-September when we had not yet lined up the performers. I wrote to Sam Katz, with whom years before I had made a sortie in the direction of film-making: "If ever I saw crazy goings on with salaries that are perfectly ridiculous—this business makes Hollywood look like a conservative old-fashioned firm. All I do is get mad every day. Jackie Gleason gets eighty-five hundred dollars for one shot, and William Bendix just asked for four thousand dollars for one appearance . . . at this moment I can't tell you who is going to be in it outside of Sinatra and the Andrews Sisters—and the show opens October 9."

Then, by one of those typical show business miracles, the situation righted itself. Besides Sinatra and the Andrews Sisters we signed Perry Como and Frankie Laine and went to work.

One consoling factor in the torturous proceedings was the professionalism of Sinatra, one of the great performers of our time. Though I had been warned that he could be temperamental and difficult, I found him generally co-operative and willing to listen. I knew he was great, and he knew that I knew it. The only time I was annoyed by him was when he rejected my suggestion that Como, Laine and he do the Florodora Sextette with the Andrews girls. I had worked out various bits of business and thought the number could be funny that way. For a while it seemed they would do it. Then Sinatra vetoed it and, as I reported to Groucho Marx, "everybody dived under the bed and it was out."

To my astonishment the show opened. The *Times* man noted that C.B.S. had made lavish use of its checkbook, but left open the question of whether or not we would be able to displace Berle. He said that Sinatra's singing had not improved with the years and that his renditions were on the routine side. However, he reported that Sinatra "does have a very real degree of stage presence and a certain likable charm, and in comedy bits he acquits himself surprisingly well." He praised Como highly and concluded, "Max Gordon, producer of many Broadway musical hits, is making his debut as a television producer . . . and the program reflected his know-how. There were no technical hitches and everyone knew what he was doing, something that could not be said for Mr. Sinatra's show last year. No doubt Mr. Gordon will see to it that on future weeks there is more diversity in the acts. Then Mr. Berle may have something to worry about."

Several days later I received a note from William S. Paley, chairman of the C.B.S. board. "I thought the Sinatra show," he said, "went very well last Tuesday night. I'm glad to see that we've got you working hard."

I did not smile at Paley's jest, however much I appreciated his letter. I was working hard, and worse, I was not enjoying it. The uncertainty of rehearsal schedules, the anxiety, the lack of co-ordination were too tough for me. I prayed for the weeks to pass as quickly as possible. Indeed, Milton Berle had not too much to worry about from the Sinatra show. We managed all right, but we set no fires. On November 5, I wrote to Paley.

My dear Bill:

As you probably know, my agreement to produce the Sinatra show ends in ten days, and I am writing you this letter because I fear you will be too busy for us to get together. I won't pull any punches because I wouldn't be any good to you if I did. Let me begin by saying that I consider Frank Sinatra one of the great actors of our time. I have rarely seen an actor with such repose, economy of gesture, a comedian who lands comedy points with so little effort. Frank must have read Hamlet's advice to the players. At least he acts as if he did. If I am right about Sinatra's talents, he is worth a big bet. If I am wrong, then he shouldn't have been signed in the first place. Before I relate my experiences for the past seven weeks, I would like to make this constructive suggestion. If I had the television future of Sinatra in my hands, I would try to find for him a play with music (not a musical comedy) with a theme that would carry over from week to week. There's nothing new about this form of entertainment, although no one in television is doing it. George Cohan did it with *Forty-five Minutes from Broadway*. Not only did this have human appeal, it also had about ten song hits.

Now, then, to a résumé of what's happened with the shows I produced. I am not ashamed of any of them, and considering the limitations imposed, I am rather proud of them. Let's take the first show. We started off by believing we had Jack Benny. The writers and I tossed around a number of ideas and then found we couldn't get him. We then set about to do a show for Perry Como and Frankie Laine. After I worked with the authors for a couple of weeks, I was told that before Como and Laine would sign, they would have to approve the script. I personally went to their agent and read him the material and convinced him to advise Como and Laine to sign for the show. I spent the final day of rehearsal rehearsing these two boys personally. You know, of course, that they never acted in their lives. I must say that I have never found two more grateful people, and they sent me a message through their agent that if I ever wanted them for a show, all I had to do was whistle.

Now, then, here's what has happened since. Because the writers don't know in advance whom to write for, they have two days to write the scripts and about two full days for rehearsal. Shows put on under these circumstances do not merit serious criticism. Take the fourth show for example: with Jules Munshin, Eddie Mayehoff and Georgia Gibbs. On that show Eddie Mayehoff was one of my choices and scored a big hit. He could have a chance with the right program. I read some of the sketches submitted for the first time on Thursday before the show. I rejected one completely, and another one we couldn't do because of legal complications.

I had to get two new sketches written and went on with the third one that flopped. I take all the blame for this one because it was my idea, but I couldn't ask for a rewrite job with that one because if I did, we wouldn't have had the other two good ones.

I produced two of the greatest revues ever done in America: *Three's a Crowd,* with Fred Allen, Clifton Webb and Libby Holman; *The Band Wagon,* with Fred and Adele Astaire. These were accomplished as a result of months of hard work and meticulous care, and then all the sketches in both shows were not good. The production of both made history. How anybody can expect all the sketches to be good every week is beyond me.

Now I find myself producing shows with shoddy and flat-painted scenery and with hurried and ill-conceived ideas and very limited budgets. I go to the warehouse and give your very competent scenic designers a rough idea of the kind of scenes we intend to have for our sketches. But what inspiration can you expect from scenic designers who never read the manuscript? The casting, of course, is almost impossible. It's a last-minute rush job, and you turn up with the best you can.

Under these circumstances, the production of a revue every week cannot possibly mirror the taste of the producer and has really nothing to do with his qualities. If I do any work in television, my main business will be the unearthing of new writing talent and new acting personalities. I have done it in the theatre, and I think it can be done in television.

I thought it best to write this letter, but I still hope to see you when the opportunity presents itself and give you other ideas I have in mind.

Within forty-eight hours Paley replied. He had read my report with a great deal of interest and "looked forward to the time when you and I can have a sitdown. I would like to get the benefit of your thinking about TV, especially after the experience you have had producing the Frank Sinatra show."

I had also sent a copy of my report to Frank Stanton, president of C.B.S., who wrote back saying that he believed I would look far and wide before I would find anyone "who agrees more thoroughly with your point of view regarding the importance of good writing in the future of this great new medium of television. . . . I want to thank you for the job you did in producing the seven Frank Sinatra shows in New York. Without you, in my opinion, there would have been no Frank Sinatra program on C.B.S. this year." The letter continued in glowing terms, Stanton saying that everyone from top creative management to the studio neophytes had been made "far richer from having had the experience of working with you. . . . I hope there will be another occasion before too long for us to exchange views on the future of television."

Like a high school boy with a good report card, I showed the letters, especially Stanton's, to all my friends. What I had been hoping for in television was about to be offered to me on a golden platter.

I waited. The weeks went by. I did not hear from Robinson or Paley or Stanton. Someone said that Stanton was trying to work something out for me. But as the days lengthened into weeks, I began to have my doubts. To Sam Katz I wrote, "I feel like the soldier who got the medal but couldn't get a job."

And then one evening I met Hubbell Robinson at a party. His greeting seemed chilly. He said something about my having gone over his head to Paley and Stanton. He evidently was referring to my report. When I disavowed any such intention, he persisted. Shocked and flabbergasted, I said, "But, Hubbell, everything in that letter I discussed with you and everything that went on between Paley and me or between Stanton and me I reported verbatim to you."

"I know you did," he replied. "But you did it after you saw them."

Apparently, I had failed again to behave like an organization man. Stanton subsequently strongly defended Robinson when I reported our conversation. "I must disagree with you," he said. "I have never found Robinson sensitive about this type of thing in parallel situations."

I don't know.

What I do know is that I made up my mind then and there to forget television or, more accurately, to forget about wanting to play a role in its development.

Helping me to forget was a young man named Howard Teichmann, who had come into my office bearing both an introduction from Marcus Heiman and a play called *Howe and Hummel*. The play was badly written. But it had something that struck my imagination—a scene, perhaps, a sense of humor, a comic twist. Whatever it was, instinct told me that Teichmann in proper hands might turn out something worthwhile. I called George Kaufman. "I've read a play," I said, *"Howe and Hummel*. It's not much good, and I don't think you have to bother reading it. But

I have a feeling you ought to see the fellow who wrote it. I think he's got something."

Teichmann had. Out of that collaboration came *The Solid Gold Cadillac,* an audience comedy if ever I beheld one. It might be running yet had Josephine Hull lived.

The Solid Gold Cadillac had been sold to Columbia Pictures and I had become a consultant for that firm, reading scripts and advising on the purchase of literary properties, when I received a call from David Sarnoff. He had read the report I sent to Paley. He felt I ought to function in a consultive capacity for N.B.C. I said that I was working for Columbia Pictures, but he brushed that aside. "It doesn't make any difference," he said. "I want you to call Pat Weaver and tell him what I said."

I called Pat Weaver, president of N.B.C. at that time. After some hesitation, he agreed to see me the following Monday. It was one of the most confusing interviews in which I ever participated. I did not bother to call Sarnoff. Instead I wrote him a letter.

My dear David:
When I saw Pat Weaver the other day, the only thing he said that I understood was that he didn't want to consult anybody about anything. When I tried to tell him that a comedy version of *Meet the Press* might be a good idea for Herb Shriner, he told me he didn't want to listen to it. Oscar Hammerstein 2nd, Noël Coward, George Kaufman and others of their reputation are very happy to have my opinions—but not Mr. Weaver. Under the circumstances, my association, directly or indirectly, with Mr. Weaver could only make me unhappy and would embarrass us both. If ever you have any problems about show business and want my advice, you may have it free, and I will always be at your service.

Sometime later I was returning from a Gridiron Club dinner in Washington. Pat Weaver was among those on

the plane. When we alighted at La Guardia Airport and
rode into New York, Weaver happened to sit next to me.
Among the things he said was, "You know, when Sarnoff
sent you to see me, I was wondering which one of my jobs
you wanted."

After this I rang down the curtain on my television
dreams.

23

⌘

They Remember Me!

ONE DAY in the spring of 1961 I found myself riding up to
Providence, Rhode Island, to give a talk at Brown University on my experiences in show business. It was an
appointment resulting from a chance meeting with Professor Albert D. Van Nostrand of the University's English
Department. We had been introduced at The Players, a
theatre club to which I have belonged for many years and
to which I had gone that afternoon to browse through
some old theatrical newspapers in the club's library.

I was in need of my memories.

Professor Van Nostrand and I chatted for a few minutes
about the state of the theatre. After a pause, he said, "You
know, Mr. Gordon, I think the students at Brown as well
as my colleagues on the faculty would be fascinated to
listen to you talk about your life in the theatre." Flattered
by his interest in me, I decided to accept the invitation.
Now, as the miles passed, I berated my vanity, belabored
myself for becoming involved in a venture for which I
really had no taste.

I kept wondering what I would be able to say to these young people about myself—a producer, regarded by the general public as nothing more than a man who raises money for a show, a "no-talent" parasite, as an actor recently said of producers, feeding on the creative talents of others. Would I be able to convince them that the abuse and insult so frequently hurled at producers were mostly unmerited; that upbraiding producers for their commercialism hardly deserved attention from sensible people; that a producer's desire to present plays that would interest the public and be successful at the box office hardly was subversive; that, indeed, without successful producers there could not be any theatre at all, unless government became the producer? Would I be able to show them how ridiculous it was to shout commercialism in a society in which it was perfectly permissible for practitioners in just about every other calling to be "commercial"? Artists, musicians, opera singers, art dealers, publishers, novelists, dentists, professors, doctors, lawyers, newspaper and magazine men could be as commercial as they pleased, and not a voice was raised. Why then a different standard for producers?

But, aside from this, who was I to them? My name had disappeared from the Broadway marquees. Hardly ever now was it mentioned in the stage news columns of the daily press. Would they know who I was, what I had done? Would they care? What would I—what could I—mean to these youngsters, members of a generation sometimes beyond even the comprehension of those much closer to their intellectual climate and attitudes?

The truth is, I was hardly in the proper frame of mind for the undertaking. For a long time I had been low in spirits. Eight years had passed since the opening of *The Solid Gold Cadillac*. With the exception of a comedy I jettisoned in Philadelphia rather than face disaster in New York, I had done nothing in the theatre. Not that I had to. But the thought that the race had passed me by bothered me. I desperately needed to be in the race. There obviously is no end to the variety of knowledge a man acquires about himself in the years of his lifetime. The bread that once I thought would be all that I wanted, or needed, to give me serenity and satisfaction had turned out not to be enough.

Not that I had consciously withdrawn from the race after the success of *The Solid Gold Cadillac.* Indeed, I had changed nothing. Every morning I read scripts, took my walk, went to my office. And yet there was change—subtle, insidious change, like the slow, unseen, unfelt, ever-present erosion of time—change that succeeded in leaving me behind. Playwrights whose works I had presented over the years had died or stopped writing. Others no longer seemed able to write the sort of scripts that could rouse me to action. Projects that I nursed for months evaporated into nothingness after a half dozen lunches. Ideas failed to equal their promise. Unsolicited scripts arrived from the untried, along with those of the established. None intrigued me, though time and again after I rejected them they enticed other managers and failed.

From George there had been nothing. Not that he had stopped writing. That was not George. He wrote until he could write no longer. It was his life. But the magic was gone, the bite of his satire, the freshness of view. Nothing that he ever wrote again found its way to the stage.

I had no sense of identity, no sense of stature as I rose to speak, following the usual introduction. There were about three hundred persons in the room, mostly students. I was not nervous. I was too old for that. I had gone through too many wars for that. But I was a theatre man and I wanted to get through. I wanted to reach them.

I started slowly. I did not have any notes, having decided that it would be better to speak extemporaneously and at random. I spoke of my life on the East Side, of my brother Cliff's influence on me, of my time in burlesque and vaudeville. I recalled how, by sheer chance, I had entered the legitimate theatre as an independent producer of *Three's a Crowd*, recalled and described the budding genius of Fred Allen, Clifton Webb, Fred and Adele Astaire. I tried not to sound like the proverbial old fossil gilding the glories of the good old days, though I did recall for them the bygone glamor of the Forty-second Street of my youth, the days when Broadway belonged more to the theatre than it does now with its auction houses, souvenir stores, blaring phonograph record shops and sundry honky-tonk tourist attractions.

And, as I spoke, I was aware of that wonderful rewarding silence. They were listening. I was getting through. Buoyed now and warmed, I went on. I tried to summon for them the sentiment that still clings in the minds of those who remember such places as Rector's, Churchill's and Delmonico's; the names of Nora Bayes, the old Palace, the New Amsterdam where some of the loveliest shows ever seen on the American stage were produced.

I took the bull by the horns and began discussing the plight of the American theatre, pointing out the strangling grip of the contemporary price squeeze, the fact that Hollywood had gobbled up a whole generation of writers, drugged and destroyed them with swimming pools, sunshine and more money than they had ever seen before. I emphasized that nothing troubled the theatre more today than the lack of good writers. I told them I was certain that the crisis were merely one of transition, that there were budding playwrights on the way, that the theatre would never die.

Caught up now and enthused, I went off the deep end. I challenged the popular concept of a producer. I told them what a real producer was, that his task was not only to raise money, but as Oscar Hammerstein once said, a producer has to be a "rare paradoxical genius, hard-headed, soft-hearted, cautious, reckless, a hopeful innocent in fair weather, a stern pilot in stormy weather, a mathe-matician who prefers to ignore the laws of mathematics and trust intuition, an idealist, a realist, a practical dreamer, a sophisticated gambler, a stage-struck child."

It dawned on me as I spoke that in reality I had been all these things. A glow of pride filled me, a glow I had not felt for years. I doubt that anyone in that room realized what had happened—what was happening to me. Some-thing of that feeling must have radiated outward, trans-mitted itself to them. When I stopped, there was a burst of applause—long, loud, heart-warming applause. Many came forward to shake hands, to say thank you, to ask questions. And the questions came like the waters over the rock ledge at Niagara: fast, furious, challenging. There were those who had been old enough to have seen *The Solid Gold Cadillac,* either on the stage or in films; those who recalled seeing *Born Yesterday* on television.

Together we remembered some of the more hilarious moments. The joy of recollection was written on their faces. I could feel the reflection in the depths of my soul. Professor Van Nostrand asked me to stay until the next day to talk to smaller groups. I dined with members of the faculty who remembered many of my earlier productions. Among them, too, it was evident that there were treasured memories of evenings spent in theatres where my produc-tions had played. I had helped talent, had given play-wrights a chance to be heard, designers and directors their chance to show what they could do. I had not only made money, but it suddenly dawned on me as it never had before that I had also brought pleasure to the world—a mission far greater than I had ever perceived.

I left Providence exhilarated—how providential that name. The uselessness, the inferiority, the dejection had gone. What did it really matter that I had not produced a play on Broadway since *The Solid Gold Cadillac?* It was not necessary to produce plays to prove myself anew. I had proven myself, had made a record that in terms of quality and quantity would be difficult to surpass. I would produce again when I found a script sufficiently worthy of risk and effort. I, Mechel Salpeter, had mingled with presidents, with princes of finance, with artists. I had dear friends. I had come back from disaster to fortune and health. I had landed on top.

Index

(307)